Claude Jutra
FILMMAKER

Jim Leach

McGill-Queen's University Press
Montreal & Kingston · London · Ithaca

© McGill-Queen's University Press 1999
ISBN 0-7735-1859-2 (cloth)
ISBN 0-7735-2005-8 (paper)

Legal deposit third quarter 1999
Bibliothèque nationale du Québec

Printed in Canada on acid-free paper

This book has been published with the help of a grant from
the Humanities and Social Sciences Federation of Canada,
using funds provided by the Social Sciences and Humanities
Research Council of Canada.

Funding has also been received from the Faculty
of Social Sciences of Brock University.

McGill-Queen's University Press acknowledges the financial
support of the Government of Canada through the Book
Publishing Industry Development Program (BPIDP) for its
activities. We also acknowledge the support of the Canada
Council for the Arts for our publishing program.

Canadian Cataloguing in Publication Data

Leach, Jim
    Claude Jutra: filmmaker
    Includes bibliographical references and index.
    ISBN 0-7735-1859-2 (bound)
    ISBN 0-7735-2005-8 (pbk.)
    1. Jutra, Claude, 1930–   I. Title.
    PN1998.3.J88L43 1999   791.43'0232'092   C99-900692-4

Typeset in Minion 10/13
by Caractéra inc., Quebec City

CONTENTS

ILLUSTRATIONS

PREFACE

Although it is generally agreed that Claude Jutra was one of Canada's greatest filmmakers, there has been very little critical discussion of his films. When I set out to write about these films, my goal was to fill the gap and to draw attention to a rich body of work that had been unaccountably neglected. I soon discovered that most of the films had met with indifference or even hostility when they were first released and that Jutra had struggled throughout his career against the effects of commercial failure and critical controversy. The one major exception to this rule was *Mon oncle Antoine*, still widely accepted as "the great Canadian movie," but the enduring success of the film has not provoked a renewed interest in Jutra's other films.

I realized that, if I was going to account for my own pleasure in watching Jutra's films, I would also have to account for why the pleasure had not been widely shared by critics during the filmmaker's lifetime. How could I do this without arguing that the critics were simply "wrong"? I decided that it was not a question of right and wrong but of norms and expectations that encouraged critics to look for certain qualities and cinematic pleasures that Jutra's films did not provide. Fortunately, with most of his films, there were one or two critics who wrote sympathetic and suggestive reviews that corresponded closely to my own responses. I took this to mean not that I was "right" but that, at the time of their release, there were other possible ways of reading the films. What was it in the cultural context of the time that ensured these enthusiastic critical responses would remain a small minority?

I also realized that Jutra's case was far from exceptional and that his films and career raise issues that are endemic to Canadian cinema and indeed to many other areas of Canadian cultural experience. My project thus broadened to encompass not just a critical reassessment of a body of film texts but also an exploration of the relations between these texts and their cinematic and cultural contexts.

The meanings and effects of any text are shaped by the contexts in which it is made and received by audiences, and which no textual analysis can afford to ignore. However, identifying the appropriate contexts and tracing their effects within and on film texts is a task that soon makes the critic aware of the difficulty of deciding what meanings would have been communicated to contemporary audiences. In Jutra's case, as I soon discovered, there are some especially tricky questions involved in defining contextual parameters.

One of the most significant contextual strategies in film studies has been to situate the work of a filmmaker in relation to general trends in the "national cinema." It is not easy to define the boundaries of any national cinema, but it is far from certain Canada even has a single national cinema. Jutra worked in both official languages, but he always insisted that the culture of Quebec provided the most vital context within which to view his films. As we shall see, however, some Quebec critics objected that he did not engage with the key issues of cultural nationalism, and his films figure prominently in all histories of Canadian cinema.

In my discussion of Jutra's films, I will argue that the unstable context of the national culture (or cultures) helps to explain the ways in which they work but also that the films (and the critical discourses about them) help to illuminate the cultural issues. I will also discuss the films in the context of "film language," dealing with the choices Jutra made in constructing them and with the assumptions and expectations that led many critics to reject his choices.

In recent years, the already complex interweaving of cinematic and cultural contexts in which Canadian filmmakers operate has become even more complicated because of political and technological developments that call into question traditional ideas about national identity and image making. Although Jutra died before the full impact of a transnational economy and electronic communications had become apparent, Canadian cultural experience has always been deeply marked by images coming from elsewhere, and Jutra's films engage with issues of personal and cultural identity in ways that prefigure much contemporary cultural theory.

Jutra's career as a filmmaker spanned four decades (from 1948 to 1985), and he had to negotiate his way through the choices and constraints offered by his changing cultural environment. A biographical account would no doubt throw light on the ways he responded to these challenges. It would be fascinating to know to what extent the recurring themes and motifs in the films evolved from the filmmaker's personal experience, but I have not attempted to write a biography. I have drawn on the "legend" that grew up around Jutra and that incorporated the scraps of personal information that appeared in the media. The numerous interviews with the filmmaker throughout his career depict him as an artist with a personal vision but offer only vague hints about his private life.

In any case, films are never simply reflections of the personal vision of an individual artist. There is, first of all, the fact that filmmaking is a collective process, and many others were involved in the production of Jutra's films. For the most part, I have not dwelt on their contributions, but I certainly do not assume that Jutra's voice is the only one to be heard in the films I will be discussing. Films are also embedded in industrial and cultural processes that affect the work of all those involved in their production and shape the ways that audiences respond to them.

I do not want to suggest that film texts can be reduced to their contexts. Most of this book consists of close readings that attend to the images and narrative structures whose effect cannot be fully explained by the cultural environment in which the films were made. In any case, the meanings and effects of films are never fixed and permanent and, consequently, value judgments are always open to revision. Jutra's films explore the experience of living in a culture without a confident sense of identity and thus work against the easy assumptions that allowed critics to dismiss them. I cannot claim that mine are the only possible readings, but I hope to demonstrate that they *are* possible readings. By doing so, I want to provoke discussion about the films themselves, about how people respond to films, and about why Canadian critics responded to Jutra's films in the way they did.

A note on translations: all translations from the French, unless otherwise stated, are my own. I have aimed for accuracy rather than elegance. Except where I make a point about the meaning of the title, I have not translated the titles of Jutra's French-language films in the text, but English versions are included in the filmography. For films by other directors, translations are provided when the title is first mentioned in the text. If possible, I have used the titles under which the films were released in English.

A note on photographs: I have included a selection of production stills to provide a visual impression of the cinematic texts I am discussing. In the current state of Canadian film archives and copyright laws, it is virtually impossible to illustrate a film book with frame enlargements that would offer a more accurate illustration of a critical argument. Jutra's films will eventually become more accessible, I hope, at least in video or other electronic formats, so that readers may judge for themselves.

I would like to acknowledge the support of Brock University for allowing me two sabbatical leaves during which I worked on this book and for keeping me on my toes in the intervening years. I am also grateful for the moral and collegial support of my colleagues in the Film Studies Program: Barry Grant, Joan Nicks, and Jeannette Sloniowski. Joan Harcourt, Joan McGilvray, and Claire Gigantes at McGill-Queen's University Press provided invaluable encouragement and editorial contributions. Thanks to Jean Bruce and Leslie Bell for their help with the photographs. This book is dedicated to Jenny, Aphra, and Nat.

Claude Jutra
FILMMAKER

Above: Claude Jutra on the set of *Les Mains nettes* (Photo Library of the National Film Board of Canada, All rights reserved)

Below: Jutra performs a balancing act in *À tout prendre* (Collection Cinémathèque Québécoise)

"JE SUIS CLAUDE JUTRA"

One of the most eagerly anticipated events at the 1963 Montreal Film Festival was the screening of Claude Jutra's first feature film, *À tout prendre*. Jutra had already become "a hero to French-Canadian youth" through his frequent appearances on television, most notably as the host of two series about cinema broadcast in 1954 and 1961.[1] He had been active as a filmmaker for almost fifteen years, first coming to the attention of the public in 1949 when, at the age of nineteen, he won a Canadian Film Award for best amateur film. During the 1950s, Jutra had been a key figure in the development of a new approach to documentary at the National Film Board (NFB). Now he was the director and star of a feature film that promised to open up new possibilities for the Canadian film industry.

The production of any feature film in Canada at the time was a rare and newsworthy event. Montreal was certainly not Hollywood, but in its own much more modest way, Jutra's new film may have reminded some observers of *Citizen Kane* (1940), the first feature film directed by Orson Welles. Both directors had already established themselves as "stars" and both appeared on screen as the main characters in their own films. The films themselves aroused considerable controversy, and the subsequent careers of the two filmmakers involved a constant struggle to develop their cinematic visions in the face of cultural and economic discouragement. Of course, *Citizen Kane* is now generally accepted as one of the great films of all time and has been frequently revived and discussed at great length by many critics; Jutra's film has not quite disappeared but is rarely seen and has received little critical attention.

À tout prendre is a colloquial French phrase most accurately rendered into English as "All Things Considered," a title that, according to Jutra, evoked his desire to express everything he had to say in case he would be unable to make another film.[2] In the opening credits, the actors are introduced not by printed captions but (in a variation on a device often used by Welles) by the director's voice accompanying images taken from the film. The only actor not so intro-duced is Jutra himself, but there was really no need to introduce a man whose voice would be instantly recognizable to many in the audience. In any case, Jutra immediately appears on screen in the film's provocative opening shot, sitting on the floor and reading a copy of *Life* magazine. His voice is again heard on the soundtrack describing the pleasures of the glossy images in the American magazine, so different from the film's own low-budget images. He then turns the magazine towards the camera, which zooms in on a double-page spread of one of the famous publicity shots of Marilyn Monroe on the set of her last, uncompleted film.

Since Monroe had died in mysterious circumstances during the shooting of *À tout prendre*, this opening shot suggests the pressures as well as the pleasures associated with American popular culture and Hollywood cinema. It also blurs the distinction between Jutra the filmmaker and Claude the character in a fiction film whose story was based on recent events in Jutra's personal life. As we shall see, its autobiographical premise and Jutra's evident pleasure in exploring the possibilities of the medium led some reviewers to dismiss the film as narcissistic and self-indulgent. The critical controversy at least generated publicity, but Jutra was unable to find a cinema willing to show the film until some months after the festival screening. Instead of the anticipated success, he found himself struggling to pay off his bank loan and to find funding for a new film.

In contrast to the lukewarm, sometimes downright hostile, reception of *À tout prendre*, Jutra's *Mon oncle Antoine* (1971) was immediately welcomed as "the great Canadian movie," and it established the director's reputation as "the most gifted moviemaker who has ever worked in this country."[3] The film quickly became a classic and has been repeatedly voted the best film ever made in Quebec or Canada.[4] In 1997 a restored print was released and the film was included in a set of postage stamps honouring Canadian cinema. Unfortunately, its success was an exception to the rule in Jutra's career and *Mon oncle Antoine* has tended to overshadow his other films, which deserve to be much better known.

Jutra's next film, *Kamouraska* (1973), an adaptation of the novel by Anne Hébert, was the most expensive Canadian film yet made, but it was released in a mutilated version and failed commercially. Like Welles after his difficul-ties with Hollywood producers, Jutra went into "exile" – in his case in English

Canada – and worked on projects that were often not of his own devising. When he returned to Quebec to make *La Dame en couleurs* (1984), the result was another disappointing commercial setback. The reception of this film, which proved to be Jutra's last, raised disturbing questions about why a filmmaker of such recognized stature should so often make films that seemed to be out of touch with critics and audiences.

These questions cannot be answered just by looking at the films, although I will argue that the films do often reflect on the cultural circumstances that always made "failure" a likely outcome. In this introductory chapter, I explore some of the issues involved in Jutra's relations with the cinematic and cultural contexts in which he made his films. The following two chapters examine the evolution of Jutra's approach to filmmaking in the years before *À tout prendre*, and the rest of the book is devoted to close readings of the major films. In discussing the ways critics persistently misrecognized these films, I suggest that they still have much to offer to contemporary viewers and that they address cultural issues that have become even more urgent (and more global) in the years since they were made.

Death Watch

In December 1986 Jutra disappeared from his Montreal home. A few months later, during the spring thaw, a body was pulled from the St Lawrence River east of Quebec City and identified by a note that simply stated, "Je suis Claude Jutra." The news media soon reported that the well-known filmmaker had committed suicide because he was suffering from Alzheimer's disease, but this explanation did not completely allay suspicions that he had been worn down by the constant struggle to make films in an unsupportive cultural climate.

Jutra himself once asked an interviewer, "If I'm so great why am I having problems financing my next film?"[5] The effect of these problems was frequently mentioned in the tributes that appeared after his death. Jay Scott, for example, called Jutra "one of the enduring monuments of Canadian film history" but added that "the discontinuous nature" of his career "was sadly typical of filmmaking in Canada during his lifetime."[6] As Scott made clear, Jutra's problems were hardly unique in the history of Canadian cinema, but this only made it easier to think that his "sad fade-out" was less a personal response to a medical condition than a symptom of a cultural condition.[7]

The sudden death of a public figure always creates a demand for explanations. Factual answers about the how and why of the death are rarely enough, and there is usually an attempt to explain it in cultural terms. The events surrounding the death of Marilyn Monroe, to which Jutra had alluded in the opening of À tout prendre, are still under investigation, but the mystery only reinforces the apparent compulsion to use the star as "a representative character through whom to approach the political cultural condition of our time."[8] The death of a Hollywood star under any circumstances would make bigger headlines – even in Canada – than the death of a Canadian filmmaker, but in a much less publicized way, Jutra's death also exposed the complexity of the cultural conditions in which he had worked.

The revelation that Jutra had been a victim of Alzheimer's was especially newsworthy at a time when the ravages of the disease were only just becoming apparent, and his refusal to live with the deterioration of his memory had both a personal and a cultural significance. He had prided himself on the power of his memory, and his films had stressed the importance of memory both in their narrative structures and in their characters' sense of identity. This emphasis on memory also situated the films within powerful cultural traditions in Quebec, whose official motto is "Je me souviens." While he did not refer specifically to Jutra, Heinz Weinmann may have had the filmmaker's death in mind when he wrote, in his book on the cultural implications of Quebec cinema, that "nations also die of Alzheimer's disease."[9]

In this sense, Jutra's death may have made him into a "representative character," but there was considerable uncertainty about how to remember him. Two other recent deaths had raised similar questions but the cultural implications were quite different. When German filmmaker Rainer Werner Fassbinder died of a drug overdose in 1982, his death was seen not only as the outcome of a lifestyle that had received at least as much media coverage as his films but also as an extreme acting out of tensions in German culture. The relations between Fassbinder's public image, his films, and recent German history have been explored by many critics, most notably Thomas Elsaesser in a book significantly titled Fassbinder's Germany (1996). As Elsaesser admits, to treat Fassbinder as "representing Germany" is somewhat problematic, but the idea of Jutra "representing Canada" seems almost unthinkable, for reasons that I shall discuss later.[10]

Both Jutra and Fassbinder frequently appeared as actors in their own films, and both were gay men whose sexual orientation became fully apparent only

6

after they had had relationships with women who also appeared in their films. After *À tout prendre*, Jutra avoided obvious autobiographical allusions, but Fassbinder's films were often thinly veiled reflections on events in his personal life. It was hard not to see Fassbinder's death as in some way an outcome of his personal and cultural situation, but it was difficult to know what to make of Jutra's suicide. His films had received much less publicity, they had been much less widely distributed, and he worked in a nation whose cultural identity was notoriously divided and ill defined.

The response to Jutra's death may also have been coloured by memories of the suicide of the Quebec novelist Hubert Aquin in 1977. Aquin's act was widely viewed both as a response to the pressures of living in a colonized culture and as a symbolic protest against these conditions. Because he had explored the tensions in Quebec in his novels and had worked actively for the separatist movement, Aquin was often seen as a "martyr" to the cause, even if the significance of his work and his final act remained open to debate.[11] On the other hand, although Jutra always identified himself as a separatist, many Quebec critics felt that his films should have dealt more directly with the political situation, and the response to his suicide was accordingly more complicated. How could a self-avowed separatist have found himself in what Martin Knelman described as "the embarrassing position of being English Canada's favourite Quebec filmmaker"?[12]

This awkward question masked the even more disturbing question how such a respected, if controversial, filmmaker could die in such miserable circumstances. His medical condition made it difficult to blame the culture; nonetheless, the shock of his death acted as a reminder of the tensions and contradictions with which Jutra struggled throughout his life. Of course, raising these questions in the context of Jutra's death places the emphasis on the negative dimensions of Canadian culture. This is certainly not the only picture that emerges from a study of Jutra's films, and, before discussing cultural and cinematic contexts, it will be useful to look at the public image of the filmmaker and his work as it developed in the media during his lifetime.

The Legend of Claude Jutra

Shortly after Jutra's death, one English-Canadian critic described him as "a modern age Renaissance man" whose last days were "lived in the shadow of his own legend."[13] Although he was a qualified doctor, he had chosen to pursue a precarious career as an actor, writer, and director for theatre, film, and television. There were frequent references in the media to the range of his talents and interests, but such observations often carried the implication that he was unable to settle down in one area of expertise. The sense of Jutra's personal instability became a central motif in the legend and contributed to the shadow that it cast over his career.

The effects of Jutra's legend can be explored more precisely by drawing on the idea of the artist's "biographical legend," a concept developed in the 1920s by Boris Tomashevsky, a Russian formalist critic, and later applied to cinema by David Bordwell in a study of the Danish filmmaker Carl Dreyer. According to Bordwell, the biographical legend is "created by the filmmaker and other forces (the press, cinephiles)" and allows the critic to "situate a filmmaker's work in film history by studying the persona created by the artist in his public pronouncements, in his writings, and in his dealings with the film industry."[14]

Apart from the autobiographical revelations in À tout prendre, Jutra made few public references to his private life. No doubt an intimate biographical account could provide a context that would explain some features of his films. However, as Bordwell suggests, the important thing is not to seek the reality behind the legend, "as if we could replace it with an easy truth, but rather to analyze the legend's historical and aesthetic functions."[15] From this perspective, we need to establish how the name Jutra, attached to a film, encouraged a certain kind of response and to suggest how the legend was shaped by, and interacted with, the broader cultural context in which the films were made.

Although I will make frequent use of the many published interviews with Jutra when they can throw light on strategies adopted in the films, the film-maker's words will be used not to reveal the "true meaning" of the films but to provide evidence of his own sense of their relationship to the cultural environment. Not unexpectedly, Jutra tended to discuss his films as expressions of his personal vision, and I will follow his lead by organizing my discussion of his early career around his encounters with the filmmakers, Norman McLaren and Jean Rouch, who most influenced him. Jutra consistently contrasted his approach to filmmaking with the "impersonal" attitudes that prevailed in the film industry. He was also well aware, however, that his films were shaped by cultural forces that also affected the ways critics and audiences responded to them.[16]

Although Jutra often had more control over the final product than film-makers working in a studio system, the question of authorship is extremely complicated in many of his films.[17] They raise questions about "who is speaking" that undermine our confidence in an omniscient author and disturb traditional notions of personal and cultural identity, and the relations between them. Jutra's legend can help us to identify these questions, precisely because it was the product of the interaction between Jutra's own sense of his personal project and the public institutions within which he worked.

Of course, personal experience and public image can rarely be completely separated, as Jutra demonstrated in À tout prendre. Although the later films did not blur the boundaries between life and art in quite the same way, the accounts of Jutra published in the media constantly assumed a close relationship between his art and his personality. The main elements in Jutra's legendary persona as it emerged in the media were a preoccupation with the experiences of youth and adolescence, an ability to combine scientific thinking with an artistic sensibility, and a fascination with film form. I shall discuss each of these intertwined elements in turn in order to suggest how they helped to frame the reception of the films.

Jutra was not entirely comfortable with the image of himself as a director who made "those nice growing-up stories of adolescence."[18] His two best-known films, however, Mon oncle Antoine and Dreamspeaker (1976), deal with adolescent boys struggling to find a sense of personal identity in adverse circumstances. The difficult transition from childhood to adulthood is also the focus of several other films, including À tout prendre, in which Claude is an admittedly rather old adolescent. The films thus seemed to confirm Jutra's own sense of his "fixation on youth" and encouraged descriptions of the filmmaker as "poet-child" and "perpetual child."[19]

Not surprisingly, his own childhood was a frequent topic in interviews. Although young people in his films are usually victims of an indifferent or oppressive adult world, he insisted that he enjoyed "a golden childhood."[20] This was certainly true in a material sense and, as Knelman pointed out, Jutra's "upper middle class background" was often held against him by those who felt that his films failed to reflect "the climate of the new Quebec."[21] He seemed to share their doubts, wondering whether his happy childhood might disqualify him from being an artist since "works of art are born from unhappiness."[22]

The Jutras family was well known in Quebec. Although Claude dropped the final "s" from the family surname early in his career, the original form continued to turn up in the Quebec media for many years and is even found in the credits of the first film on which he worked at the NFB. His father was a successful radiologist and patron of the arts, and his older sister Mimi enjoyed some fame as a singer in the mid-1930s. Jutra described her as "almost the Shirley Temple of Montreal," and he apparently appeared on stage with her when he was five. His parents encouraged him to take courses in painting, dance, and dramatic arts and even bought him his first film camera when he was sixteen; but the ultimate goal was that he should become a doctor, like his father.[23]

While he always insisted that his childhood was "extraordinary," Jutra did sometimes hint at "a lot of dark things underneath that I repressed."[24] He apparently idolized his father but was less close to his mother, whose fictional counterpart in *À tout prendre* is extremely cold and calculating – but then the father is a disturbingly absent figure in this film. If the troubled couple in *Pour le meilleur et pour le pire* (1975) represented Jutra's parents, as Pierre Lamy once claimed, then the material comforts and cultural urbanity of the Jutras household must have coexisted with some severe psychological tensions.[25] Perhaps this is what Jutra meant when he claimed that his own youth was "simultaneously unhappy (like all youths) and especially happy when compared with all those that I have since come to know."[26]

Jutra himself never married and, through the fictional "confessions" of *À tout prendre*, suggested that he was unwilling to take on the responsibilities of fatherhood. The issue is complicated by Jutra's homosexuality (or bisexuality), to which he also "confessed" in *À tout prendre*. His sexual orientation, like the whole of Jutra's private life after the period depicted in *À tout prendre*, hardly figured at all in his legend, although it must have shaped both films and legend in indirect ways.[27] Despite the constant depiction of the sexual anxieties and fantasies of the adolescents in the films, the poet-child persona often deflected questions of sexuality into a more general sense of a refusal to conform to the norms of adult life. Thus, John Hofsess described the director in mid-career as a man who had refused to settle down and raise a family because he wanted to keep alive "a perilous childlike wonder and impressionability."[28]

According to the legend, this perpetual child resisted the fixed categories by which adults regulate their lives. The result was an "instability" that liberated his cinematic vision from established conventions but also contributed to his difficulties in dealing with the complex "adult" reality of the Canadian film industry. A similar tension also appeared in discussions of Jutra's scientific background in which he was often described as a kind of child prodigy who excelled equally in the arts and sciences. "There are two men in Claude Jutra: the man of science and the artist," wrote Léo Bonneville, who felt that this "double personality" contributed to the specific qualities of his films.[29]

If his fixation on youth suggested regressive tendencies in Jutra's life and work, his scientific interests associated him with progressive trends in Quebec culture. Looking back on his childhood, Jutra remembered frequent visits by many of the key figures who paved the way for the Quiet Revolution to the Jutras home on rue Saint-Famille, a site whose name was an ironic reminder of the old Quebec. He recalled visits by "the whole artistic colony of Montreal," including painters (Alfred Pellan and Paul-Émile Borduas) and writers (Gratien Gélinas and Félix Leclerc) whose work helped to overthrow the traditional conservative and Catholic values that had dominated cultural life in Quebec. Scientists were also present, and Jutra specifically mentioned the visits of Warren McCulloch, whom he described as "the father of cybernetics" and who would later be the subject of the second part of *The Living Machine* (1961), Roman Kroitor's NFB documentary on the implications of the new technology.[30]

Jutra's family background thus encouraged the possibility of reconciling science and the arts, two activities that, in the culture at large, seemed to be "diametrically opposed."[31] However, as in Quebec as a whole, there must have been some tension in Jutra's domestic environment between the orientation towards a new technological future and "a bourgeois atmosphere where the social and cultural standards were from France."[32] Although Jutra's parents encouraged his early artistic endeavours, they (especially his mother, it seems) also expected him to follow in his father's footsteps and become a doctor. He must have pleased his parents when he received special permission to enrol at the Université de Montréal at the age of sixteen and when he qualified as a doctor in 1952, at the age of twenty-one.

In keeping with his credentials as a scientist, Jutra aligned himself with the cause of "progress" in many interviews and in some of his NFB documentaries, notably *Le Niger: jeune république* (1961), *Petit discours de la méthode* (1963, codirected with Pierre Patry), and *Comment savoir* (1966). These films seek to allay fears about the dehumanizing effects of technology and imply that the artist and the scientist must work together to create a cultural environment responsive to human needs. Although many felt that the new information society posed a threat to Quebec's distinctive culture, Jutra hoped that the resulting intellectual ferment would have a liberating effect and was optimistic about the cultural impact of technological change.

Despite his commitment to the cause of progress, there were some darker overtones to the way his scientific background functioned in Jutra's legendary persona. His medical training was supposedly responsible for an interest in madness, in which the scientific pursuit of objective knowledge came into conflict with the artistic exploration of subjective experience. Jutra's films sometimes seemed unbalanced to critics because of the apparently contradictory demands for detachment from and identification with the many so-called mad characters that inhabit them.

The unsettling effect of madness first appeared in Jutra's first amateur film, *Le Dément du Lac Jean-Jeunes* (1948), made when he was still himself an adolescent, in which a troop of boy scouts are disturbed by the lurking figure of the "madman" referred to in its title. As his first official assignment for the NFB, Jutra was assistant director on Stanley Jackson's *To Serve the Mind* (1954), a short fictionalized documentary about a doctor who suffers a nervous breakdown. Mad or disturbed characters appeared in many of the later films, and they often provoked allusions to the director's own experiences as a medical student. When he was making *Ada* (1976), a television film set in a modern psychiatric hospital, Jutra himself claimed that he had drawn on his familiarity with the "miserable conditions" faced by mental patients "during the Duplessis period."[33] At the end of his career, critics responded to *La Dame en couleurs*, set in a mental hospital run by nuns before the Quiet Revolution, as a return not only to an earlier phase of Quebec culture but also to Jutra's own past.

If Jutra's scientific knowledge equipped him to explore the experiences of the mad, critics often implied that the effects spilled over into the artistic domain through his refusal to settle for the "normal" cinematic conventions. Despite the supposedly personal roots of these tensions, however, the conflict between progress and regression in Jutra's films could also be seen as a response to what he called "a kind of 'crise de conscience' of the Quebec people and their culture" during the Quiet Revolution.[34] The result was an unsettled but stimulating cultural climate that Jutra, using a cinematic metaphor, characterized as "the 'cross-fade' between tradition and next week."[35]

Jutra himself translated these "two tendencies" into cinematic terms when he referred to the opposition between his "very documentary" and "very 'subjective'" films. He claimed to find "objective things … marvellously comfortable," but the tension between the objective and subjective in his films often made critics distinctly uncomfortable.[36] Yet this tension is inherent in a medium that makes use of technology for aesthetic purposes, and it was Jutra's fascination with the medium that provided the third component of the legend.

As we have already seen, Jutra's reputation as Quebec's "man of cinema" was an early illustration of the power of television.[37] After writing *L'École de la peur* (1953), the first television play broadcast by Radio-Canada, he really established himself as a presence in the new medium in 1954 as the host of "Images en boîte," a series of thirteen half-hour programs on film history (followed in 1961 by a series on Canadian cinema).

His willingness to exploit the possibilities of television, a medium usually perceived as a threat to the survival of cinema, is in keeping with the progressive aspects of the Jutra legend. Yet his fascination with cinema also carried regressive connotations because, as Jean-Louis Baudry has put it, film spectatorship is often associated with "a state of artificial regression."[38] The conflict between progress and regression is, from this perspective, a defining characteristic of all cinema, but it is especially important to Jutra's films (and his legend) because of the way it connects with his interest in childhood and madness.

Jutra indeed traced his love of cinema back to childhood experiences. He remembered being "thunderstruck," at the age of eight, by the first moving image he ever saw, an eight-millimetre film of a sailing boat shown at a friend's house. From that moment on, he saw films whenever he could, even though he lived in what he called a "cinematographic desert."[39] As a student during World War II, he "absorbed as many films as possible" despite the need for identity cards and the Quebec censorship law that prohibited cinemas from admitting anyone under sixteen.[40] Later on, he travelled to New York to see films that had been banned in Quebec, but filmgoing of any kind was virtually illicit in Jutra's cultural environment and perhaps even within his liberal family, given the relatively low status of film in comparison with the fine arts.[41]

Whatever problems Jutra may have run into with his new enthusiasm, he was soon able to see most of the important works of film history at the Montreal Film Club, and his parents did buy him a sixteen-millimetre film camera for his sixteenth birthday. With this camera, Jutra and his friend Michel Brault shot *Le Dément du Lac Jean-Jeunes*, which he described as "a quick sketch, with the naiveté of children's drawings."[42] The frequent collaboration between Jutra and Brault, who would himself become a major figure in Canadian film as a cinematographer and director, thus began as a result of their childhood friendship, again linking "the man of cinema" to the "perpetual child."

Jutra's next effort, *Mouvement perpétuel ...* (1949), earned him his first public recognition when it won the prize for best amateur film at that year's Canadian Film Awards. It was, as he later described it, a "formalist, impressionist" film, "a sponge, saturated with all the influences: the French classics of the thirties, the American moderns, Bunuel, Maya Deren." Jutra's enthusiasm for the avant-garde filmmakers, whose work he had recently seen in New York, resulted in an eclectic style whose effect he later tied into another aspect of the legend by calling it "total madness."[43] This judgment may be the product of Jutra's attempt to disavow the excesses of a youthful work in the light of his later, less overtly transgressive films, but he could never live down the image of himself as an artist who refused to recognize "normal" constraints, a quality that might give his work a fresh, "childlike" vision but that suggested, at least potentially, a lack of discipline or stability.

The interweaving of the different elements of the legend thus built up the image of a filmmaker whose achievements were inseparable from a certain lack of responsibility. This image is summed up in an anecdote told by Pierre Lamy to illustrate Jutra's well-known love of "gadgets." According to Lamy, he once spent several weeks filming a one-minute television commercial because he insisted on finding a way to create huge close-ups of the insides of a watch.[44] Scientific curiosity and "childlike wonder" combine to overcome a cinematic challenge in total disregard of practical and economic considerations. Lamy fondly recalled this episode just after Jutra's death: as a legendary image, it no doubt simplifies and misrepresents important aspects of Jutra's character and his films, but it does illustrate the perceptual framework that Jutra himself helped to construct and that formed the background against which his films were viewed.

Where Is Here?

The legend that grew up around Jutra in the media was, in part, an attempt to account for qualities in his films and in his presentation of himself that critics found troubling. Although the films do not engage openly with political issues and may not seem to be formally complex, they nevertheless raise disturbing questions about personal and cultural identity and thus have much in common with developments in contemporary cultural theory. I discuss Jutra's relationship to these developments at the end of the chapter, but the problem of identity is also a characteristic of the specific cultural context in which he worked, and this is never more apparent than when his films are viewed as contributions to a "national cinema."

Studies of national cinemas tend to assume that there is a national identity that films reflect and help to construct. This assumption has been challenged by the new thinking about identity, to which I have just alluded, but also by political events that have eroded national boundaries. Nations are being absorbed into larger multinational institutions (such as the European Community) and fragmented by ethnic separatist movements (as in the former Yugoslavia). Other important factors include the growing economic power of multinational corporations and the technology of electronic communications that enables virtually unrestricted image flows across national borders. Partly because it is geographically so close to the United States, Canada experienced many of these problems of national definition before many other nations, but discussions of the national cinema must also deal with the relations between French- and English-language production.[45]

Andrew Higson has suggested that "to identify a national cinema is first of all to specify a coherence and a unity; it is to proclaim a unique identity and a stable set of meanings."[46] The production of this sense of coherence inevitably does violence to what Tom O'Regan has called "the intrinsic noisiness and mixed character" of any national cinema.[47] Yet a sense of national identity does play an important part in the complex mixture of cultural knowledge and myths that enables audiences to find meaning (or coherence) in films, and filmmakers are often discussed in the context of national film traditions.

In discussing the relationship between Fassbinder and German culture, Elsaesser declares that his aim is to show "how a film can, at one and the same time, have a degree of internal coherence, form part of an ongoing authorial project, and intervene in a number of public histories."[48] My argument in this book is that the richness and complexity of Jutra's films are the outcome of a struggle to achieve "internal coherence" within cinematic and cultural contexts, or "public histories," that were themselves highly fragmented if not incoherent. This kind of approach is not unusual in film studies, but it does raise some very difficult issues. These include the uncertain boundaries between public and private in the age of electronic media, but there are also some quite specific obstacles to coherence when the subject is a Canadian filmmaker.

Northrop Frye has suggested that the "Canadian sensibility ... is less perplexed by the question 'Who am I?' than by some such riddle as 'Where is here?'"[49] This formula is in danger of becoming a cliché, but it has perhaps not been taken seriously enough, especially in dealing with films that represent what Margaret Atwood has called "Canada as a state of mind."[50] Frye stresses the importance of landmarks in creating a sense of identity and argues that Canadians live mainly in urban centres that seem to be indistinguishable from modern cities throughout the world. He also suggests that most Canadians live their predominantly urban lives in the shadow of a northern wilderness whose vastness defies the imagination, and that, taken together, both kinds of space create the effect of an "obliterated environment."[51]

The problem of national identity in Canada is further complicated by the difficulty of deciding exactly which "here" Frye's question refers to. It seems designed to encompass the experience of all Canadians, but it may mean something different in each of the cultural contexts associated with the country's two official languages (and clearly has a different meaning for aboriginal peoples). For English-Canadian filmmakers, it involves the practical problem of whether and how to distinguish Canadian settings from those south of the border, and many English-Canadian films have contributed to the sense of an "obliterated environment" by systematically concealing their Canadian origins for the sake of the international market. Although the Québécois identity is culturally more distinct, the sense of "here" on which it is based involves a delicate balance between French traditions and the North American context. In both cases, film production becomes caught up in a complex interplay between accommodation and resistance to powerful cultural influences from outside the national borders, however these are defined.

Do Jutra's films "represent" Canada as a whole or can they only be fully understood in the context of an emerging national identity in Quebec? If the latter position is adopted, how should we treat the English-language films? Is it possible to combine the two perspectives in ways that will illuminate the films? I shall try to do that here, adopting a "double vision" similar to that which I find in many of Jutra's films. But there will inevitably be times when an emphasis on one will do violence to the other.

This dilemma is characteristic of the experience of living in a country whose political future remains uncertain. However, even if we accept that Canada's two official linguistic communities have developed distinct cultural identities, we need to remember that, like all forms of identity, these are "constructed in and through their relations to each other."[52] Whatever the eventual political outcome, Canadian films in both languages must, in different ways and with different purposes, inhabit these in-between spaces of cultural identity, just as they are shaped by and react against the conventions of Hollywood cinema, European art cinema, documentary, and other possible cinematic models. In this sense, Jutra's films raise important questions about "where is here" in ways that interact with the "public histories" that shape contemporary Canadian experience.

However, it is difficult to argue that any Canadian films reflect patterns and tensions in the culture at large (however this is defined) when the Canadian public remains apparently indifferent to Canadian cinema. As Higson pertinently asks: "What is a national cinema if it doesn't have a national audience?"[53] My own allusions to Orson Welles and Marilyn Monroe have already demonstrated that Canadian films are often discussed in the context of the popular Hollywood cinema with which the Canadian public is much more familiar. Although this is also true of other national cinemas, the problem is especially acute in Canada, not only because of the continuing instability of the national context but also because of Hollywood's insistence that Canada is part of its domestic market.

Despite constant laments by many filmmakers and critics, Canadian audiences have historically seen no real contradiction between their sense of belonging to a national culture and a massive preference for films produced elsewhere. Audiences in Quebec have certainly been rather more supportive of domestic films than audiences in the rest of Canada, but Jutra's films achieved only limited commercial success there. Although many critics recognized Jutra as one of Quebec's major filmmakers, others felt that his films were out of touch with the new cultural environment. These critics were no doubt confirmed in their views whenever English-Canadian critics responded to the films as contributions to the development of Canadian cinema and culture. John Hofsess, for example, described *À tout prendre* as "a life-changing film" that made him aware that "a Canadian film industry" was possible, and, of course, *Mon oncle Antoine* has become a Canadian classic.[54]

This ambiguous and shifting national context presents obstacles to the application of methods such as those developed by Siegfried Kracauer in *From Caligari to Hitler* (1947). Kracauer attempted to account for the appeal of Nazism to the German people by examining the ideological implications of the national cinema. He argued that films are "never the product of an individual" and that "the technique, the story content, and the evolution of the films of a nation are fully understandable only in relation to the actual psychological pattern" of the nation. The cultural significance of films thus emerges from the recurrence of "popular screen motifs" that appeal to, and thus reveal, "those deep layers of collective mentality which extend more or less below the dimension of consciousness."[55]

Although this appeal to a "collective mentality" depends on some questionable assumptions and can lead to rather reductive readings of individual films, Kracauer's attentiveness to film form made a strong case for a symptomatic approach to the study of national cinemas. As I have already suggested, however, the relations between audiences and films in the case of Canadian cinema and the uncertainties about the national context make the attempt to apply this model even more risky than it is in Kracauer's own work. But it is also difficult not to see some connection between films and the culture in which they are made, even if the question is transformed into one of identifying the cultural attitudes that prevent Canadian films from becoming popular.

There have been a few attempts to interpret Canadian cinema along these lines. Most notably, Heinz Weinmann (a historian born in Germany at about the same time that Kracauer, in exile in the United States, was completing his book on German cinema) has produced an ambitious cultural analysis of Quebec cinema. The acknowledged inspiration for *Cinéma de l'imaginaire québécois* (1990), however, was not Kracauer but Edgar Morin, the French anthropologist, whose ideas provide the basis for an examination of Quebec cinema as a reflection of "the collective imaginary of a people."[56] Weinmann undertakes close readings of a number of films, including *Mon oncle Antoine*, to demonstrate the emergence of a new Québécois cultural identity to replace the old hybrid French-Canadian identity. Although he clearly supports the arguments of the nationalist movement in Quebec, Weinmann sees the defeat of the separatist option in the 1980 referendum as a sign of regression towards "an infantile mentality" that had been characteristic of Quebec before the Quiet Revolution. His book thus becomes an attempt to locate "the sources of this almost constitutive indecision of the Québécois people."[57]

As we have seen, some critics found symptoms of an "infantile mentality" in Jutra's films, and "indecision" is an appropriate term to describe the cultural climate to which they respond, whether this is regarded as Québécois, Canadian, or something awkwardly in between. Weinmann and many other critics deplore the debilitating effect of such tendencies, and there is no doubt that the perceived lack of any clearly defined national identity does have negative consequences. However, the instability and uncertainty of the national context may also be seen as a distinguishing feature and not always a liablity.

In an article first published in 1976, Peter Harcourt argued that Canadian films are not inferior to the products of more highly regarded cultural traditions but that they operate in their own "mode," one that is "more tentative" and reflects "our own social uncertainties." According to Harcourt, this is a mode that "touches on fable, that *implies* more than it says" but "does not spell out with great psychological authority a specific social problem."[58] Although it would be foolhardy, and certainly unCanadian, to apply this model indiscriminately to the entire output of a diverse and divided national cinema, it is suggestive with regard to Jutra's films, which often "touch on fable" and depend on an "instability" of vision that disturbs conventional expectations.

Critics have often rejected this "tentative" and "indecisive" mode, especially when comparing Canadian films to the overwhelmingly positive outlook of Hollywood cinema. In my approach to Jutra's films, I want to develop what, in the context of Canadian literature, D.G. Jones has called "a general way of looking ... which would allow us to acknowledge the many negative characteristics and yet maintain that the literature has a basically positive character."[59] Thus, I appropriate negative critical assessments and read them against the grain to reveal qualities that often disappointed the critics but that make Jutra's films distinctive.

The issues of film language and cultural context cannot, of course, be divorced from the economic problems of the Canadian film industry. The cost of film production, even on a modest scale, requires a level of investment that has rarely been available in Canada without government support. Since the late 1960s, federal and provincial governments have supported film production, but the films produced have rarely been widely distributed in a domestic market virtually controlled by the major Hollywood studios. Only in very rare cases have Canadian films attracted large audiences or serious critical attention in their own country, and frequent shifts in government policy have left Canadian filmmakers even more vulnerable than their colleagues in other nations to economic, political, and cultural pressures.

The Canadian domestic market, already relatively small, is further reduced by the country's linguistic divisions. Films are not always subtitled or dubbed in the other language, and when they are, the process of translation often distorts the effect of the original versions, as was the case with *À tout prendre* whose English-language version omitted all reference to homosexuality. Although the language barrier clearly adds to the costs of production, the main issue is a cultural one: are the problems of translation (cultural as well as linguistic) so great that we should be talking of *two* national cinemas rather than one? In Jutra's case, as we have seen, this is a crucial question, and it raises the further question whether the psychological divisions and tensions in his films are in some way analogous to the social and political tensions that shape Canadian culture.

The Career of a Canadian Filmmaker

These tensions must have been very apparent around 1950 when Jutra surveyed the limited options open to him if he wished to pursue his interest in filmmaking. Apart from leaving the country, which never seems to have occurred to him, he would have been aware of two major initiatives in Canadian cinema whose ideological perspectives seemed to be diametrically opposed. On the one hand, there was the NFB, established ten years earlier under the leadership of John Grierson, with its headquarters in Ottawa, producing documentaries "designed to interpret Canada to Canadians and to other nations."[60] On the other hand, there were two commercial studios in Quebec that produced a series of popular feature films during the postwar years but were unable to withstand the competition from television in the early 1950s.[61]

The NFB was undergoing its own identity crisis after World War II as it tried to adjust to the less urgent propaganda needs of peacetime.[62] Grierson himself had resigned as commissioner in 1945, but his ideas on documentary and public service remained a powerful influence on policy and production. NFB films promoted the benefits of technology and cultural modernity, and their ideological project proved especially controversial in Quebec where it conflicted with the conservative policies of the Union Nationale government under Maurice Duplessis. The melodramas and comedies produced at the Quebec studios were much more in keeping with the outlook of the government and the Catholic church.

The ideological boundaries, however, were not as clearly drawn as this account might suggest. Alongside its wartime propaganda films and its advocacy of a progressive outlook, the NFB produced films like *Alexis Tremblay, Habitant* (Jane Marsh, 1943), which depicted a rural Quebec community whose traditional way of life continued virtually unchanged despite the adoption of modern agricultural methods. Meanwhile, as Weinmann effectively demonstrates, two of the most successful productions of the Quebec studios, *La Petite Aurore l'enfant martyre* (*Little Aurore's Tragedy*, Jean-Yves Bigras, 1952) and *Tit-Coq* (Gratien Gélinas and René Delacroix, 1953), were highly critical of the traditional iconography and anticipated the new perspective of the Quiet Revolution.[63]

Jutra's own commitment to the idea of progress drew him towards the NFB, and he accepted an invitation to work in Ottawa from Norman McLaren, who had been one of the judges when Jutra won his Canadian Film Award. Although he never became a permanent staff member, Jutra quickly became involved in the development of direct cinema, a new approach to documentary filmmaking developed by the filmmakers of the NFB's Unit B under the leadership of Tom Daly.[64] This approach, which stressed the filmmakers' response to an evolving situation rather than the exposition of a preconceived argument, appealed to the francophone filmmakers at the NFB who also became freer to develop their own projects when the headquarters moved to Montreal in 1956. They were able to explore the changes in Quebec society in ways that often embarrassed the NFB bureaucracy, and Jutra participated in many of their collective endeavours, including *La Lutte* (*Wrestling*, 1961) and *À Saint-Henri le cinq septembre* (*September 5 at Saint-Henri*, 1962).[65]

The strategies of direct cinema were developed in response to the increasing demand for television programming. Many of Unit B's most innovative films were made for the Canadian Broadcasting Corporation (CBC), and Jutra contributed to several NFB French-langauge television series produced for Radio-Canada. His involvement with direct cinema eventually led to his encounter with Jean Rouch, an anthropologist who used new lightweight film equipment to document his work in Africa. With Rouch's help, Jutra made his own African documentary, *Le Niger jeune république*, and this experience fed into *À tout prendre*, in which Jutra adapted Rouch's strategy of placing non-actors in fictional situations closely related to the reality of their own lives.

Although a group of students from the Université de Montréal had already produced *Seul ou avec d'autres* (*Alone or With Others*, 1962), Jutra's film preceded Gilles Groulx's *Le Chat dans le sac* (*The Cat in the Bag*) and Don Owen's *Nobody Waved Good-bye*, both made at the NFB in 1964.[66] These films and a few others formed a new wave of small-budget films that helped to pave the way for the emergence of a feature-film industry in Canada. Jutra's contribution, however, was soon overshadowed by the films of Groulx and Owen, which received somewhat better distribution because they were, after all, made at the NFB, even if they did not have the full support of the organization.

In response to the relative success of these low-budget films, the federal government established the Canadian Film Development Corporation (CFDC) in 1967 to encourage the growth of the Canadian film industry. The NFB also produced a small number of feature films, including *Mon oncle Antoine*, and this film, along with several CFDC-supported films released in the early 1970s, raised the prospect of a critical and commercial breakthrough for Canadian cinema.[67] As noted earlier, *Mon oncle Antoine* was immediately recognized as a major achievement, but it also provoked some controversy in Quebec. The film was made just before, and released just after, the federal government invoked the War Measures Act in October 1970 in response to the kidnapping by the Front de libération du Québec (FLQ) of British diplomat James Cross and Quebec cabinet minister Pierre Laporte. After the suspension of civil liberties in Quebec led to the arrest and imprisonment of many innocent people, Laporte's body was discovered in the trunk of a car and Cross was released following tense negotiations with his captors. In such a context, the film's depiction of life in rural Quebec during the Duplessis era seemed to be out of touch with the political and cultural issues of the day.

Despite this criticism, the film's success established Jutra as one of Canada's leading filmmakers at a time of some optimism about the future of the national cinema. However, he soon fell victim to a combination of economic, political, and cultural problems that halted the momentum created by the direct cinema films of the 1960s. His next film, *Kamouraska*, was an international coproduction and came under attack as a threat to the economic stability and cultural distinctiveness of a film industry founded on small-budget productions. Although his critics accused Jutra of selling out, the film was in fact a commercial failure, and his career received a further blow when he made *Pour le meilleur et pour le pire*, a more modest personal film that also failed at the box office after being viciously panned by reviewers.

Since low-budget Canadian films lacked the production values of popular Hollywood films, and since higher budgets required international markets, Canadian film policy began to stress economic rather than cultural objectives, encouraging the production of imitation Hollywood films that often went to great lengths to conceal their Canadian origins.[68] By the end of the 1970s, Jutra, like many of his colleagues, could not find support for his projects in Quebec, and he accepted an invitation to make English-language television "docudramas" for the CBC. He also directed two English-language feature films: the ill-fated adaptation of Margaret Atwood's *Surfacing* (1980) and the underrated comedy *By Design* (1981). Although this period of "exile" was involuntary, Jutra came under fire in Quebec for betraying his cultural roots. Yet when he did return to make *La Dame en couleurs*, the film also failed to impress the critics and received only limited distribution.

Despite the indifference and incomprehension that greeted so many of Jutra's films, they are nevertheless expressions of what Weinmann calls the Quebec "imaginary" and they also maintain a clear, but often uncomfortable, significance in a broader Canadian context. In terms of his "legend," Jutra emerges as someone who sought to immerse himself in the "imaginary" plenitude of the film image to compensate for a failure to situate himself adequately in the "symbolic" order of law and language. While such an account is clearly relevant to a body of films populated with "marginal" figures – troubled children, adolescents, and "mad" women – who struggle to define themselves against an adult and male symbolic order, I want to stress the way it also reflects the divided culture in which the films were produced.

According to Jacques Lacan, the movement into the symbolic order takes place with the acquisition of language and demands an acceptance of "lack," because language is fundamentally a way of representing things when they are absent.[69] Society depends on language and on the willingness of reasonable adults to accept that they cannot have everything they desire. For francophones in Quebec, the experience of lack involves the added difficulty of becoming an adult in a culture in which authority seems to be located elsewhere and speaks a foreign language. For anglophone Canada, a similar sense of cultural lack is created by the enormous influence of American popular culture, although in this case the problem is not the imposition of a different language but the difficulty of asserting difference in a shared language. Jutra, a filmmaker who worked in both official languages and whose films have been treated as both Québécois and Canadian, had to confront the problems of working with the myths and codes of a linguistically and culturally divided nation.

Film as a Political Act

Jutra's account of his earliest memory of film images associated the medium with the prelinguistic imaginary, but it also alluded to the changes in Quebec society that took place during the Quiet Revolution. He claimed that his friend's eight-millimetre film deflected him from his goal of following in the footsteps of an uncle who was a missionary in China.[70] This "conversion" from religious faith to cinematic fascination aligned Jutra, somewhat uneasily, with the shift from a religious to a technological society. In terms of cultural identity, the submissive French Canadian, whose faith offered protection against the hostile influences and temptations of English-speaking North America, gave way to the dynamic Québécois, ready to use modern technological resources to bring Quebec into the twentieth century.

At least, that was the theory; and the feeling of euphoria resulting from the new cultural identity did lead to major achievements in film and the other arts. But the drive towards a new and progressive vision of Quebec often resulted in an underlying uncertainty about what exactly the new identity involved. Jutra belonged to what Dominique Noguez called "the lost generation of those who were twenty in 1950," who rejected traditional Christian values but were still uncertain about what could replace them.[71] Gilles Marsolais similarly referred to "the crisis of identity of a whole people who were being liberated from the dictatorship of divine right."[72] Gilles Groulx gave this crisis cinematic form in *Le Chat dans le sac*, a film hailed as "the image of our most recent awakenings" and in which the hero declares, "I am Québécois, therefore I am searching."[73]

The problem of finding a stable basis for identity in the new cultural context provoked Yves Lever to argue that there is more evidence of a "great darkness" in the Quebec fiction films of the 1960s than in those produced at the end of the Duplessis era, to which the phrase is normally applied.[74] This is certainly an exaggeration, but it does point to the need to account for the negative terms in which many filmmakers depicted life in contemporary Quebec.

For many, the answer lay in Quebec's dependent status, which meant that its filmmakers had to confront "the problem of the existence of a national cinema in a colonized country."[75] Jutra would have agreed with this assessment. He saw himself as an "ardent separatist" and insisted that in Quebec "film is just the tool we are using for nationalistic purposes."[76] However, while critics generally regarded the early films of Groulx and Jean Pierre Lefebvre (despite their extremely hesitant heroes) as significant contributions to Quebec's cultural needs, Jutra was "not regarded as conspicuously *engagé*," and his films were viewed with suspicion because they did not deal explicitly with political issues.[77]

English-Canadian critics were more likely to regard Jutra's avoidance of explicitly political themes as a sign of maturity rather than a childlike vision. John Hofsess, for example, described *Kamouraska* as a fable in which "Jutra's political feelings are a sublimated form of eroticism" that depicts "the new Quebec wresting herself free from the ancient priest-ridden one."[78] In a similar vein, Martin Knelman suggested that, although Jutra's films are not political in "the same narrow didactic terms" as films like Denys Arcand's *Réjeanne Padovani* (1973) and Michel Brault's *Les Ordres* (*Orders*, 1974), "maybe Jutra is political in a deeper way."[79]

In Quebec, the depiction of the October Crisis in *Les Ordres*, which Knelman found "narrow" and "didactic," often came under attack for not being political enough because of its stress on the personal experiences of the victims rather than on the underlying causes of the situation. Jutra's own response to the invocation of the War Measures Act revealed his tendency to mediate political issues through "personal" memories of childhood. He claimed that he was "really shaken" by events that he associated with feelings of "fear and guilt" linked to World War II "which I lived through as a child."[80] This translation of the disturbing political reality of the present into the subjective experience of a poet-child could only seem evasive – a slippage from symbolic struggle to imaginary impotence – to critics who saw film as a force for political change.

Jutra's own sense of the political was much too diffuse to satisfy such critics, but he responded by insisting that the effort involved in making a film in Quebec was in itself "a political act." He did not want to make didactic films but rather films that would allow people to think for themselves. Despite his commitment to Quebec's independence, he pointed out that "the worst collective crimes have been committed in the name of nationalism" and warned against "the spectacle of the political trance" that releases people from responsibility for their own decisions and actions. Given his belief in "the right of a people to govern themselves" and in "everyone's need for a cultural and national identity," he declared that his goal as a filmmaker was "to define the contradictions, and to share the anguish," as a contribution to cultural understanding and communal feeling.[81]

He asserted his political convictions publicly in 1972 when, along with actress Geneviève Bujold, he refused to accept the Order of Canada and wrote an open letter to the Governor General expressing his concern for "the survival of Quebec."[82] In an interview published at the time, a journalist described Jutra as one of the few Quebec filmmakers to "circulate" in the "extremely internationalized art" of cinema. Jutra nonetheless insisted that he would not go to Hollywood and wanted to make smaller-budget films "dealing with the Quebec reality."[83] He thus reaffirmed his earlier categorical statement that, "outside Quebec, I have absolutely nothing to say."[84]

After dealing with the Quebec reality in *Mon oncle Antoine*, *Kamouraska*, and *Pour le meilleur et pour le pire* in ways that many nationalists found unacceptable, Jutra had to look outside Quebec in order to continue making films. He discussed the state of his career in an interview given in 1978, when he had just arrived back from California where he had attended a preview of Francis Ford Coppola's *Apocalypse Now*. He looked back nostalgically to the beginning of the Quiet Revolution, a time when the postwar boom in feature-film production and the beginnings of television sustained a vision of "a new world that extended to the horizon like a new America." This utopian vision now seemed highly ironic because the emphasis on success in the "international" market had created a very different "new America" in which Jutra, like other Quebec filmmakers, found it virtually impossible to interest producers in French-language film projects.[85]

Despite being forced to find work outside Quebec, Jutra did not change his political attitudes. In 1980, the year of Quebec's referendum on "sovereignty association" (the qualified version of independence proposed by the Parti Québécois government), he insisted that he had been a separatist for twenty years and that, if he lived in Uruguay, he would be a *tupamaro* guerrilla. "But Quebec is not Uruguay," he added, and he refused to believe that "the authoritarianism of the countries of Eastern Europe" would be an improvement on the existing "liberalism." He expressed support for Quebec's separatist premier, René Lévesque, "the only politician whom I have taken seriously in my whole life," but repeated his antipathy towards politics, claiming that "all political mechanisms escape me, even on the dramatic level."[86] Although Jutra admired Lévesque, he had little hope that the Parti Québécois would find a solution to the problems that prevented him from making films in Quebec. He thought that Quebec cinema could thrive if the government had "the same concern for cinema as for asbestos" but doubted that this would ever be the case because "asbestos is economically more important than cinema."[87]

Jutra's period of exile in English Canada, at a time when the election of a Parti Québécois government had given new hope to the nationalist cause, might seem to contradict Gilles Marsolais's assertion that Canadian cinema is "in fact composed of *two* cinemas: the 'Canadian' and the Québécois, whose interests are divergent."[88] The impact of Jutra's films on Canadians outside Quebec suggests that this claim is somewhat exaggerated. Yet it is equally exaggerated to argue, as David Clandfield does, that Jutra's career was "divided between a Quebec that blew hot and cold about his films and an English Canada that welcomed him and gave him work for half a decade."[89] The welcome given to Jutra in English Canada was by no means unequivocal. Although *Mon oncle Antoine* was celebrated as "the great Canadian movie," *Kamouraska* and *Pour le meilleur et pour le pire* were no more successful than in Quebec, and his two English-Canadian theatrical films were commercial failures. Both Marsolais and Clandfield simplify what was, for Jutra, the messy and uncomfortable reality of working in a context in which cultural boundaries were ill defined and constantly shifting.

Jutra himself would certainly have supported Marsolais rather than Cland-field. In his letter outlining his reasons for refusing the Order of Canada, he insisted that he did not believe in the idea of a "bilingual" and "united" Canada. A few months later, he supported the boycott by Quebec filmmakers of the 1973 Canadian Film Awards ceremony, an action that he justified as an asser-tion of the existence of "two cultures" that did not belong "under one roof."[90] The boycott in turn led to a protest outside the cinema in Toronto that was showing *Kamouraska*, with picketers urging filmgoers not to see the film.

In the circumstances, it is not surprising that Jutra felt that working in Toronto was "like working in a foreign country," although he added that it was "a very *friendly* foreign country."[91] His needs as a filmmaker were in conflict with his cultural and political convictions. Making a film "every four or five years in Quebec" was "not enough," so he came to Toronto to avoid "getting rusty" and was now even prepared to work in Hollywood. Although he frequently returned to his home base in Montreal and regarded himself as an exile, his work in Toronto gave him a "financial and cinematic stability" that he had not found in Quebec, relieving him of the material and psycho-logical pressures that had been weighing on him since the failure of *Pour le meilleur et pour le pire.*[92]

As we have seen, however, one of the components of Jutra's legend was precisely the instability of both his personal life and his cinematic style. Although he welcomed the stability that he found in Toronto, he thought that the city was "extremely dull."[93] By viewing himself as an exile working in a foreign country, Jutra could reassert a degree of instability in his situation, but his resistance to the idea of settling down was increasingly difficult to distinguish from his frustration at not being able to find work in Quebec. The (relative) material security that he gained by making English-language television films for the CBC only served to highlight Jutra's precarious posi-tion as a francophone filmmaker whose work rarely fitted comfortably into the prevailing categories of ideological debate, cultural policy, or production practice.

Postmodern Jutra?

In terms that are highly relevant to my discussion so far, Stuart Hall has argued that "identity is formed at the unstable point where the 'unspeakable' stories of a subjectivity meet the narratives of history, of a culture."[94] Hall's suggestive formula is part of his contribution to a collective work on "postmodernism and the question of identity," and I shall now explore the experience of instability in Jutra's films in the context of postmodernist theories of subjectivity and culture. My speculations about the postmodern strategies at work in the films provide a theoretical context that remains (for the most part) implicit in my readings of the films in the rest of the book.

Jutra himself was an outspoken opponent of the discourses of cultural theory associated with "structuralism" that originated in France and had a powerful effect on intellectual life in Quebec (while remaining a marginal influence in English Canada). Nevertheless, he did share the new theory's distrust of the humanist tradition in Western culture. He denounced "the whole sclerotic, fossilized humanism of Greco-Latin culture" and argued that "humanism," treated as an "absolute, obligatory, exclusive value," denied the value of the language and culture of Quebec.[95] Yet he also dismissed the new theory in the same terms, condemning "sclerotic European intellectual structuration."[96]

In keeping with Jutra's scientific background, his argument against traditional values found support not in the new theoretical models but in the "cybernetic" revolution. He rejected what he saw as the denunciation of technology in Jean-Luc Godard's *Alphaville* (1965), a film that he accused of contributing to a "collective panic."[97] During the 1960s, when Godard's films increasingly adopted an ideological perspective from which science was viewed as complicit with a reactionary political order, they became models for the growing protest movement in France and elsewhere. Jutra, as we know, came under attack for refusing to make explicitly political films, and he certainly did not endorse the nexus of political and theoretical ideas that led to the uprising that almost toppled the French government in May 1968.

One critic has suggested that Jutra was "too much the gently mocking humanist for those who want tough political statements."[98] It would be more accurate to say that he was a mocking anti-humanist who refused to see even his own convictions as fixed and final. His commitment to progress aligned him with the "modernist" desire to sweep away outmoded traditions, but his films are much more ambivalent about the relations between past and present. In this respect, his resistance to the structuralist version of theory amounted to a refusal to be pinned down to one position, and he would certainly have been more comfortable with "poststructuralist" theory, which (drawing especially on the work of Lacan) stressed the artificiality and fragility of the structures that provide the basis for cultural patterns.

The idea that all structures are fictions underpins Jean-François Lyotard's account of the "postmodern condition" as one in which meaning derives from "language games" rather than from "grand narratives" that claim absolute authority.[99] According to Linda Hutcheon, "Canada has a privileged place in postmodernism" because its unstable cultural identity is one that calls into question "the possibility of a centred, coherent subjectivity." The questioning of this possibility is also central to the way Jutra unsettles cinematic conventions, and he would have welcomed Hutcheon's belief that "the postmodern 'different' … is starting to replace the humanist 'universal' as a prime cultural value."[100]

Hutcheon distinguishes between "a *modernist* search for order in the face of moral and social chaos" and "a *postmodern* urge to trouble, to question, to make both problematic and provisional any such desire for order or truth through the powers of the human imagination."[101] Whereas modernists argue that new forms are needed because traditional forms cannot be separated from the traditional values that they were designed to serve, postmodernists insist that there are no "pure" forms free of ideological contamination. As Sylvia Söderlind and others have suggested, postmodernism's "simultaneous reliance on and contestation of existing patterns explain the frequent accusations levelled at its perceived lack of political engagement."[102] Jutra was often attacked in much the same terms, but it may be possible to apply to his films Hutcheon's conviction that "postmodernism is fundamentally contradictory, resolutely historical, and inescapably political."[103]

One of the major strategies of postmodernist texts, again according to Hutcheon, is an irony that depends on "an unwillingness to make decisions about meaning that would imply singularity or fixity."[104] Whereas modernists insist on art as serious "work," postmodernists celebrate the "play" of the text as it interacts with other texts in its cultural environment. It is this playful approach that links Jutra, who once told an interviewer that he saw "life as a game," not only to the postmodernist outlook discussed by Hutcheon but also to the work of Roland Barthes, a writer closely identified with the structuralist theory that Jutra hated but who developed some of the key ideas that inspired postmodern theory.[105]

Barthes first came to prominence in the 1960s, and he may well have met Jutra, either in France or during Barthes's visit to Montreal in 1961 to work with Aquin on the NFB documentary *Le Sport et les hommes* (*Of Sport and Men*). Barthes's name also appears in the final credits of *La Lutte*, presumably as an acknowledgment of the film's indebtedness to his famous essay on the cultural myths of wrestling.[106]

The acknowledged influence of Barthes on this film, which Jutra codirected, is only the most obvious sign of a relationship that is not so much one of influence but of affinity. Their active careers spanned the period from the end of World War II to the early 1980s, although Barthes was fifteen years older. Both men were gay and, in both cases, their sexual orientation bore an uneasy relation to a stress on instability in their biographical legends. Bjornar Olsen, for example, refers to the way Barthes's "refusal to be tied down is articulated in his repeated shifts and by his mocking his own previous procedures," and Barthes himself referred to a "restless relation to language" that led him to prefer a "precarious position" to complacency.[107]

As John Sturrock has noted, Barthes preferred "plural and centrifugal" texts to "singular and coherent" ones, and this preference had implications for the experience of subjectivity, since "the presumed unity of any individual is dissolved into a plurality and we each of us turn out to be many instead of one."[108] In his analysis of the "mythologies" that shaped everyday life in France in the 1950s, Barthes showed how myths work to justify the social order by translating it into a "natural" order that is assumed to be stable, unified and whole. Yet the Barthesian "myth" is not simply a lie; it is a sign that points to cultural needs for which it offers an "imaginary" satisfaction. To shake up this mythic order, Barthes promoted texts that call attention to their origins, their constructedness, and to the necessary incompleteness of their representation.

This resistance to traditional aesthetic and psychological notions of "wholeness" is also a key element in Jutra's cinema and in the problems it creates for many spectators. The preference for instability and incompleteness shared by Barthes and Jutra links their work to "the radical instability of the aesthetic" that, according to Steven Connor, distinguishes postmodernist texts from the modernist insistence that the artwork must be "complete in itself."[109] In Jutra's case, however, this perspective also situated his films as part of a national cinema whose small-budget films were often experienced as incomplete in comparison to Hollywood films because of their rough visual style and their fragmentary and unresolved narrative structures.

On this unstable ground, which unites his biographical legend, Canadian cinema, and the postmodern condition, Jutra's films develop what I will call an aesthetics of failure. This term does not imply an evaluation of the films, although it cannot be separated from the critical and commercial failure of most of them. Rather, I am using it in the spirit of Slavoj Zizek's claim that the greatness of Roberto Rossellini, the Italian neorealist filmmaker, "lies in the fact that he intentionally included in his films traces of their own failure."[110] In this sense, Rossellini's films "fail" because they adopt a strategy that acknowledges, as Barthes's theory demanded, the necessary incompleteness of any representation in relation to the reality with which it engages.

This aesthetics of failure is an important factor in the negative dimension in Canadian culture that I mentioned earlier, and the commercial problems of the Canadian film industry certainly have a great deal to do with the refusal or inability to deliver the Hollywood happy ending.[111] The prevalence of the negative in Canadian cinema implies a modernist critique of mainstream popular culture similar to the one mounted by the cultural theorists of the Frankfurt School, who argued that one of the main functions of the modern mass media is "to translate the negative into the positive."[112] According to this line of argument, mass culture eliminates the critical dimension that was an important factor in the major cultural texts of the past and that encouraged a negative view of the established social order, however complicit the texts may have been in other ways. The "negative" vision thus has a utopian thrust since it encourages a search for the seeds of possible alternatives within existing social conditions.

The Frankfurt School attitude to mass culture also has much in common with the "high culture" rhetoric that has profoundly influenced cultural policy in Canada. However, the aesthetics of failure implies a negative reaction not only to popular (Hollywood) cinema but also to the high culture and modernist belief that formal order and completion can compensate for a fragmented social order. In Lacanian terms, Canadian cinema does not "suture" the "imaginary" desire for plenitude with the symbolic (legal, moral) codes to create pleasure and meanings that have the authority of either the Hollywood or the so-called European art cinema.

Despite the intense cultural and economic problems caused by this state of affairs, it is possible to respond to the aesthetics of failure in a more productive way. My focus here, of course, is on the films of Claude Jutra, but the argument applies to much of Canadian cinema (in both official languages) as well as to other areas of Canadian culture. My approach to Jutra's films thus becomes a case study for developing a general way of looking at Canadian cultural production and its relations to the postmodern condition. The goal is not to reverse the traditional value judgments by claiming that Canadian cinema is superior to Hollywood cinema (which is, in any case, far more complex than the Frankfurt School analysis assumes) or to a modernist art cinema (which can accommodate, if uneasily, films like Rossellini's that include "traces of their own failure"). Such a move would itself simply translate the negative into a positive value. Rather the aim is to suggest that Jutra's films, and Canadian cinema in general, should not automatically be condemned for what John Hofsess has called a failure to create "a character with the brains, balls, will or gall to master life as it must be lived in the twentieth century."[113]

In response to Hofsess, Jutra's aesthetics of failure can be seen as an attempt to explore the implications of a series of questions put by Barthes: "Is it not the characteristic of reality to be *unmasterable*? And is it not the characteristic of any system to *master* it? What then, confronting reality, can one do who rejects mastery?"[114] Jutra's response to these questions was first fully developed in *À tout prendre*, a film dedicated to Norman McLaren and Jean Rouch, two filmmakers whose work seems to embody the opposite poles of the medium (fantasy and reality) but who enabled Jutra to begin to see the possibilities and limits of cinema.

As we shall see, *À tout prendre* is a highly reflexive film that links the problem of producing adequate images of reality to the subjective quest for a sense of cultural identity. In the next two chapters, I examine Jutra's early work in relation to the influence of the filmmakers who most helped to shape his aesthetics of failure.

Above: Jutra takes a tumble in *A Chairy Tale* (Photo Library of the National Film Board of Canada, All rights reserved)

Below: Félix Leclerc rehearses with Monique Leyrac in *Félix Leclerc troubadour* (Photo Library of the National Film Board of Canada, All rights reserved)

THE PRECISE IMAGE
Encounter with McLaren

The dual allegiance that Jutra declared in dedicating *À tout prendre* to McLaren and Rouch appealed to his legendary ability to combine artistic and scientific interests. McLaren, as a leading exponent of animated film, explored the abstract/artistic possibilities of the medium while Rouch, who turned to film as an extension of his ethnographic fieldwork, epitomized the apparently opposed documentary/scientific approach. Jutra saw them as representing "two different polarities" with McLaren standing for "the formal side of things, the understanding of the medium, its physical dimension," and Rouch for "the *cinéma-vérité* side, the contact with people, the integration of a lived experience into a work that, once made, takes on an independent existence."[1]

The dedication was thus an act of personal homage that simultaneously drew attention to the two polarities and, by bringing them together, announced the film's intention to unsettle the opposition between them. McLaren was Jutra's sponsor and mentor at the NFB during the 1950s, while his encounter with Rouch took place over a shorter period of time in the early 1960s. The influence of these two filmmakers certainly does not explain everything about Jutra's development, but his early films work through the implications of the polarities that they represented for him.

McLaren: Animating the NFB

Norman McLaren was a member of the jury at the 1949 Canadian Film Awards that selected *Mouvement perpétuel ...* as best amateur film, and Jutra's short film so impressed him that he invited its director to make an experimental film at the NFB. Their encounter was a virtual replay of McLaren's own first meeting with John Grierson at an amateur film festival in Glasgow in 1936. Grierson, who pioneered the theory and practice of documentary film-making in Britain, had produced some of the most important films in the evolution of documentary cinema, under the sponsorship of government institutions (the Empire Marketing Board, the General Post Office, or GPO). As one of the judges at the festival, Grierson awarded a prize to a short film by McLaren and invited him to London to work for the GPO Film Unit.

Although Grierson's enthusiasm for what McLaren called "a little abstract film in colour" may seem surprising in view of his commitment to the documentary movement, he was also responsible for an even more important step in McLaren's career.[2] As commissioner of the newly established National Film Board of Canada, Grierson invited a number of experienced British filmmakers, including McLaren, to join his staff. The animation department set up on McLaren's arrival in 1941 quickly became one of the most respected and influential in the world.

In keeping with the NFB's contribution to the war effort, the role of animation was initially a functional one and consisted mainly of the insertion of maps into newsreels and the production of public service messages. Peter Harcourt has pointed out, however, that "for all [Grierson's] belief in propaganda, he believed that there should be this section where film could be used like clay, for its own sake," and McLaren was allowed, relatively undisturbed, to experiment with the possibilities of the medium until his retirement in the early 1980s.[3] The legend that grew up around him at the NFB pictured him as an isolated genius pursuing his own interests outside the mainstream of the institution's activities. Thus Sidney Newman, film commissioner from 1970 to 1975, claimed that "since the end of the War" the NFB had never told McLaren what to do, "which is a great testimony to the kind of idiotic place the Board is that allows a genius like that to just live and do what the hell he wants."[4]

There is strong evidence, however, that the presence of McLaren and his innovative approach to animation were not as remote from the central documentary thrust of the NFB as the legend suggests. In the postwar restructuring of the board, animation became part of Unit B, whose filmmakers revitalized the documentary tradition during the 1950s. Many of the Unit B filmmakers, notably Colin Low and Wolf Koenig, worked both in animation and documentary, and this dual focus certainly contributed to the questioning of the traditional assumptions of documentary practice found in many of the key films produced by Unit B.

According to Harcourt, "the discipline involved in animation ... can be seen in the highly disciplined and formal work of Unit B."[5] D.B. Jones has also argued that McLaren's presence in Unit B encouraged a new awareness of the implications of Grierson's famous definition of documentary as "the creative treatment of actuality." He describes the Unit B documentaries as the product of "a finely honed tension between the ultimately inseparable qualities of form and content," a tension that brought together "Grierson's sense of the whole and McLaren's sense of detail."[6]

The Unit B films were of great interest to the francophone filmmakers who were also growing impatient with the traditional ways of doing things. There was a good deal of contact between the two groups: Michel Brault and Georges Dufaux, for example, were cinematographers on *The Days before Christmas* (1958), the first of the Candid Eye films. Jutra does not seem to have worked on any of the Unit B films, but he also brought the experience of working in animation to his documentary work. As Pierre Lamy put it, what Jutra learnt from McLaren was primarily the "precision and quality" of the image.[7] McLaren himself defined animation as "the art of controlling the difference between one frame and the next," a process that always involves a decision about "how much you're going to change."[8] This precision and the commitment to what Jutra called the "physical dimension" of the medium were most apparent in the films McLaren made without a camera, by drawing directly on the celluloid. Such films emphasized the contribution of each frame to the film as a whole and helped Jutra to grasp "the formal side of things."

In a comment that perhaps helps to explain Grierson's interest in McLaren's work, Jutra referred to McLaren's "direct" approach to filmmaking.[9] Although McLaren often found inspiration in the other arts, especially music, painting, and dance, the cinematic element is primary and creates its own structures and forms. In drawing attention to McLaren's use of film language, Jutra almost certainly chose the term "direct" to suggest a provocative connection, across the "two different polarities," between McLaren's abstract use of the medium and the documentary practices often referred to as direct cinema.

McLaren's "direct" approach had further implications for the new developments in documentary. According to Dominique Noguez, McLaren freed cinema not only from its dependence on the other arts but also from its apparently inherent "subservience to the real."[10] Although documentary is the cinematic mode most clearly grounded in the real, the fact that McLaren's films do not depend on a pre-existing reality encouraged reflection on the role of the cinematic apparatus in constructing the meanings that documentary filmmakers often claimed to have found in reality. As we shall see, this resulted in a sense of direct cinema not as a neutral record of a lived reality but as an intervention in the social and cultural processes that shaped that reality.

Many of the documentaries produced at the NFB in the late 1950s actively questioned the relationship between the cinematic and the real. In so doing, they also revealed a distrust of the omniscient or voice-of-God commentator who guided the spectator's responses in most previous documentaries. The elimination or downplaying of the commentary is a key element in the aesthetic of direct cinema, although not always carried through consistently in the Unit B films, and implies a resistance to traditional forms of authority. In these films, the camera sets out to explore reality rather than to illustrate ideas developed verbally and approved in advance.

For francophone filmmakers, *Les Raquetteurs* (*The Snowshoers*, Gilles Groulx and Michel Brault, 1958), a short documentary on a snowshoers' convention in Sherbrooke, showed the possibilities of the direct approach. The filmmakers simply took their equipment to the convention and improvised the shooting as the events unfolded around them. Their example not only encouraged a more flexible response to local conditions but also showed how to evade the censorship of the English-Canadian bureaucracy at the NFB. As Fernand Dansereau put it, "When you made a direct cinema film you did not have to prepare a treatment," which meant that "you didn't have to translate it and submit it to the judgment of the producer."[11]

If the primary reasons for breaking with the voice-of-God commentary were ideological, the effect is analogous to what René Jodoin has called "the absence of voice" in McLaren's films. McLaren often called attention to this aspect of his work by using multilingual credits that set up a contrast between the freedom of visual (and musical) language and the complications and divisions of linguistic discourse. For Jodoin, McLaren's refusal to depend on verbal language meant that "animation is something that is continually invented," an approach that paralleled the efforts of the direct cinema filmmakers to liberate the documentary from the tyranny of the omniscient commentator and the pre-existing script.[12]

Jutra Meets McLaren

When Jutra started to work at the NFB in 1952, McLaren had just completed *Neighbours* using the "pixillation" technique that allowed him to treat human actors as if they were animated figures. The film established McLaren's international reputation when it won an Oscar, but the violent imagery used to enforce its anti-war message generated a great deal of controversy. Two male neighbours destroy their property, their families, and finally themselves in their struggle to possess a flower. In the context of the Cold War, the film sought to expose the horrifying implications of dominant political attitudes, its violence being the obverse of the experience of beauty and harmony offered by the more "abstract" films that McLaren was making at the same time.

Several years after the departure of Grierson, the traditional approach to documentary still dominated the output of the NFB; but new developments were in the air. In 1954 Colin Low, who had been working at the board on animated films since 1945, directed *Corral*, his first documentary. This short film is a lyrical evocation of a lone cowboy rounding up wild horses on a ranch in Alberta, its images accompanied only by quiet guitar music. It does not set out to provide information on ranching but to create an impression of a way of life, a rural utopia opposed to the suburban dystopia depicted in *Neighbours*. The fluid movement of men and animals contrasts with the mechanical, pixillated movements of the dehumanized figures in McLaren's film, but the choreography of image and music in *Corral* bears witness to Low's background in animation.

Jutra was very much aware of the significance of *Corral*, which he called "a precursor of all sorts of things to come."[13] His own film work at this time consisted of official assignments to fairly conventional documentary projects as well as the experimental work that had gained him his invitation to the NFB. He completed two short films, presumably in consultation with McLaren. *Trio-brio* (1953) was apparently lost when the NFB moved from Ottawa to Montreal in 1956, but Jutra described it as a film in which paintings were animated to the accompaniment of synthetic music that he himself composed and performed on "an apparatus invented and constructed" by McLaren.[14] *Pierrot des bois* (1955) was produced independently and features a clown who plays with a rose until it dies (a reversal of the situation at the end of *Neighbours* when the people die but the flower survives).[15]

The culmination of Jutra's experience with McLaren was undoubtedly *A Chairy Tale* (1957). Apart from his performance as a man engaged in a battle of wills with an unruly chair, it is not clear exactly what Jutra contributed to this film, on which he was credited as codirector along with McLaren, but he later stated that he was "the actor and McLaren's perpetual acolyte at all stages of the film."[16] The basic situation motivates the absence of voice since, obviously, speech would be useless in dealing with a chair. Jutra is able to display his talents as a mime, while sitar music played by Ravi Shankar comments on the action. Like *Neighbours*, *A Chairy Tale* uses the pixillation technique, but the effect is less to dehumanize the man than to humanize the chair, which, at the level of the film's action, is granted the equality it evidently seeks in its relationship with the man.

As Janick Beaulieu has suggested, *A Chairy Tale* depicts not the revolt of the material world against human pretenses but the "fantasies" of a chair that demands respect.[17] The film opens with the title, "Once upon a time ..." and the chair alone on an empty stage. When the man enters he moves normally and, engrossed in a book, goes to sit down on the chair. Only after the chair has repeatedly evaded his attempts to sit on it does the man, in his anger, become pixillated. At one point, the chair "watches" from beside the camera as the man distractedly races back and forth across the screen. This shot aligns our point of view with that of the chair and underlines the way his loss of self-control has mechanized the man's behaviour.

The man's struggle with the chair gains a new meaning, however, when he decides to give up and sits on the floor. Now the chair begins to court the man, but it still refuses to allow him to sit. Apparently intrigued by the chair's behaviour, the man tries to amuse it by playing out various roles, cradling it like a child, playing hopscotch, presenting arms as a soldier, and dancing a passionate tango with the chair as his partner. None of this seems to work, and the man tries to leave. However, the chair now blocks his way and then "watches" as the man paces up and down. Suddenly, he seems to realize what the chair wants and crouches down so that the chair can sit on him. The chair dances for joy at the prospect and, after briefly experiencing the pleasure of sitting on the man, it allows the man to sit down. The final title informs us that "they lived happily ever after."

The moral of this fairy tale is less obvious than that of *Neighbours*, but it implies the need to adopt the point of view of the "other." The return to a normal state of affairs at the end seems to suggest that a brief overthrow of the accepted order, as in the medieval carnival days, allows things to continue as usual. The image of a chair sitting on a man both surprises through its subversion of the accepted order of things and, through its absurdity, risks suggesting that any change in the way things are would be equally absurd. In *Neighbours* the struggle over the flower turns the same – the neighbours are identical – into the hated other with deadly consequences; in *A Chairy Tale* the struggle leads to an awareness of the desires of the other and to a peaceful coexistence based on a return to the *status quo*.

What Jutra learned from McLaren, along with the precision of the image, was a way of creating narrative structures using the possibilities of fable as an alternative to the dominant realist approach. Other influences (most notably the rich tradition of storytelling in Quebec culture) certainly reinforced McLaren's example, but the ending of *A Chairy Tale* also raised some doubts about this approach. There was a risk that the stability provided by the fable (here in the adherence to the conventions of the fairy tale) could solidify into a complacent acceptance of the way of life that the fable (through the animation of the chair) initially called into question. Although critics sometimes accused Jutra's films of just this kind of complacency, his fables always involve a degree of instability whose significance became fully apparent only after he discovered the films of Jean Rouch.

Serving the NFB

Jutra's encounter with McLaren left its mark in the traces of animation that remain in many of his feature films. The most immediate effect, though, was the introduction it afforded him to the opportunities provided by the NFB. But while the NFB produced most of Jutra's films up to and including *Mon oncle Antoine*, his position within the institution remained somewhat marginal. He always insisted that he was never a "permanent member," and thus he never enjoyed the stability that such an appointment would have provided.[18]

Jutra's own view of the history of the NFB and its relationship to Quebec cinema was quite negative. He arrived in 1952 during what he called "the prehistory of the French unit" when its members worked like "negro pen-pushers" in a climate of "total and colonialist incomprehension." According to Jutra, the arrival of Pierre Juneau in 1954 and the move from Ottawa to Montreal in 1956 did create an atmosphere within which francophone film-makers were able to work productively. However, he felt that the situation quickly "degenerated" to the point where the NFB became, like the Comédie-Française in Paris, "an institution devoted to tradition" producing "a sort of ignoble folklore, financed by the State."[19] He made these comments shortly after working independently on *À tout prendre*, but the reference to "folklore" would return to haunt him when critics accused him of complying with the NFB's devotion to tradition in *Mon oncle Antoine*.

As his own historical summary makes clear, Jutra began his apprenticeship at the NFB just before the emergence of francophone filmmakers as a signif-icant force for change. In the postwar years, the urgency that had inspired Grierson's approach to documentary filmmaking had largely evaporated and no viable alternatives had yet emerged. Peter Morris, however, has identified a group of films, produced at the NFB between 1945 and 1953, whose approach "straddles the ground between fiction and documentary, drawing on the syntax or conventions of both."[20] Jutra's first official assignment for the NFB in 1954 was as assistant director on Stanley Jackson's *To Serve the Mind*, a late example of this kind of film.

The film opens with (at least partially staged) shots of city streets while a commentary spoken by Jackson introduces the topic of mental illness. The techniques of fiction cinema come to the fore in the re-enactment of the case history of a doctor who suffered a nervous breakdown because of the pres-sures of his profession. A flashback explains why he attempted to commit suicide, and the documentary commentator gives way to the doctor's inner voice. The shift from a public to a private voice is also apparent in the first shot of the flashback in which the doctor moves away from a brightly lit room full of guests at a party into dark shadows that envelop him.

This effect recalls the shadows of the *film noir* style, which had been prev-alent in Hollywood during the previous ten years. The dramatic lighting violates the principle that "lighting … never draws attention to itself," which most Hollywood films adhered to and which contributes to the "transparent and natural" look usually found in the NFB's dramatized documentaries.[21] The main effect in *To Serve the Mind*, however, is to make the documentary look seem healthy and clear-sighted in comparison to the distorted and subjective seeing that fiction provokes. Fiction may be necessary to allow insights into the workings of a diseased mind, but it is the documentary frame that is associated with the "cure." This contrast loses some of its force when the commentator admits that science is not yet able to help all the mentally ill, and the film itself often blurs the distinction between documentary and fiction.

Jutra's own first NFB documentary, *Jeunesses musicales* (1956), is apparently more conventional. Its structure is based on an alternation between an interview with the Canadian director of the organization to which the title refers and activities at a summer camp on Lake Magog. But Jutra undercuts the documentary claim to objectivity by locating the interview at a radio station where interviewer and interviewee compete with each other for control over what will be said (and thus shown). The interview provides a commentary but frequently cues images that illustrate its points in excessive or playful ways. When the director speaks of providing opportunities for exceptional children who would otherwise be misfits in the classroom, the camera offers a distorted image of a boy tapping his fingers impatiently during a lesson. After he describes an educational project that involves distributing records with commentaries to young people, a young woman listens to a piece of "modern music" and, taken aback by the unusual sounds that emerge from the record player, examines the record to see if it is damaged.

Although *Jeunesses musicales* includes many striking camera, editing, and sound effects, Jutra was apparently uncomfortable with the "academic" approach of the NFB crew. He thus invited Michel Brault, who had himself left the NFB after a brief exposure to its "francophobic" atmosphere in 1950, to return to work on his next film.[22] *Les Mains nettes* (1958) was originally presented in four thirty-minute episodes as the final instalment of the television series "Panoramique" and then re-edited into a seventy-five-minute feature film (on which the following analysis will be based). It thus became Jutra's first feature-length fiction film, although he clearly regarded it as an assignment rather than his own personal project. The screenplay was by Fernand Dansereau, the producer of the series, who had directed two of the earlier films.

C. Rodney James has compared "Panoramique" (1957–58) with the contemporary series of "Candid Eye" films (1958–59) produced by Unit B, arguing that "Panoramique" was equally "a reaction against the reportages and half-hour dramas that preceded it" but that the Quebec series opted for "the dramatic format" rather than *cinéma-vérité*.[23] In fact, the distinction is not quite as clear-cut as this suggests. As we have seen, the genre of the dramatized documentary was already well established at the NFB, and "Panoramique" was itself preceded by a series called "Passe-partout" (1955–57), which mixed documentaries and docudramas. Meanwhile, the NFB also provided the CBC with its own English-language series of thirty-minute dramas in "Perspective" (1955–58).

"Panoramique" was certainly the most ambitious of these series, its six stories providing a chronicle of recent Quebec history from the Depression through to the present. As the final instalment, *Les Mains nettes* deals with what the opening quotation from C. Wright Mills describes as the "psychological misery" of white-collar workers in contemporary society. While this quotation functions conventionally by providing the film's documentary "alibi," defining it as an investigation of a significant social issue, it also licenses an interest in psychological tensions that goes beyond the typical situations and characters required by the genre.

The film deals with the plight of workers in the personnel department of a trucking company who resent the demands made by their new manager. They consider setting up a union to deal with their grievances, and a new sense of solidarity emerges, despite the resistance of some of the older workers. The plan for a union never gets off the ground, however, because the manager announces that the company intends to replace the workers with machines.

As the opening quotation suggests, the film's treatment of the situation of the office workers draws on the ideas of Mills, a sociologist who had published *White Collar*, his study of "the American middle classes," in 1953. Mills argued that "the material hardship of nineteenth-century industrial workers finds its parallel on the psychological level among twentieth-century white-collar employees." In a world in which traditional "certainties ... have disintegrated and been destroyed," the white-collar worker becomes prey to "anxiety" and "insecurity."[24]

The film depicts the social issues primarily through their impact on Marguerite, who is appointed as the manager's secretary because he finds her attractive. His open admission of the basis for his decision initially intrigues her, and she agrees to give him information on the other workers on whom they spy through his half-open office door. When the camera pans across the office, picking out the workers as she describes them (introducing them to us as well as to him), we see a male worker run his hand along the back of another female employee, Monique, as she bends over a filing cabinet. This casual sexual harassment is apparently habitual (nobody comments on it), and it provides the link between the social implications of the situation in the office and Marguerite's own problems with her personal and sexual identity.

She is tempted by the attentions of the manager (even when she discovers that he is married), but she rejects his advances when he tries to make love to her in his car. In the attempt to unionize the employees, she works with Jean-Paul, a young colleague (who is also married), but angrily rejects him when he suddenly tries to embrace her in the street. Her situation becomes even more uncomfortable when Monique, with whom she shares an apartment, announces that she has just become engaged. While Monique is content to accept traditional female roles, Marguerite's response to her announcement is to insist that "all men are disgusting."

As she makes this declaration, however, she is applying make-up in front of a mirror, and she later admits to an older female colleague that she felt "jealous." This older woman thinks that she herself belongs to a "sacrificed generation" but assures Marguerite that she is still young. At the age of twenty-seven, Marguerite feels that it is now too late for her, and the film ends with a contrast between Monique at a funfair with her fiancé and Marguerite silhouetted as she stands alone in front of the closed blinds in her apartment.

Marguerite's situation anticipates that of Claude in *À tout prendre*, who also wonders if it is "too late" for him to make something of his life. The two men who lead her to the conclusion that "men are disgusting" also prefigure Claude in their use of sexual adventure to compensate for their inability to impose themselves on their social environment. The manager seems initially to be in control of his situation, but we soon discover that his power is illusory. We do not see the upper management from whom he receives his orders, just as we do not see the workers whose activities the personnel department presumably administers. The office workers, as the "middle class," produce nothing and are vulnerable to orders from above, which seem to come from nowhere, and the confrontation between the employees and the manager evaporates when it becomes clear that he is as powerless as they are. They are all the victims of what Mills called "an impersonalized and ... anonymous system of control" in which it is difficult to know "who really has power, for often the tangled and hidden system seems a complex yet organized irresponsibility."[25]

Early in the film, when he takes Marguerite to a bar after they have been working late at the office, the manager tells her that he needs "risks" and "challenge" in his life. At this point, he attributes his frustrations to the constraints of marriage, but by the end, when Marguerite has come to feel pity for him, he tells her that he is simply not capable of being a "hero." That the erosion of the traditional basis of male identity is endemic to the system is underlined by the parallels that the film establishes between the manager and Jean-Paul, despite their apparent opposition. Both make clumsy attempts to seduce Marguerite, and both are shown in one sequence of strained communication with their wives. The affinity between the two men emerges most clearly when Jean-Paul confronts the manager as the delegate of the workers. He is taken aback when the manager asks about his past and then proceeds to describe it as if it had been his own, guessing correctly that Jean-Paul did not go to university because his mother wanted him to be a priest, even though he lacked the vocation.

The image of the priest in Quebec, of course, had traditionally been one in which male authority could be affirmed without the economic and sexual complications of the secular world. When Marguerite confesses her problems to a priest, he tells her that the solution lies in "militant action through Christ." This advice seems irrelevant in the new Quebec where the break with traditional values and roles has apparently led only to a sense of alienation, which, according to Mills, had become prevalent in the United States.

The dynamism implied by the priest's formula conflicts with the lethargy among the office workers who lounge around the office in the opening sequence, none of them even bothering to answer the telephone. In the new order, dynamism is associated not with religion or politics but with "personality," and the film examines the implications of this change when some of the workers attend a "personality course." An old employee, intimidated by the prospect of public speaking, finally speaks, movingly if hesitantly, about his childhood. But the effect of this intrusion of private memory into public utterance is immediately negated when the instructor asks the entire class to recite a text that asserts that only people with ambition will succeed in life.

The "militant action" that Marguerite and Jean-Paul try to organize in support of the old man whom the manager intends to fire does promote new feelings of friendship among the workers. However, the old man himself refuses to endorse a revolt against authority, and the final verdict seems to be that of the manager who insists that company policy cannot be "human" because "the world is not human."

In reaching this conclusion, the film seems to do little to adapt Mills's vision of alienation in the modern technological society to the specific problems of Quebec during the Quiet Revolution. The references to the priesthood, however, act as a reminder that in Quebec the attempt to affirm purely human values ran counter to a still-active theological tradition as well as to the logic of advanced capitalism. In addition, the company's English name – the General Transport Company – provides at least a hint that the state of inertia depicted in the film derives from Quebec's "colonial" status, implying a parallel between the alienation of middle-class workers and that of a people unable to affect their own destiny.

In developing these tensions, *Les Mains nettes* draws on the tradition of dramatized documentaries at the NFB, although the absence of a voice-over commentary inclines the film to the fiction side of the equation, as does the extensive use of studio sets. Brault was apparently bored at having to work in a studio, but the virtual absence of exteriors effectively evokes the claustrophobic atmosphere in which the workers live (the few exteriors lack horizons and appear mainly at night).[26] There are many long takes in which the camera observes the characters, sometimes moving in to a close-up that isolates a character from the environment, but emotional confrontations are usually filmed in shot/reverse-shot constructions typical of classical narrative cinema.[27]

A certain restrained instability does creep into the *mise en scène* during the confrontation between Marguerite and the manager shortly after she rejects his advances. He sits at his desk and tells her that he has decided to let her go, but she remains standing and retorts that she has asked for a transfer. The shot/reverse-shot structure means that low-angle shots of Marguerite alternate with high-angle shots of the manager, but while this apparent reversal of the power relations does point to the manager's actual weakness, the effect is complicated by the tilted camera, which unbalances the end of their exchange. A more "correct" use of angles occurs in the manager's confrontation with Jean-Paul during which he sits on his desk and is thus able to look down on his employee.

The shadows that envelop the film suggest the influence of the postwar Hollywood *film noir*, but Brault stressed his efforts to break with "traditional lighting methods" in this film.[28] His innovative approach is most evident in the use of silhouettes in a way that prefigures similar effects in *À tout prendre*. In one sequence, Marguerite and Jean-Paul are silhouetted against a wall in the street just before he tries to embrace her; and in the final sequence, Marguerite is silhouetted against the bright light that seeps through the closed blinds in her apartment.

These shots reveal Brault's tendency to create images that even Jean Rouch, despite his enthusiasm for Brault's work, found "too beautiful."[29] This excessive "beauty" offends against the requirements of realism in both documentary and classical narrative cinema, although the lighting effects in *Les Mains nettes* call attention to themselves in a way that goes only slightly beyond the common use of shadows to signify social or psychological pressures. These slight deviations from the norms do suggest, however, that the filmmakers responded to cinematic constraints in much the same way that Marguerite does to her situation as a female white-collar worker.

While *Les Mains nettes* remains a fairly conventional fiction film despite its documentary roots, Jutra did challenge established practices more radically in two thirty-minute episodes that he contributed to another television series produced by the NFB. "Profils et paysages" (1958–59) was a series of documentaries about people who had contributed to Quebec culture. As its title implies, the series set out to relate its subjects to the environments that had shaped their work. Typically, the films did this by "intercutting recent film material with a studio interview."[30] Jutra's films subvert this process in two ways: by shifting the interview from the controlled world of the studio into the subject's environment, and by referring to the process of making the film within the film itself.

In *Fred Barry comédien* (1959), Jutra meets the old actor who is the film's subject in an empty theatre and then films him discussing the past with some of his friends. Their reminiscences are intercut with extracts from films in which Barry appeared. By appearing in his own film, Jutra mediates between the theatrical environment within which Barry has operated (even when working in cinema) and the documentary search for "truth" to which the NFB filmmakers are necessarily committed. The effect is to raise questions about the relationship between the documentary look and the theatrical presentation of self. Does the actor create a façade behind which the documentary camera can find a hidden truth? Or do theatrical (or fictional) masks make possible the expression of states of mind to which documentary techniques do not provide access (as, apparently, in the NFB's dramatized documentaries)?

These questions are raised again, in a more provoking way, in Jutra's other profile, *Félix Leclerc troubadour* (1959). Leclerc was well-known as a writer and as performer of his own songs, and he had just enjoyed some success as an actor in Bernard Devlin's *Les Brûlés* (*The Promised Land*, 1957), the first film in the "Panoramique" series. He functions as actor, singer, and commentator in Jutra's film in ways that challenge traditional notions of documentary "truth."

In the opening sequence, the camera is in a car that arrives at the house where Leclerc is emptying his mail box. However, even before the car arrives, Leclerc introduces himself on the soundtrack and describes the whole project as "the worst kind of fraud." After he has greeted the filmmakers, his voice then describes this meeting as "the first lie," because the shooting had already been going on for several days and because what we are seeing is the third take of a carefully rehearsed action.

The exposure of the documentary "lie" continues in the constant allusions to the presence of the filmmakers (who keep getting in the way of the illusion that Leclerc is addressing us). Thus, after Leclerc has shown us around his barn in normal documentary fashion, we see the filmmakers unloading their equipment from the car. Leclerc points out that the director works as hard as the rest of the crew but adds that Jutra was obviously aware that he was being filmed.

The equipment that has just been unloaded is not visible when Leclerc invites us to make ourselves at home and we (by means of an invisible hand-held camera) follow him upstairs to his workroom. Before he can demonstrate a new song, however, the filmmakers interrupt him, and a cumbersome camera is pushed into the room. When Leclerc's wife arrives to announce that supper is ready, it seems that the film's structure is being dictated by the routines of domestic life. As he sits at the table with his wife and son, Leclerc invites us (the camera? the filmmakers?) to sit down with them. However, the camera discreetly withdraws to another room before the image fades to black.

In the evening, Monique, a young woman whom Leclerc earlier telephoned to announce the arrival of the filmmakers, drops in to pay an apparently unexpected visit. Leclerc comments on the false spontaneity of her "acting," and we later learn that she is an actress needed for the dramatization of one of his songs. However, she also takes on some of the functions of an interviewer when she asks Leclerc to respond to a questionnaire in a French magazine. The magazine refers to the *chanson* as a "minor mode," but Leclerc's responses cause her to tear it up and to agree that his songs are a mixture of "philosophy, fantasy, and love." The film then proceeds to underline this definition through two visual fantasies illustrating the imagery of Leclerc's songs (in a style that anticipates music videos and harks back to McLaren's animated films on French-Canadian folk-songs).

After drinking a toast to the success of the film, Monique goes off to a bedroom to change for her performance. Leclerc, slyly addressing us (the camera), declares, "Honni soit qui mal y pense" ("Shame on he who thinks evil thoughts").We are then suddenly plunged into a fantasy world, but one that takes us out into the natural world where we see birds flying as the camera swoops over a frozen stream. The camera also peers at a pensive young woman (Monique) standing at a window in her nightdress, giving the sequence an uneasy eroticism considering Leclerc's previous comment.

We return to "reality" as we see the equipment being put back into the car, but the camera stays with the Leclercs as they wave to the departing filmmakers. As his wife puts their son to bed, Leclerc remains alone in a dark room where he begins to sing the new song that he had rehearsed earlier. In a dreamlike sequence, the song's protagonist, a tramp called Bozo, drifts on a raft in a moonlit marsh while eighteenth-century aristocrats enjoy an entertainment from which he is excluded. The film ends with a return to the living-room where Leclerc turns out the light and goes upstairs.

Instead of the usual "objective" account of a subject in relation to milieu, *Félix Leclerc troubadour* allows the actual environment in which Leclerc lives, the fantasy world that he constructs, and the filmmaking process to contaminate each other. The result is that the spectator can never settle into a secure position with regard to the film, caught between Leclerc's viewpoint and that of the filmmakers, frequently invited to identify with the camera but then thrust out of that identification as the camera intrudes into the visual field. The constant playful disruption of the spectator's position through the exposure of the documentary lie suggests that Jutra was already exploring issues central to the work of Jean Rouch, whom he met shortly after making this film.

Above: Native drummers perform in *Le Niger jeune république* (Photo Library of the National Film Board of Canada, All rights reserved)

Below: Absorbed spectators at a wrestling match in *La Lutte* (Photo Library of the National Film Board of Canada, All rights reserved)

THE UNSTABLE EYE
Encounter with Rouch

When *Mouvement perpétuel ...* was shown at the Antibes festival in 1950, the program also included *Les Magiciens de Wanzerbe* (*The Wanzerbe Magicians*, 1948), a short film by Jean Rouch. Nevertheless, Jutra apparently did not grasp the significance of Rouch's ethnographic documentary films until he saw *Moi, un noir* (*I, a Negro*, 1957) during a visit to Paris in 1958. As the legend has it, this film so impressed Jutra that he went to Africa to meet the filmmaker and accompanied him on a Central African journey. He described his travels with Rouch in a long article published in three issues of *Cahiers du cinéma*, and Rouch later helped him to make his own African documentary, *Le Niger jeune république* (1961).[1]

Before he set out from Paris in pursuit of Rouch, Jutra met a younger French filmmaker with whom he would later often be compared. After making his name as an acerbic critic of traditional French cinema, François Truffaut helped to establish the French New Wave with his autobiographical film, *Les Quatre Cent Coups* (*The Four Hundred Blows*, 1958). In their assault on the literary and theatrical values that dominated French cinema, Truffaut and his colleagues used the lightweight equipment developed by documentary filmmakers like Rouch. However, when Truffaut and Jutra decided to make a short film together, they chose a project that seemed to have little in common with these new developments.

The screenplay for *Anna la bonne* (1959) was a twenty-year-old theatrical poem (or "*poème-chanson*," as Robert Daudelin called it) written by Jean Cocteau.[2] Cocteau was a poet, novelist, and dramatist, but he had also made several films that were admired by the New Wave filmmakers for their personal use of the medium. The admiration was apparently mutual since Cocteau was president of the jury at the 1959 Cannes festival that awarded Truffaut the prize for best director.

Despite its poetic language and theatrical setting, *Anna la bonne* reflects the interest of both Truffaut and Jutra in blurring the boundaries between documentary and fiction. Jutra described the film as a documentary on an actor, shot "not in a studio, but in a real hotel, a real theatre."[3] As in *Fred Barry comédien*, his earlier theatrical documentary, the actor came from an earlier generation, in this case Marianne Oswald for whom Cocteau originally wrote the text.

At the beginning of the film, the camera penetrates a theatre curtain but enters a dreamlike space that oscillates between the stage, on which Oswald is an actress reciting Cocteau's words, and a hotel room, in which she becomes Anna, the maid who poisons the beautiful Annabel Lee. It is the poem recited by the actress in *Anna la bonne* that challenges the limits of documentary observation: while it expresses the feelings of resentment that drive the maid to murder, its artificial language constantly reminds us that we are witnessing a "performance." In a similar way, in *Les Magiciens de Wanzerbe*, Rouch's camera observes states of trance that, to some extent, it provokes and shares but that it cannot explain.

Jutra described Cocteau as a "priest and magician" whose work had much in common with Rouch's ethnographic documentation of African rituals.[4] Despite the apparent opposition of their methods, both filmmakers challenged the claims of immediate access to the "truth" implicit in traditional documentaries and classical narrative cinema. Instead, they acknowledged the artifice of the medium in ways that simultaneously respected and partially overcame the otherness of their subjects.

Rouch and Ethnographic Cinema

Rouch began making films in 1947 as a way of documenting the cultures of the African tribes he was studying. The use of the camera to provide detailed records of cultural practices was already a common part of the fieldwork of anthropologists at this time. Rouch's approach to filmmaking, however, became part of his polemic against the traditional methods of anthropology, a discipline in which, he argued, privileged social scientists questioned "primitive" people. He felt that this approach was complicit with colonialism and advocated an alternative conception of an "anthropological dialogue between people belonging to different cultures."[5] The implications of Rouch's critique of anthropological methods would have a strong influence on the documentary movement that became known as "direct cinema."

This movement depended on the portable sixteen-millimetre equipment developed for use by anthropologists working in remote areas. When documentary filmmakers in many countries (including Canada) started to use this equipment in the 1950s, the debate that ensued raised issues closely related to Rouch's questions about established anthropological practices. In their influential survey of the ideological implications of various forms of cinema, Jean-Luc Comolli and Jean Narboni distinguished between two kinds of direct cinema. The first kind, which used the new equipment as a means of achieving a greater realism or "authenticity," assumed that "seeing is understanding." Like the anthropological practices that Rouch criticized, Comolli and Narboni argued, this approach to direct cinema did not question the role of the filmmakers in constructing the reality that they claimed to be recording, and it thus simply reinforced the dominant ideology. It is not surprising that Rouch was a key figure in the development of a second kind of direct cinema that "attacks the basic problem of depiction" so that it "becomes productive of meaning and not just a passive receptacle for meaning produced outside it (in the ideology)."[6]

Many of the filmmakers and critics who supported this critical approach to direct cinema objected to the term *cinéma-vérité*, the first name proposed for the films made with the new equipemnt. Like the term "candid eye" applied to the Unit B films, the equation of "cinema" and "truth" seemed to imply an immediate access to a reality unaffected by the practices of the filmmaker. They preferred the term "direct cinema" (which Comolli and Narboni use for both kinds) because it acknowledged the participation of the filmmaker in the events depicted in the film. Rouch, however, continued to use the term *cinéma-vérité*, emphasizing its derivation from the term *kinopravda* used by the Soviet filmmaker Dziga Vertov. He argued that the truth (*vérité*) that emerges is specifically cinematic, "a new truth … which has nothing to do with normal reality" but is the product of the camera's presence as "an incredible stimulant for the observed as well as the observer."[7]

The new lightweight equipment enabled filmmakers to respond quickly to changes in the situations being filmed. Rouch was especially interested in the possibilities of the hand-held camera, and this interest brought him into contact with Canadian filmmakers. Although Pierre Lamy claimed that Jutra learnt the use of the "mobile camera" from Rouch, both Jutra and Rouch also acknowledged the influence of Unit B's "Candid Eye" films.[8] Jutra admired the use of the hand-held camera in *Pilgrimage* (1958) to film a crowd of pilgrims filing up to Brother André's tomb; and Rouch credited the NFB with first freeing the camera from the tripod, stressing the impact of a shot in *The Days before Christmas* "when the camera follows the revolver of the bank guard."[9]

Both of these films were directed by Terence Macartney-Filgate, but several cinematographers made important contributions. The two shots in question were often attributed to Michel Brault (although the shot in which a hand-held camera follows a bank guard from inside a story to a security van in the street was actually improvised by Roman Kroitor).[10] Rouch met Brault at the 1958 Flaherty Seminar in California and was highly impressed by his work on *Les Raquetteurs* (1958). Later, when Rouch needed a cinematographer willing to experiment with the possibilities of a newly developed lightweight sixteen-millimetre camera, he remembered Brault and invited him to Paris to work on *Chronique d'un été* (*Chronicle of a Summer*, 1960). As Rouch himself suggested, the result was a film "in which the camera itself becomes just as much alive as the people it is filming."[11]

After a three-day conference on *cinéma-vérité* at Lyon in 1963, British critic Ian Cameron commented that "taking the camera off the tripod is like being cured of a paralysis" and that this new freedom allowed the documentary to present "real events with the immediacy which has previously been lacking." But this gain in immediacy inevitably led to a loss of stability. Cameron himself felt that "the instability of the picture" in one of Rouch's early films was a slight drawback; in fact, the unstable image is at the core of Rouch's project.[12] It challenged the tradition of the centred eye in Western perspective painting, which stressed that seeing is understanding and which had greatly influenced the visual style of classical narrative cinema and documentary filmmaking.[13] The prevalence of hand-held camera work in contemporary television news programs testifies to the ultimate triumph of Rouch's aesthetic, but television initially adopted cinematic norms and rejected "films shot without a tripod ... because of the consequent lack of stability."[14]

The unstable eye in Rouch's films affirms the value of doubt. He argued that "the moment you have doubts, everything is possible."[15] Jutra very much shared this attitude; characteristically, he even had doubts about Rouch. He insisted that he did not admire Rouch "without reservations" and claimed that "every act of homage includes an element of denunciation."[16] In particular, he thought that Rouch's influence in Canada led to a period of "psychological, almost sexual, fixation on the camera."[17] Despite these doubts, the unstable tension between fiction and documentary in Rouch's films, and the way he used this tension to unsettle colonialist attitudes, deeply influenced Jutra's thinking about cinema.

Jutra described Rouch as behaving like "a truant schoolboy" amusing himself "like a madman all the time," thereby investing Rouch with the ambivalence and fascination associated with childhood and madness in many of Jutra's later films. This playful approach involved a refusal to adopt the professional persona of the mature intellectual and challenged the detachment that separates traditional ethnographers from their "primitive" subjects. Jutra accurately characterized Rouch's cinema as a repudiation of an "ethnography that consists of taking snapshots of a civilization, of mummifying living beings" and an attempt to construct "new relationships between men previously unknown to each other ... breaking down ... geographic, cultural, linguistic, and racial divisions."[18]

Rouch's anti-colonial perspective offered an alternative to what Bruce Elder has called the "colonized outlook" of the Unit B filmmakers, an outlook grounded in "a form of consciousness which is alienated from the world and ... limited to passive observation."[19] In films like *Moi, un noir* and *Jaguar* (1967), Rouch collaborated with his subjects to develop fictional narratives based on their own everyday lives. As Jutra noted, Rouch placed his nonprofessional actors in familiar situations and filmed their responses. In the process of making the film, "new situations emerged which were as true as the first," with the result that the story "really unfolded in front of the camera, but ... unfolded because the camera was there."[20]

Jutra insisted that the tension between fiction and reality is vital to the dual perspective that emerges from Rouch's films, bringing together views from inside and outside the culture. He argued that Rouch used the camera as "a catalyst that releases authentic human reactions," while the fictional elements in his films worked to promote "new relationships."[21] Just as the hand-held camera leads to a visual instability, the films expose the contradictions in the colonial experience and undermine the ideological stability of the dominant cultural attitudes.

Jutra's account of Rouch's methods foreshadows his own approach in *À tout prendre*. The transgression of the boundaries between documentary and fiction, however, inevitably led to criticism both from supporters of traditional documentary and from critics accustomed to the norms of classical narrative cinema. From a documentary perspective, Claude Lévi-Strauss (who was himself an anthropologist) reasserted the opposition between truth and fiction that Rouch was trying to undermine when he warned against the danger of "prostituting" truth to fiction by transforming it into "spectacle."[22] On the other hand, as Jean-André Fieschi has pointed out, the unconventional fictional elements in Rouch's films caused "discomfort" for unprepared audiences who regarded him as a "film maker unacquainted with continuity, dramatic construction, rounded characters."[23]

These criticisms are precisely those that would later be directed at *À tout prendre*, and Fieschi's discussion of Rouch illuminates the underlying attitudes that affected the reception of many of Jutra's films. According to Fieschi, Rouch's films reveal "the *materiality* of the cinema itself" through the creation of "an elusive subjectivity that is simultaneously present and withdrawn as it is being formulated." Rouch films "not just behaviour, or dreams, or subjective themes, but the indissoluble amalgam binding them together."[24] This unstable vision is often disturbing for spectators precisely because it opposes what Mick Eaton calls "those discourses which are at the disposal of those who have so much invested in a world which can be easily rendered visible and available for our gaze."[25]

Jutra in Africa

The major product of Jutra's experiences with Rouch was *Le Niger jeune république*, a film nominally produced by the NFB but whose final form owed a great deal to Rouch. Jutra acknowledged that Rouch had taught him all that he knew about Niger and that, "in several sequences, he told me what to film."[26] Rouch also acted as a "catalyst" and "demiurge" during the shooting of an animist ceremony, but the film presents itself as Jutra's personal view of the African country, a more detached and organized perspective than that found in Rouch's films on Africa.[27] Although he had originally intended to include interviews with local politicians and bureaucrats to whom Rouch had introduced him, he decided to cut most of this interview material "in order to focus his attention on the people."[28]

The film's "unusual simplicity" led Robert Daudelin to declare (in 1967) that *Le Niger jeune république* was Jutra's best film, preferring its restraint to the formalist excesses that he found in *À tout prendre*.[29] The film's opening sequence signals its basic strategy. After a cut from native drummers to a plane landing, Jutra describes himself arriving to "find the secret of the country." However, unlike the active investigator that the pursuit of a secret implies, Jutra claims that he "abandoned" himself to "the torrent of impressions" and let himself "be carried away by the vitality" around him. It is as if the "vitality" of the subject matter discourages the filmmaker from embellishing the material through cinematic means, although the editing constantly imposes structure on what we see and Jutra frequently offers his opinions in the commentary.

The contrast between the flow of African life and the shape that the film imposes on it implicitly acknowledges the documentary lie that *Félix Leclerc troubadour* explicitly unmasked. As filmmaker and commentator, Jutra mediates between Niger and Quebec, focusing attention on what the commentary describes as a process of "decolonization" that involves the passage "from childhood to adulthood" and the attempt to "harmonize the traditional and the modern." In discussing the film with Michel Brulé, Jutra insisted on his concern with "the phenomenon of decolonization" and claimed to feel "more African than Canadian."[30] At least one reviewer felt that Jutra's claim that he let himself be carried along by "the torrent of impressions" also applied to the effect of the film on the spectator with the result that "for a while, one feels more African than Canadian."[31]

Since Jutra presents himself as an outsider exploring an alien culture, the sense of being "more African than Canadian" is not only a case of cross-cultural identification but an implicit allusion to the "colonial" experience in Quebec.[32] The film's depiction of the struggle to overcome traditional ways of seeing and colonial attitudes in Africa suggests that a similar struggle is needed in Quebec. In his commentary, Jutra claims that the two major challenges facing Niger are "education and the economy," and the film stresses the importance of "progress" in decolonizing the country. It implies the need for an acceleration of the Quiet Revolution in Quebec, although its treatment of the contradictions of modern life in Niger sometimes seems to undercut a simple advocacy of industrial and technological development.

When a former resistance fighter unexpectedly speaks of the good things that the white rulers brought to Niger, these things can presumably be summarized under the heading of progress. However, the film's utopian vision of Niger's future places more emphasis on a synthesis of contradictions than on the linear model of sweeping away the old ways through the introduction of modern technology. The march of progress has its costs, and Jutra insists in the commentary that "Niger cannot become a modern country until it overcomes the giant problem of the industrial irrigation of the whole land," thereby destroying the traditional nomadic way of life of the Tuareg people.

The unwillingness of nomadic peoples to settle down contributes to the sense of flow that Jutra found in Africa, and he also describes the matriarchal Tuareg culture as "feminism before the letter." Their tribal customs must give way not just to technological developments such as irrigation schemes and the intrusion of motorized vehicles into the desert but also to the political need of newly independent nations like Niger to assert their boundaries. Jutra's rather brutal comment that the Tuareg must "assimilate or disappear" has clear relevance to Quebec, although its implications in the Canadian context remain uncertain.

The processes leading to the destruction of the Tuareg culture also conflict with what Jutra calls "the resignation of the collective," inherent in the religious teachings of Islam. Although he shows regret for the decline of the nomadic way of life, he is less sympathetic to what he sees as fixed and dogmatic religious attitudes. The relationship between the old and the new, which the film often highlights through montage, emerges as an inherently unstable one further complicated by the contrast between the "lunar landscape" of the desert and the "great fecund river" from which the country takes its name. The "vitality" of the country that produces "the torrent of impressions" owes much to the diverse environments that it encompasses and to what the commentary calls the "ethnic complexity of the people," their "cross-breeding" (*métissage*).

The implications of *métissage* become highly visible in a sequence that contrasts the religious practices of the Islamic community with "the ancient religion of the blacks." Despite the opposition of Islam to the spirit of progress, the traditional muezzin call is broadcast by radio, and Jutra comments that "the minarets change their form but Islam remains the same." The coexistence of old and new is both less stable and more productive in the indigenous animist rituals that, according to Jutra, evolved from the confrontation with "hostile nature." After we witness a possessed man dancing in a ceremony to contact the "souls of the departed," there is an abrupt cut to a medical building where one of the priests works as a "technical agent." We also learn that he is the secretary of a political party, while at home his four wives and nine children live together in the family compound.

The *métissage* that we see in the film is between the traditional and the modern rather than among the various groups who make up the nation. It involves productive use of contradictions between new and old ways. Although the commentary stresses the need for industrial progress, the film as a whole implies that the new nation can become unified only through the acceptance of hybrid cultural forms. In this spirit, a montage effect, near the end of the film, juxtaposes traditional chanting in an African village, recently reconstructed as a museum, with jazz being performed on traditional African instruments in a modern nightclub.

The tension between the film's official progressive ideology and its contradictory discourse emerges clearly in its treatment of education. Education is necessary to modernize the country but resisted by the Tuareg people who, Jutra informs us, tell their children that school is evil. When Jutra finally shows us a school, we see black youths in a philosophy class being taught by a white teacher. Black teachers appear in a montage sequence that shows several different classrooms, but the depiction of the school ends in a classroom where young pupils are watched over by their mothers who pound grain in the traditional manner as the lesson proceeds. On the soundtrack, Jutra comments wryly that there is "still a lot to do."

After shots of the opening of a new bridge across the river and of modern urban buildings, we see the president in an open car. Jutra declares (to him? to us?) that "freedom is also responsibility" and that Niger must now speak for itself. The film ends with a shot of children rushing towards the camera, providing what one reviewer called "an image-symbol of the new Niger."[33] This image also implies that the passage to adulthood still has to be completed, but the tensions at work within *Le Niger jeune république* (despite its relatively straightforward documentary approach) suggest reservations about the terms in which adulthood is defined in modern Western ideology. Despite Jutra's lifelong commitment to the separatist option, the analogy between

Niger and Quebec also suggests that independence will not by itself resolve the complex cultural issues to which the film draws our attention.

Rouchian Filmmaking at the NFB

On his return to Canada, where he finished editing *Le Niger jeune république*, Jutra found himself caught up in the collective spirit that animated the French Unit at the NFB. He was involved in the two most ambitious collective films made at this time, *La Lutte* and *A Saint-Henri le cinq Septembre*, and also assisted in the making of two other key films: he was one of four cameramen on Gilles Groulx's *Golden Gloves* (1961), and, according to Rouch, he assisted Pierre Perrault in editing *Pour la suite du monde* (1963).[34] He was also one of the main targets of an attack on Rouch's influence on Quebec filmmakers.

In 1962 Jean Pierre Lefebvre and Jean-Claude Pilon published an article condemning the recent documentary films produced by the French Unit and placing the blame for the problems on Rouch's influence. They suggested that the films suffered from a disease called "Roucheole," a rather laboured pun on the French word for measles. After succinctly defining Rouch's concept of *cinéma-vérité* as "the desire to make the camera *present* and thus to provoke in the non-professional actor an artificial reaction supposedly closer to the truth," the authors point out that this approach is different from that of the Unit B filmmakers whom they describe as "photographing people unawares." Nevertheless, they attribute the "dissipation that currently characterizes the output of the French Unit at the NFB" to the "simultaneous influence of the 'candid eye,' of Rouchian '*cinéma-vérité*,' and of a certain bastard cinema destined for television."[35]

The bulk of the article was devoted to an attack on *Québec-USA* (1962), codirected by Jutra and Brault, the two Quebec filmmakers most closely associated with Rouch. Lefebvre and Pilon used this film to illustrate what they regarded as three interconnected problems in the films of the French Unit: first, an apparent delight in ridiculing the people depicted in the films; second, a tendency to make films in collaboration, which, the authors suggested, might work well for English-Canadian filmmakers but is incompatible with "the individualism characteristic of the Latin temperament"; and third, a rejection of the constraints of a script, leading to irresponsibility, laziness, and a lack of artistic unity. As an illustration of these charges, the critics condemned *Québec-USA* as "a film from which love is literally absent" in which Jutra and Brault "amuse themselves ... like two young adolescents" at the expense of American tourists in Quebec City.[36]

Rouch's influence is vaguely defined in the article and only loosely linked to the alleged deficiencies of *Québec-USA*. Brault's virtuoso use of the hand-held camera does perhaps illustrate the fetishization of the camera that Jutra himself (who only contributed to the editing of this film) saw as a side effect of the new freedom. However, its playful depiction of American tourists "invading" Quebec City does expose the colonial basis of Quebec culture. A francophone student speaks English as he acts as guide to the historical sites for a middle-class black couple from the United States. Sound recorded in a language laboratory acts as a counterpoint to touristic images of the city. The film's satiric thrust centres on the implications of Quebec as a site/sight for the tourist gaze, and the alleged absence of "love" is best seen as the product of a colonized culture rather than as a component of the playfully "irresponsible" way in which the filmmakers disrupt documentary conventions.

What is at stake in this attack on *Québec-USA* is clearly a conflict between two different approaches to filmmaking soon to become apparent in the feature films of Jutra and Lefebvre. A more sympathetic view of the work of the French Unit at this time emerges from David Clandfield's comparison of this approach to direct cinema with the work of Unit B. Using terms close to those of Comolli and Narboni, Clandfield distinguishes between "the dispassionate empiricism" of the "Candid Eye" filmmakers, for whom "the subject of the film was its subject-matter rooted in objective reality," and "the overt personal involvement" of the French Unit filmmakers, for whom "the point of departure is the filmmaking process in which the filmmaker is deeply implicated as a consciousness, individual or collective."[37]

Clandfield describes the approach of the French Unit in terms that bring out the parallels with Rouch: "Instead of effacing his presence, the filmmaker will affirm it. Instead of rendering the technical process transparent (supposedly), he will emphasize its materiality. Instead of standing apart from his object of study or inquiry, he will implicate himself within it."[38] Contrary to the objections made by Lefebvre and Pilon, Clandfield argues that, by rejecting any claims to objectivity and "immediacy," the French Unit filmmakers bridged the gap between the personal and the collective and created what Gilles Carle called "a passionate appropriation of the cultural environment [*milieu*]" in which "the picturesque (the outsider's view) has yielded to the familiar."[39]

According to Clandfield, these goals were most fully achieved "in the two years, 1961 and 1962, when the French Unit operated as a tightly-knit team."[40] Through his involvement in the two major collective projects undertaken in these years, Jutra must have been very much aware of the ongoing debates over the implications of the direct cinema approach.

La Lutte is a film about professional wrestling in which ten cameras were used to film an evening's entertainment. Jutra's assignment was to film the spectators, whose responses are more important than the action in the ring to a film that, like many of those produced by the French Unit, dealt with "the rituals of the urban masses."[41] He was also apparently responsible for the episode in which the excited interjections of a supposedly Russian wrestler are subtitled in Russian.[42] The film has no commentary, and its playful attitude to its subject comes through in such ironic devices as the use of harpsichord music by Bach to accompany the wrestling in a sequence edited by Jutra.[43]

A Saint-Henri le Cinq Septembre was a very different kind of project in which thirty NFB filmmakers descended on a working-class district in Montreal to record a day in the life of its inhabitants. The aim was to inject a more political engagement with Quebec culture into the work of the French Unit. The film's producer, Fernand Dansereau, later disowned its methods on the grounds that they still "involved an *outsider's* observations, despite the makers' good intentions."[44] However, this judgment is already incorporated into the film itself through its self-reflexive commentary, written by Jacques Godbout, which raises the issue of the relationship of the filmmakers to the people they are filming and admits at the end that "Saint-Henri has still not yielded its secret."

The differences between these two films have to do with the problem of how to organize the perceptions made possible through the techniques of direct cinema. Both strain towards fiction, *La Lutte* in its formalistic tendencies and *A Saint-Henri le Cinq Septembre* in its "literary" commentary. While each film offers a fascinating vision of a milieu, neither completely succeeds in bringing about the appropriation that would allow the filmmaker (and the spectator) to assume a position other than that of the outsider. Despite their very different approaches, both films generate an unstable tension between the picturesque and the familiar. Neither could be described simply as a Rouchian film, but a similar tension is at work in Rouch's ethnographic explorations of everyday life in Africa and Paris.

At the same time as the French Unit was making these films, several NFB filmmakers were already exploring the possibilities of direct cinema for fiction filmmaking in another collective project that would eventually become Jutra's *À tout prendre*.

Above: Claude (Jutra) and Victor (Désy) discuss Proust and human relationships (Collection Cinémathèque Québécoise)

Below: Claude comforts Johanne (Johanne Harelle) after her confession (Collection Cinémathèque Québécoise)

PHANTOM OF REALITY
À tout prendre

By making an independent feature film in Quebec, when there was little cultural and virtually no industrial support, Jutra felt that he was doing the impossible. Yet the effect was strangely euphoric: "everything became possible," and he found himself working with "an incredible freedom."[1] He later remarked that he began *À tout prendre* "in a vacuum" and that "because I had nothing to lose, I put everything into it."[2] As Jacques Lacan suggested, however, "saying it all is literally impossible: words fail," although Lacan was careful to add that "it's through this very impossibility that the truth holds onto the real."[3] The impossibility of Quebec cinema and the impossibility of total communication set the terms of the aesthetics of failure in *À tout prendre*. It is an attempt to say it all and to make the production of a film into the utopian emblem of a free society, while at the same time reflecting on the necessary impossibility of this task.

Usually (mis)translated into English as *Take It All*, the film's title is more accurately rendered as "All Things Considered" or "When All's Said and Done." It is a colloquial phrase, a kind of verbal shrug, spoken in the film by Claude when, unable to cope with the prospect of becoming a father, he decides to apply for a bank loan to finance an abortion. The title thus links the demands of an all-or-nothing logic to the failure of the protagonist (which eventually results in his disappearance from the film); but the pressures on the character also reflect the film's "failure" to find a coherent way of saying "everything" about Claude's dilemma.

Since Jutra not only directed but played the central character in a narrative based on his recently ended affair with a black woman, many critics understandably treated it as a personal and autobiographical statement. They saw little or no difference between the character and the director and, using standards that the film itself explicitly rejects as inappropriate to its cultural context, declared *À tout prendre* a failure. Claude's humiliating visit to the bank mirrored Jutra's need to take out a personal loan (of fifteen thousand dollars) to finance the project. However, the director wanted the money not for an abortion but to create a rich and complex film that uses the idea of failure to explore the contradictions involved in living and working in a culture in which "success" is possible only by imitating models imported from elsewhere.

Although it won the prize for best Canadian film at the Montreal Film Festival in August 1963, *À tout prendre* was not a commercial success when it finally opened to the public in Montreal in May 1964. Jutra was frustrated by the delays in obtaining a commercial release and by the lack of interest shown by distributors and exhibitors, and he was never able to raise the money to revise the somewhat provisional version of the film that he had prepared for the Film Festival.

Despite its disappointing initial reception, a few critics have defended *À tout prendre* as a significant cultural and cinematic achievement. After seeing the film at the festival, Colin Young wrote a review for *Film Quarterly* in which he enthusiastically, if rather oddly, described it as "the only thoroughly *contemporary* American (albeit French-Canadian) film of my generation."[4] Dominique Noguez, a French critic who spent some time in Quebec in the 1960s, protested against the "scandalous … misrecognition" of the film in Europe, and Jean Rouch remained committed to a film that he regarded as "one of the major films not only of Quebec cinema but of world cinema."[5]

I do not intend to try to substantiate Rouch's claim (the history of the film's reception ensures that it will always have a marginal place in "world cinema") but rather to identify the causes of its "misrecognition" and to explore the way the film relates to its cultural context through its aesthetics of failure.

Production and Reception

It started out in 1961 as a collective project involving Jutra, Claude Fournier, and Michel Brault. All three had worked at the NFB, but they now wanted to apply the lessons of direct cinema to the production of a fiction film. The project soon began to look impossible, and the economic difficulties frequently brought the production to a halt. Fournier left for New York to work with Richard Leacock, and Brault was also absent for extended periods, working with Rouch in France and on *Pour la suite du monde* with Pierre Perrault. The original group thus "gradually disintegrated."[6]

What Jutra called "an adventure in objectivity," a fiction film using the methods of direct cinema, gradually became a "subjective" film with "an obvious narcissistic element."[7] One reviewer thought that the film became a "self-indulgent sarabande" in which Jutra performed a kind of "moral strip-tease."[8] Yet Jutra always insisted that the film remained "a collective creation" to which everybody involved (in front of and behind the camera) contributed, causing the film to deviate from his own reality. During the production process, "no function was defined" and ideas were exchanged in a spirit of give and take.[9]

Jutra called the film a "re-happening" because "it reproduced something that had in effect already happened," but this term also implies that, as with the theatrical "happening," the film's final shape could only be roughly planned in advance. The tension between the impossible attempt to replicate past events and an openness to the evolving situation in front of the camera is characteristic of the Rouchian approach to direct cinema. In *À tout prendre*, improvised performances complemented the fluidity of the production process, but since these performances were being created by people who had lived through the events depicted, which had "ended badly," the result was that old tensions resurfaced and new ones developed during the shooting.[10]

These tensions weighed most heavily on Johanne Harelle, who played herself in a narrative based on the breakdown of her relationship with Jutra. In what Jutra called "one of the crucial scenes in the film," she confesses to Claude that she is not Haitian, as she had claimed, but was born in Montreal. The pressures of re-enacting this emotional episode were so great that she could not bring herself to do it under Jutra's direction. A few days later, Brault stepped in and "directed" the sequence: he apparently placed the camera in front of the couple, set it running with a half-hour reel of film, and then left them alone.[11] Although this long take was broken up in the film by a number of jump cuts, the sequence has a concentrated quality that, as Young noted in his review, sets it apart from the instability of the images and the editing in the rest of the film.[12] The shift in style underlines the significance of the moment, but the visible pressures hover uncomfortably between fiction and reality.

Such pressures and tensions led to questions about the basic strategy of applying the techniques of direct cinema to a fiction film. Although he valued the comment of Edgar Morin, the French anthropologist and film theorist (who later married Johanne Harelle), that the film "found the right tone for speaking of oneself in cinema," Jutra came to wish that he could "efface all the information that exists about *À tout prendre* and not say that it is a film about myself."[13]

Morin had collaborated with Rouch on *Chronique d'un été* and his approval suggests that *À tout prendre* succeeded in creating a Rouchian blend of subjective and objective, fiction and documentary. However, while he set out to make a film "in the manner of Rouch," Jutra came to the conclusion that *À tout prendre* is "cinéma-vérité only insofar as it is autobiographical." He now felt that Rouch's "obsession with truth [*vérité*] ... is questionable" and claimed that he was "searching for another truth, that of memory." Even this truth was not self-evident because the actors had grown older since the original events occurred, and Jutra found that the production took on a life of its own. The truth of memory came up against "the terrible precision of the image" about which Jutra had learned while working with McLaren.[14]

The pressures and tensions at work in the production process probably contributed to the disruptive formal effects that alienated many critics. Louis Marcorelles complained that the film contained "too many pirouettes" and that the blending of documentary and fiction techniques led to a disconcerting "mannerism."[15] In his book on the "Young Canadian Cinema," René Prédal also objected that "its style hesitates ... between *cinéma-vérité* and dramatic cinema."[16] In his devastating review of the film on its US release, John Simon called it "a vastly self-indulgent and derivative film" in which "the story is too much Jutra's own, and the technique too much everybody else's," concluding that the film, like its protagonist, "lacks center."[17]

On the other hand, Colin Young valued the film precisely because of its refusal to adopt "the usual one-track concentration of a conventional scenario." Young rejected the idea that "'art' must abstract from 'life'" and expressed a preference for films that are true to "the multivalence of an actual, untidy event." But he insisted that the film does not lack form and argued that the "directorial and editorial flourishes" help to make the film "revolutionary (in its structure and narrative form)."[18]

Young was clearly very much in tune with the film's project, and Jutra appreciated his attempt to demonstrate that the film is "North American in spirit, rather than European." He contrasted Young's review with the largely negative review that appeared in a Quebec film journal. The journal was called *Objectif* but Jutra complained that this review was far from objective because it did not even "take the trouble to justify" its "supremely contemptuous insinuations."[19]

In effect, the *Objectif* review, written by Michel Patenaude, took the same position as Simon, objecting that the film tries out "all styles imaginable, without ever adopting its own." As a result of this formal instability, Patenaude claimed, the audience is unable to identify with the characters, who seem like "distant beings" whom we cannot "get to know" because "the process of integration which turns an actor into a film character is incomplete."[20] As both Patenaude and Simon made clear, *À tout prendre* must be judged a failure in terms of the practices of classical narrative cinema.

As we have seen, however, Jutra claimed that making a film in Quebec was in itself "a political act."[21] The formal strategies of *À tout prendre* thus imply that the tensions and contradictions of contemporary Quebec culture simply could not be expressed through the conventions of classical narrative cinema. Opinion was divided, to say the least, about the ideological implications of Jutra's alternative approach.

Jean Basile and Gilles Marsolais both thought that the film reflected recent changes in Quebec culture. Basile argued that the urban setting represented a "definitive" break with the "folklore" image of Quebec.[22] Marsolais linked the film's break with the past to its subjective approach by suggesting that, "before moving on," Claude "must first disengage himself from an oppressive and cherished past." He argued that the film's depiction of this process accurately reflected "our situation in Quebec."[23]

Other critics expressed disappointment that *À tout prendre* did not directly address the political situation. The film's refusal to relate Claude's experience explicitly to the separatist debate, and the ambiguity generated by the film's formal play with the codes of documentary and fiction cinema, led to attacks from critics who usually supported new cinematic initiatives in Quebec. Léo Bonneville, for example, felt that the only rebellion in the film takes place "at the level of the individual," suggesting that Claude remains dissatisfied despite the "freedom" that he achieves, just as Jutra's "free" style only leads to an "impasse."[24] In an article on "cinema and sexuality" published in the radical cultural review *Parti Pris*, Denys Arcand also raised doubts about whether the film really broke with the ideology of the old Quebec, arguing that the rejection of "the farms and rural churches of our ancestors" was only superficial and that Claude's affair with Johanne showed the traditional French-Canadian male's attraction to "foreign" women.[25]

Despite Arcand's insistence that the film did not really challenge sexual and cultural stereotypes, the Catholic church condemned the film because of its depiction of an adulterous relationship. Most reviewers, however, ignored the issues of sexual morality and identity. Some did suggest that the autobiographical perspective was unfair to Johanne, and Jutra himself said that he would like to have "got closer to the character of Johanne."[26] It was not until twenty years later that a feminist critic related the "mythic presentation of the black woman" to Jutra's homosexuality.[27]

Given the public awareness of the film's autobiographical origins, Claude's homosexual experience was a virtual confession on Jutra's part at a time when Canadian society had only just begun to question traditional gender codes. When an English-language version (prepared by Jutra with the help of Leonard Cohen) was shown on CBC television in April 1965, a number of cuts were made, ostensibly for reasons of time but actually to remove all references to Claude's homosexual tendencies. Ironically, when a complete English-language version was released in the United States in April 1966, Bosley Crowther felt that Jutra had felt obliged "to work ... in" a homosexual episode just to show that this is "an avant-garde picture."[28] In Quebec the question of Claude's sexual orientation was not subject to censorship or dismissed as modish but simply ignored, although it may lie behind frequent references to Jutra's lack of "presence" as an actor and to the "clumsiness" of certain (unspecified) sequences.[29]

Apart from the few defenders of the film mentioned above, the critical consensus on *À tout prendre* has been that it is historically important but suffers from major formal and ideological weaknesses that diminish its impact. Gilles Groulx's *Le Chat dans le sac*, released in the following year, is usually regarded as the first major film of the new Quebec cinema. I will argue that this assessment is based on a misunderstanding of *À tout prendre* that derives from the cinematic and cultural context in which the film was made, and that the film anticipates (perhaps even invites?) this misunderstanding.

Life after Life

The opening sequences cue the spectator to expect a film that will not operate according to the norms of classical narrative cinema. We are immediately confronted with an image of a young man (played by Jutra and soon to be identified as "Claude") sitting on the floor, reading a copy of *Life* magazine.

On the soundtrack, we hear him describe the pleasure he receives from reading the magazine every week. He claims that it offers an image of modern life as "beautiful," "fascinating," and "easy." To emphasize his point, he turns the magazine towards the camera to reveal a double-page photograph of Marilyn Monroe, on which the camera zooms in, accompanied by a "wolf-whistle." An off-screen voice then asks Claude if he is going to a party (in hindsight, we can identify this voice with Victor, an actor who lives next door but whom we will not see until later in the film). Claude replies that he will not go, but a debate ensues between two "inner voices" that ends when he changes his mind.

Claude's immersion in *Life* identifies him with the new Quebec, shaped by the Quiet Revolution, for whom the United States represented a progressive and dynamic culture opposed to the inward-looking moral values of traditional Quebec society. Yet the fact that Claude reads about "life" in an English-language magazine while commenting on it in French begins to suggest that the richness of life that fascinates him is "elsewhere," and the film will quickly confirm the comparative poverty of Claude's experience in Quebec.

Since *Life* is not life, however, but glossy images that claim to represent life (the Monroe image is a publicity photograph taken on a film set), this opening shot also questions the validity of the media images to which the reality of life in Quebec is compared and found wanting. The film later explores the problematic relationship of image to life more fully, but the complexity of the initial image, the product of a "poor" cinema with its roots in the direct cinema tradition, suggests that richness is not a question of material and technical resources but of openness to the contradictions and pressures of modern cultural experience.

The image of Monroe relates the film's cultural politics to its treatment of sexuality. Claude draws attention to the erotic power of the glamour image, and the whistle (presumably Claude's but seeming to act as a stand-in for the spectator's response) invites us to share his appreciation. This attitude to women reappears during his (and our) first encounter with Johanne, but the allusion to Monroe already introduces some disturbing overtones. The image shown is one of the famous stills from the "nude" bathing sequence in the star's last, uncompleted film, *Something's Got to Give*. Monroe died while *À tout prendre* was in production, and the gaze invited by the titillating image (the woman's supposedly naked body coyly concealed by the edge of the pool) foreshadows the pressures on Johanne that lead her to the verge of suicide when Claude breaks off their relationship.

Claude's acknowledgment of the camera's presence when he holds up the magazine also defies the codes of classical narrative cinema in which the camera functions both as an invisible observer of events and as a means of involving the spectator with a character's viewpoint. Although direct address to the camera does not occur again, the effect is to set up an unsettled relationship between spectator and camera/screen that does not allow the spectator to identify with Claude in the way that Hollywood cinema has made familiar.[30]

In addition to this disruption of the expected smooth alignment of the looks of camera, character, and spectator, those aware of Jutra's multiple roles in the making of the film could find a similar tension in his involvement as director, actor, and character in a work based on his own recent experiences. These tensions sometimes went unnoticed, as when Joan Fox simply referred to the "hero" as "Jutra … a Frenchman."[31] However, the original audience in Quebec included Jutra's "friends" (as Marcorelles stressed in his review), as well as many people who were aware of the autobiographical premise and some who were familiar only with Jutra's public image, and these varied levels of awareness inevitably complicated the film's play with the relationship of the spectator to camera and character.[32]

Claude's voice can initially be taken either as an inner voice expressing his thoughts as he reads the magazine or as a documentary voice commenting on the image at a later time (a frequent device in Rouch's films and in the NFB's direct cinema documentaries). The introduction of another voice emerging from an undefined off-screen space indicates that we are dealing with "dramatic" fiction, but the lack of a cut-away to reveal the source of this voice leaves us disoriented. After Claude says goodbye to the owner of the voice, the situation becomes even more complicated when another voice interrupts what we now take to be his inner voice. The first voice insists that Claude hates "surprise parties" and has a lot of work to do, but the other convinces him that he hates work more than he hates parties.

In this opening shot, the uncertain status of image and sound in the film becomes associated with Claude's indecisiveness, itself a product of his inability to define himself in relation to the world around him. A rapid montage of shots extends this unsettling effect. Several extreme close-ups show various parts of Claude's body as he prepares to go out, and the two voices discuss his "fear of work," one of them suddenly rendered unintelligible because he is brushing his teeth. When Claude looks at himself in a mirror, one of the voices comments that he always seems to be running away, but the other reminds him that he still has his "youth." The camera immediately zooms in on his face in the mirror, and choral music swells up briefly on the soundtrack. These effects, which amount to a cinematic underlining of the word youth, emphasize that Claude is an adolescent faced with the difficult passage into adulthood.

In fact, Jutra was already in his thirties when he made *À tout prendre*, and Claude now suggests that he may be faced with his "last chance." But because the zoom and the burst of music are so obtrusive, the spectator is cued to expect that the film will not make its points subtly, allowing them to arise naturally from the narrative (as, ideally, in classical narrative cinema). The experience of the film encourages an awareness that Claude's dilemmas, whatever personal or cultural "truth" they may represent, are images constructed by a cinematic apparatus.

As he stands in front of the mirror, Claude refers to "all these characters inside me," and we then see some of these characters reflected in the mirror, as if he is trying out various roles. First, we see him as a "rebel" in a leather jacket, declaring his hatred of the world; then he appears as an aristocratic figure, with a monocle and a moustache, who enjoys seeing others suffer. The final image is that of a gangster, wearing dark glasses, who shoots at the mirror, but before this figure appears, we indistinctly hear a baby crying and Claude appears briefly in the mirror dressed as a clown. Because the clown does not speak and because the image is registered almost subliminally, it seems that this role has been forcibly suppressed, suggesting that it is too uncomfortable for Claude, the product of a self that recognizes the immaturity behind his narcissistic concern with his image.

Although the gunshot shatters the mirror, the sequence ends as Claude unconcernedly finishes his preparations in front of an unbroken mirror. The next sequence restates his problem in poetic fashion as he rides his moped through the city at night and his (now single) inner voice expatiates on his lack of experience. Since he has not experienced fear, misery, war, suffering, or a "great love," he fears that he may have nothing to say. His anguished lyricism is abruptly interrupted by a female voice apparently telling him to shut up, followed by laughter. As we soon discover, these sounds are anticipations of the party sequence that follows, but their disruptive effect emphasizes the gap between Claude's attempts to invest his concerns with poetic significance and the inconsequential chatter at the party.

It is at this party that Claude first meets Johanne, but as we have come to expect by now, her introduction into the film defies classical cinematic grammar. After an establishing shot of the guests standing around chatting, a close-up shows the metal bracelets on the arm of a black woman, but this brief shot of a fragment of the woman's body remains unexplained as our attention is shifted back to the party (with jump cuts reducing the trivial conversation to total nonsense; in the English-language version, the subtitles read simply, "Blah, blah, blah" and "Yap, yap, yap"). The arm will soon be identified as Johanne's, but its abrupt insertion into the narrative at this point is not clearly motivated by Claude's consciousness. He does not yet seem to be aware of her presence, but the fragmentary image that anticipates narrative developments functions, like the image of the clown in the mirror and the misplaced laughter from the party, as evidence that Claude is not in control of all that we will see and hear in the film.

The party activities are soon suspended so that the guests can listen to Johanne's song, which is introduced by a woman (off-screen) who explains that it is in Creole and there is little point in trying to understand the lyrics. The performance begins with a shot of Johanne's other arm, which the camera follows as she places it on her forehead and begins to sing. This close-up is then held through the first verses of the song, and it thus becomes the first truly stable shot in the film. Like the opening shot, it is a relatively long take, but here the synchronous sound allows us to focus on the performer. Johanne's image thus seems to respond to the spectator's desire for meaning (even if we have been told not to worry about the meaning of her song), frustrated by the disruptive strategies of the preceding sequences.

In some ways this shot functions in a conventional manner, since Claude's affair with Johanne will offer him a much-needed sense of purpose and become the focus of the film's narrative structure. Yet the shot is not related to Claude's viewpoint until midway through the song, when a reverse shot shows him watching intently. The spectator's desire for meaning is retroactively identified with Claude's and both are tied to the intensity of the gaze he fixes on the woman. Now the film moves quickly to distance itself from the voyeuristic gaze as Claude leans back to ask another guest for the singer's name; the guest replies that he does not know, but the word JOHANNE flashes on a blank screen before we are returned to a close-up of the singer. The film playfully reminds us that it can satisfy or frustrate our desire for meaning in ways that may or may not implicate us in Claude's search.

Style and Narrative

These opening sequences make clear that image making will be one of the film's main concerns, and it is hardly surprising that Johanne turns out to be a fashion model and Claude a filmmaker. What is also clear by now, however, is that this concern with images will be conveyed in a style that constantly disrupts continuity and leaves the spectator scrambling to make sense of the film's own images (and sounds). The narrative core is Claude's relationship with Johanne, which is complicated by his fantasy life, his attraction to other women, and his discovery of his homosexual desires. Despite these problems, they become engaged when Johanne finds that she is pregnant. Claude's mother and a priest both try to persuade him that the marriage cannot work, and he eventually ends the relationship. He raises the money for an abortion, but the pregnancy ends "naturally" as a result of a miscarriage. Although Johanne is distraught and threatens suicide, it is Claude who finally disappears.

Claude's disappearance, in response to the breakdown of his relationship with Johanne, brings the narrative to a bleak end. The film's controversial deployment of mannerist effects seems to support this final sense of loss and failure, since they apparently express Claude's defective subjectivity and (as I will argue shortly) the film's "failure" to achieve the stability associated with conventional film language. However, as my analysis of the opening sequences already suggests, the frequent disruptions of continuity also have a playful quality. Freeze-frames, zooms, and focus shifts are just the most frequent devices that the film uses to provide emphasis and, at the same time, to draw attention to its own workings. The obtrusive visual style, in counterpoint with an equally unconventional soundtrack, distances the spectator from the narrative and creates new cinematic patterns even as it laments the film's inability to conform to the old ones.

The sequence in which Claude applies for a bank loan is an especially remarkable example of the film's deviant strategies. It defies not only the norms of classical cinema but also the terms in which some critics were calling for a new kind of political cinema. The depiction of the bank in this sequence does not fit comfortably into the categories developed by Yves de Laurot in an essay on the different ways cinema can express the statement "In America, the only real temples are banks." He suggests that a filmmaker like Luis Buñuel would "reach for symbols" and "dress up a bank, put a cross here and there, have officiating gestures, ecclesiastical music, and so on." As an alternative to including "things that do not normally belong in a bank," de Laurot advocates an approach that would depend on "a *manner* of seeing the bank as a temple," built up through "the angle we employ for the camera, the hushed footsteps, the shafts of light falling through the window in a certain way, the manner of photographing the teller's bar." De Laurot prefers this approach because it avoids "giving the viewer the impression that he is being masterminded, being given a statement already packaged."[33]

Although de Laurot offers this example in a discussion of radical approaches to political cinema, his preferred option is suspiciously close to classical narrative cinema. The aim is to influence the spectator without giving the impression of doing so. The bank sequence in *À tout prendre* employs cinematic language to construct a way of seeing the bank, as recommended by de Laurot, and does not include things that "do not normally belong" (except for a burst of "ecclesiastical music"). Yet the camera movement and the point of view that it adopts during the interview with the bank manager are so unusual that the spectator must take these strategies into account in trying to assign meaning to the sequence.

It opens with a rapid montage, accompanied by drum beats, in which the camera looks up at and pans wildly over the façade of a high-rise building on which the word BANK is seen. The camera then tracks in front of Claude as he walks up to the door, but instead of entering with him, it withdraws around the corner, following Claude who is barely visible through the dark glass of the bank's windows. As we hear the interview taking place inside in English, the camera remains still, showing the wall of the bank that almost completely obscures a church on the other side of a busy street. A jump cut changes the angle slightly so that cars appear to collide with their own reflections in the wall of the bank. Another cut returns the camera to its original position before it tracks forward to capture Claude's emergence, accompanied by exultant choral music to celebrate his success in obtaining a loan.

Although the opening shots of this sequence may represent Claude's excitement and disorientation, they are not tied to his optical point of view. The device of keeping the camera outside the bank while Claude is inside also suggests that Claude is an outsider in the English-speaking halls of power even when he is physically inside them, but the detachment of the camera from Claude's position invites the spectator to consider the implications of the idea of "bank as temple" for modern Quebec society. Claude is turning to the bank to finance an abortion, after consulting with a priest, and is refusing to become a father in a situation in which his own father is absent from his life as we see it, and in which the power of the Church gives way to the paternalistic authority of the (unseen and thus godlike) English-speaking bank manager (who addresses him paternalistically as "my boy").

The effect of this sequence, and of many similar devices throughout the film, is to create an unstable relationship between the camera's look and Claude's consciousness. This refusal to elide the differences between character and camera encourages a spectatorship based not on being told what to think, as in de Laurot's "Buñuelian" scenario or in voice-of-God documentary, nor on being given the impression of finding out for oneself, as in de Laurot's non-didactic political cinema or in classical narrative cinema. Instead Jutra develops an intricate and playful approach to the contradictions of Quebec's cultural experience and to the conventions of cinematic realism.

Hanging On to the Real

The disruptive strategies through which *À tout prendre* tells Claude's story imply a crisis in cultural and cinematic codes. Just as the film calls into question traditional notions of subjectivity and identity, it places an enormous strain on film language itself. The problem of the "real" and its relationship to the (cinematic and self) image becomes a key issue in the film's depiction of modern urban life in Quebec.

In 1965 Jean Pierre Lefebvre, who had just embarked on his own prolific career as a filmmaker, published an article on the "crisis of language" in Canadian cinema. He begins with a description of a collective "crisis of consciousness" that could easily be applied to Claude's dilemma in *À tout prendre*:

"Incapable of defining ourselves, it is normal that we should be incapable of expressing ourselves."[34] However, Lefebvre rejects the kind of realism with which Jutra depicts Claude's search for identity.

Lefebvre argues that, just as the *chansonniers* translated the vision of Quebec's poets into terms accessible to the general public, filmmakers must combine poetic insight with the unique ability of the medium to reproduce "immediate realities." He points to two major obstacles that make it difficult for filmmakers to meet this challenge. One of these, as with the *chanson*, is the temptation to give in to merely commercial demands; but the more specific problem with which Lefebvre is most concerned derives from the special relationship between film and reality. He cites Alain Robbe-Grillet's complaint that the filmmaker has less control than the writer over the unpredictable aspects of reality, but Lefebvre argues that the unpredictable is "part of the rules of the game" and that filmmakers can move "one step closer to *the truth of the real*" by adapting the unexpected to their own needs. He regards "the candid eye and cinéma-vérité" as a "preliminary stage" that allowed Quebec filmmakers to explore their cultural environment but which ultimately "re-stated the problem of realism in the cinema," as Lefebvre had implied in his earlier attack on *Québec-USA*.[35]

According to Lefebvre, filmmakers must attempt to avoid two extremes: on the one hand, there is the danger of "allowing one's thought to depend on reality, which always appears in a disordered and confused manner"; on the other, there is "the danger of enclosing reality within the idea that one has of it so that it becomes a kind of phantom of reality." Lefebvre refers to *À tout prendre* as "flagrant proof" of the problems associated with the second extreme and cites Gilles Groulx's *Le Chat dans le sac* as the one film to have successfully gone beyond the "preliminary stage" in the journey towards "the truth of the real."[36] Unfortunately he did not go on to identify the qualities that distinguish this film from Jutra's, but many critics agreed that it was the first film to capture the new reality of "a time when French Canada is becoming Quebec."[37] On the other hand, few critics took seriously Jutra's claim that his film was a "documentary" on Quebec "during the Quiet Revolution."[38]

The narratives of the two films have much in common, since Groulx's hero (also named Claude) is searching for a sense of identity and is involved in an affair with a "foreign" woman (in this case, Barbara is English Canadian and Jewish, but her aspiration to be an actress parallels Johanne's modelling career). Although this Claude does not disappear, he does leave Montreal for the country, leading to the breakdown of his relationship with Barbara, and the last sequence shows him lost in contemplation of a young woman skating in a frozen landscape. The major difference between the two films is that Claude in *Le Chat dans le sac*, despite his disorientation, can articulate a relationship between his own problems and those of his society, while his counterpart in *À tout prendre* is so cut off from the world around him that he begins to live in his own fantasy world.

The status of the "real" in *À tout prendre*, however, is much more complex a question in its ideological implications than most of its critics have suggested. The real is a problem not only for Claude but also for the spectator, as indicated by the divergence between Lefebvre's assessment and Young's contrary claim that the film expresses the "untidiness" of actuality. Lefebvre's phrase, "phantom of reality," stripped of its pejorative intentions, does evoke the way the film's subjective, fantastic, and allusive elements create a kind of screen through which reality is filtered, quite unlike the easy conflation of reality and spectacle that Claude finds in *Life*.

The film's style is also at odds with the claims of documentary realism. As we have seen, the impetus for making *À tout prendre* came from dissatisfaction with the constraints of documentary filmmaking at the NFB, and the film explicitly raises the question of its documentary origins. At the end of a sequence that interrupts the narrative and in which Jutra uses his talents as a mime to offer a series of vignettes on the behaviour of a "young bourgeois" male, Claude's voice is heard declaring, "End of documentary. Time for real cinema." The next shot shows Claude with a clapper board, and we learn for the first time that he is a filmmaker.

But what is "real cinema"? Claude's film (from the two brief glimpses that we get of it in production) seems to draw on his own experience but represents it in the terms of a Hollywood melodrama. Jutra himself suggested that the depiction of Claude at work in a studio functions as "a negation of the studio ... in the aesthetic context of the film."[39] In any case, by showing Claude at work on his film immediately after his reference to real cinema, *À tout prendre* opens up the question of its own status in relation to the real. If Hollywood has established that real cinema is studio-bound fiction cinema, Jutra's fiction film clearly moves in a different direction from Claude's in its attempts to find a narrative mode appropriate to the Quebec cultural context.

Claude's denial that documentary is real cinema establishes an ironic distance between the film's Rouchian origins and classical narrative cinema, but the stress on memory in the reconstruction of "real" events also sets up a tension between Rouchian and Proustian concepts of reality. When Claude meets Victor at an open-air café, the latter quotes a passage he happens to be reading from *A la recherche du temps perdu*: "What we call reality is a certain relationship between sensations and memories (a relationship that is destroyed by a bare cinematographic presentation, which gets further away from the truth the more closely it claims to adhere to it)." The idea that film is a "naturalistic" medium that can only reproduce the outward signs of reality and not the complex processes through which reality is experienced is a familiar one; but in its context in the film, the allusion to Proust works against both the conception of the real that underpins the documentary tradition and the claim of classical narrative cinema that it follows in the footsteps of the novel through techniques that suggest that there is an easy fit between visible action and inner experience.

Just before Victor quotes Proust, Claude asks whether he knows the woman with whom Victor spent the previous night, but Victor evades the question by asking whether it is possible to "really know" anyone. This apparently inconsequential exchange suggests that there are three (not mutually exclusive) explanations of the problems of communication that Claude is faced with and that are foregrounded by the film's disruptive style: first, they are inherent in human nature (it is impossible to "really know" another person); second, they derive from the limitations of the cinematic apparatus (as Proust claims); and third, they are the product of the "impoverished" cultural environment in Quebec (signified perhaps by the bottle of Dow ale on the table as Victor quotes Proust).

In his discussion of the passage quoted by Victor, William V. Constanzo points out that, of course, Proust "did not know Bergman or Resnais." But he goes on to argue that "film's literal bias – its adherence to the surface of events" is opposed to Proust's use of language "to arrest the flow, to step down the pace of events below the threshold of continuity so that steadiness of action, time, and personality [is] revealed as an illusion of the mind." To make a film in the spirit of Proust would "challenge the hypnotic, captivating flow of film itself" through the use of devices such as "freeze frames and flashbacks," which, however, "seem artificial" because "they interrupt the spell."[40]

À *tout prendre* does include freeze-frames and flashbacks, and many other "artificial" devices that work against any "steadiness of action, time, and personality," and Gilles Marsolais has stressed the Proustian treatment of memory in the film. He argues that in Jutra's film, as in Proust's novels, "memory is the search for vanished feelings," although his own memory fails when he claims that Claude is reading Proust at the beginning of the film. He does plausibly suggest that the Proustian idea of "double memory," the tension between "voluntary memory and involuntary memory," can be applied to a film that seems to want to repress images that conflict with Claude's view of himself.[41]

My own argument is that the film's Proustian elements collide with its Rouchian origins and that both clash with the idea of cinema as spectacle. The film's failure to live up to any of these models is part of its meaning, and its refusal to settle into one approach again leaves open the question whether this failure is personal (the inadequacy of Claude or of Jutra), cultural (the lack of shared values in the new Quebec), or cinematic (film cannot do what this film tries to make it do). Victor accuses Claude of having a "sixteen-millimetre vision of things," but is this an attack on the limitations of Claude's (or Jutra's) "subjective" approach, or an extension of his Proustian view of cinema, or an allusion to the lack of cultural and economic resources in Quebec (which meant that À *tout prendre* was itself shot on sixteen millimetres and then blown up to thirty-five millimetres for its release)?

New Wave Allusions

The French New Wave cinema provided another possible model for the style of À *tout prendre*, which contains several in-jokes like those in which the New Wave filmmakers indulged in their early films. Victor climbs through Claude's window to find him reading a copy of *Cahiers du cinéma*, the magazine in which the young French filmmaklers had developed their ideas as critics, and François Truffaut makes a cameo appearance, showing Johanne how a character in his *Jules et Jim* (1961) imitated a steam engine with the lit end of a cigarette in her mouth. As many critics duly noted, these two moments are only the most obvious instances by which the film acknowledges its debt to the New Wave. Michel Patenaude compared it to Godard's first feature film and declared that À *tout prendre* was "a failed *A bout de souffle* (*Breathless*)," while Marsolais punned on the titles of both films by suggesting that Jutra's film leaves the spectator "breathless" because it insists on considering all things at the same time.[42]

The French New Wave had an enormous influence on world cinema, but Truffaut and Godard also developed what amounts to an aesthetics of failure. Although they proclaimed their allegiance to the ideas of André Bazin, the founder of *Cahiers du cinéma*, who advocated a cinematic realism that would respect the complexity and wholeness of reality, the rapid and fragmented editing of their films offered a vision of a world in which any such sense of "wholeness" was conspicuously absent. They enthusiastically celebrated the dynamic qualities of Hollywood cinema, which they consumed with the same enthusiasm that Claude shows for *Life*, but the vitality of their own films came from their lack of respect for the continuity rules of classical narrative cinema.

À tout prendre obviously shares, and perhaps heightens, the fragmentation and discontinuity of New Wave cinema, but the New Wave filmmakers succeeded in at least partially unifying their films through their concept of the *auteur*. Each film was thus seen as a contribution to the developing personal vision of its director. Some critics objected that Jutra was flaunting his own status as an *auteur* while neglecting the social and cultural problems facing Quebec, but the director's presence in his own film actually leads to a breakdown in his authority as its author.

The relationship between Jutra and Claude is quite different from that between Truffaut and Antoine in *Les Quatre Cent coups*. Truffaut's film is also autobiographical, but he filters his own memories through a character with a different name and played by an actor (Jean-Pierre Léaud). Although Truffaut's unorthodox filmmaking strategies implicate him in his character's resistance to authority, they also proclaim his ability to put his past behind him by expressing it through the medium of film. In *À tout prendre*, there is also an implied gap between Claude's impotence and Jutra's ability to make this film, but the boundary lines are much less clearly marked.

The film's vision can never be completely equated with Claude's, nor can it be completely dissociated from his unsettled outlook. Because of this uncertainty, it is difficult to read the film as authorial self-expression developed through character identification, although many critics did try to read it this way. What the film instead invites us to do is examine the social and cultural implications of Claude's experience and of our own experience as we look for meanings in what we see and hear.

Race and the Colonial Context

If *À tout prendre* "fails," then, to achieve the density of a Proust novel, the spectacle of a Hollywood film, or the authorial voice of New Wave cinema, the central question becomes: what is standing in the way of success? While the film does not suggest on what terms a "successful" Quebec fiction film might be possible – indeed it implies a critical attitude to all the models to which it alludes – it does suggest that its difficulties are intensified by pressures deriving from Quebec's "colonial" status. In terms of the film's narrative structure, the colonial metaphor developed in Claude's relationship with Johanne interweaves questions of racial, sexual, and cultural identity.

Johanne's status as a woman from "elsewhere" suggests that Claude's attraction to her, like his enjoyment of *Life*, is a desire for what is lacking in his own everyday life. Unlike the English-speaking Barbara in *Le Chat dans le sac*, Johanne cannot be suspected of complicity with the dominant cultural power. She is repeatedly associated with the sound of tom-toms, or native drums, like those that Jutra heard in Niger conducting a "dialogue of the deaf" with church bells.[43] A recurring image of plantation boys at work, which first accompanies her account of life in Haiti, also apparently evokes her racial background. The drums and the plantation boys are, however, soon redefined as products of Claude's imagination, as projections of his desire for the exotic onto the image of Johanne.

When Johanne finishes speaking of Haiti, the image freezes and the camera zooms in on the face of one of the "boys," followed by a montage of close-ups of faces that we soon realize are those of black customers at a nightclub to which Johanne has taken Claude. Johanne dances with another man to music that at first sounds oddly like a "civilized" minuet. Then, as Claude watches the couple, there is a white flash, and wild drumbeats accompany a "primitive" and sensual dance. The drums thus evoke Claude's jealousy even though the dance stands for the reality of a black culture in which he feels out of place.

In the next sequence, Johanne disrupts Claude's fantasies by revealing that she was born in Montreal and that she spent her childhood in orphanages because it was difficult to find foster parents for a black child. She has concealed her past in an attempt to construct an exotic image, an exaggeration of the otherness projected onto her because of her gender and her race, enabling her to feel that she is in control of situations in which she would otherwise feel powerless. This feeling of empowerment, however, is an illusion, and Johanne – like Marilyn Monroe – comes to experience her image as a trap, and she now fears that Claude loves her only because she is different and exotic. Although he assures her that he loves her for herself, his assurance is unconvincing in view of the film's concern with the complex relationship of self (or selves) and image. She insists that she does not want his pity but needs to find her own identity.

In revealing her true background to Claude, in a sequence in which, as we have seen, the pressures on Johanne during the filming are very evident, she tries to establish a relationship that will go beyond images. The film suggests that this endeavour is difficult at the best of times but virtually impossible in Quebec. As a member of a visible minority, Johanne appears foreign even though she was born in Quebec, whereas Claude (as a white male from a well-to-do family) ought to feel at home. Yet his sexual activities are as much a mask as Johanne's exotic image. He attempts to deny his impotence within a colonial culture, a situation made all the more frustrating because the marks of his difference are not visible. As Claude discovers, Johanne's gender and race do not make her into the exotic other but rather render visible the colonial mechanisms that govern cultural life in Quebec.

Language is one of the most important of these mechanisms, although one that cuts across gender and racial differences. As the opening sequence indicates, real cultural power lies elsewhere, and this elsewhere is associated with the use of English through Claude's immersion in *Life* magazine. Two later sequences confirm that English is the language of cultural authority and also suggest how the film's obtrusive cinematic language, its "pirouettes," work to undermine this authority.

One of these, of course, is the bank sequence in which the interview is conducted in English. The other occurs earlier in the film when, while Johanne is away on a modelling assignment in New York, Claude happens to meet Barbara, with whom he had once had an affair, and they apparently decide to spend the night together. Instead of showing their love making, however, the screen goes black, and we hear a male voice asking a woman (in

English) to move her hips forward. The words are presumably addressed to Johanne by an American fashion designer during a modelling session, but the black screen means that they are not clearly anchored in a context. Their sexual connotations evoke Claude's love making with Barbara (which is repressed by the black screen), but although the male voice makes us think of Claude, the language of male sexual authority is English. At the same time, the association with Johanne's work in New York points (actually or in Claude's jealous imagination) to the sexual hierarchy in the world of modelling.

If English is the language of cultural and sexual power, the film depicts a francophone culture in which language has lost much of its communicative function. The talk of the guests at the party becomes a meaningless babble, while Johanne's exotic appeal emerges from her performance of a Creole song whose words are supposedly incomprehensible and unimportant. Meanwhile Claude's voice on the soundtrack never establishes a stable position of authority from which to comment on the images. His words become garbled when he brushes his teeth; his poetic musings are interrupted by the sounds of the party and are later reduced to gurgling noises when he jumps in a river. When Claude tries to find words to describe his vision of "perfect love," he complains that his "words sound like literature."

The implication is that, in a colonial culture in which the native language lacks institutional authority, language veers wildly between babble and poetry but lacks the stable grounding in everyday life necessary for basic communicative acts. Similarly, the film's sudden shifts in tone that disturbed so many critics are signs (or symptoms) of the lack of definitions in a colonial culture.

After Johanne's "confession" brings her to the verge of tears, Claude's voice-over asks what has happened to "the carefree Johanne," and a brief flashback shows her laughing. When we return to the present, Claude cradles Johanne's head in his arms and asks her to "do the flea in agony," a nonsense rhyme that she performs, complete with crazy faces and gestures, so that the intense mood generated by the confession dissolves in laughter. The insertion of Johanne's past image suggests that the film is complicit with Claude's desire to deflect attention from the effect on their relationship of her revelation of the truth, but, as usual, the obtrusiveness of the cinematic effect only draws attention to what Claude is trying to hide.

Claude's insistence on a laughing Johanne is also symptomatic of the way laughter, throughout the film, substitutes for language, deflating tensions even as it reveals them. This sequence reinforces the idea that the role of clown is the only viable one in the colonial context. Laughter reveals the tension in many situations and gains meanings as it recurs in different contexts.

When Claude and Johanne return from the party to find Victor in Claude's bed (because his own room is being decorated), their wild laughter is explained by their inebriated state, but it also suggests their nervousness at the prospect of making love for the first time and only heightens Victor's embarrassment. The euphoria of the early stages of their relationship is conveyed in a montage sequence in which they give each other a series of gifts; the sequence ends with the couple rolling about in laughter after she has given him a mirror and a trick camera (neatly summing up his character). The laughter rebounds against Claude when he looks through the window of a café to see Johanne with Barbara. When the two women collapse in laughter, he is left to wonder whether they have compared notes on his sexual performance.

Laughter again acquires sexual and cultural connotations when we briefly see Victor on stage playing a frenetic Scotsman, dressed in a kilt. The (unseen) theatre audience roars with appreciative laughter at his antics, but this easy laughter derives from a theatrical genre (the bedroom farce) that translates sexual embarrassment into cultural terms that seem alien and old-fashioned in contemporary Quebec.

The laughter that recurs throughout À tout prendre is distinctly uneasy. Just before he breaks up with Johanne, Claude laments that the time has passed when their quarrels could be ended with a joke, creating "happy endings" that only repressed the problems that provoked the quarrels in the first place. Not unexpectedly, the film's own ending uses laughter to ambiguous and unsettling effect: as a plane apparently takes him away from Quebec, Claude's commentary dissolves into laughter. Does he really have the last laugh?

Claude's experiments with different personae in front of his mirror attempt to suppress his awareness that he is really a clown. To be a clown is to make a fool of oneself: this is how Victor earns his living in the theatre, and Johanne is afraid that she is "making a clown" of herself when she performs as a model. When she dances with another man at the nightclub, Claude immediately thinks that she is trying to make a fool of him. Although he does adopt the role of clown to amuse some children in a park, the shot appears as if in a distorting mirror and once again suggests that Claude does not want us to see this aspect of himself.

The film also relates the clown image to Claude's refusal of fatherhood through a chain of associations that begins when Johanne returns from New York. As the couple wander through the streets of the city on what appears to be Hallowe'en night, he insists that he has been faithful in her absence and proclaims that he is "the happiest man alive." At these words, they pass a clown chained to a lamp-post, an image that seems to provoke a sudden cut to a close-up of a death's head. This proves to be a mask worn by a child, but it later reappears, accompanied by a scream, just before Claude receives the letter in which Johanne informs him that she has had a miscarriage. Although Claude has sent her money for an abortion and is relieved to escape from the burdens of fatherhood, the loss of the child reminds him of his own mortality. He laments the passing of his youth as, once again, a gunshot shatters his mirror image.

Recurring images of violence evoke the pressures involved in Claude's search for identity. In the fantasy sequences that punctuate the film, gunmen pursue Claude and eventually kill him. Fantasies of regression to childhood, romantic love, and violence come together in a sequence in which Claude embraces Johanne and tells her of his longing for a perfect love. As he does so, she looks over his shoulder at some boys playing with guns in the street. One of them pretends to shoot Claude who joins in the game by pretending to die. Later, Claude has a fantasy in which masked gunmen attack the couple in a park and kill Johanne. It is uncertain whether the attack represents Claude's fears or his desire to end the affair, but after she has told him that she is pregnant, he clearly equates Johanne with the gunmen when he "sees" them as he enters the room and then greets her in reality.

Claude's fantasies of regression are also apparent in his work as a film-maker. He tries to create images of an impossible perfection that deny the complicated reality of his everyday life and only add to his dissatisfaction with that life. After he breaks off his affair with Johanne, he curls up in a foetal position on his sofa and longs for "the secret to a quiet, well-ordered life." This "secret" dates back to his childhood when he could escape into the fantasy world of Saturday matinées at the cinema, a world that has presumably shaped the boys' games as well as Claude's fantasies of being attacked by gunmen.

The two figures from Claude's past that we see in the film, his manipulative mother and the priest who warns him against the wiles of women, offer static images that are clearly irrelevant to the untidy actuality of Claude's present life. They represent a time (real or imaginary) in which boundaries were more clearly defined than they are in the present. The mother is confined within the walls of her large modern apartment where she lives alone with her dogs, and the priest lives in a dark cell-like room filled with religious objects and a television set. Their entrapment only reinforces Claude's fears that his relationship with Johanne will become a prison, while their advice does not stabilize his life since it allows him to break off with Johanne without having to make a decision on his own.

Claude's mother never explains why she opposes his marriage to Johanne, whom she has never met, nor does she comment when Claude shows her photographs of his new lover. She claims that he will not be able to cope with the responsibility, but her sidelong glance at Claude (emphasized by a freeze-frame) after she has looked at the photographs suggests that she also objects to an interracial marriage. The priest, on the other hand, is quite open in opposing the marriage not for racial reasons but because women cannot be trusted. What these figures from the past offer is thus an allegedly stable basis for value judgments that depends on categories of (racial, sexual, cultural) difference that make sense of the flow of modern life by defining boundaries that can become the walls of a prison.

Bodies and Walls

This ambivalence about the collapse of the old order leads to an association between bodies being seduced and walls being demolished. The film explores a dynamics of seeing in which subjectivity is constructed through seeing other people's bodies as objects and that encourages people to turn their own bodies into images. Images, by defining the terms in which the body can be seen, simultaneously intensify the objectification of the body and deny the body's physical reality.

In focusing on the relationship between Claude and Johanne, the film places this process in the context of racial and sexual difference. After they have made love for the first time, they compare the colour of their skins as he strokes her arm, the first part of her body seen in the film. He is fascinated by Johanne's "foreign body" but is soon equally tempted by the attractions of Barbara's "heavenly body," which is present when Johanne's is absent. As Joan Fox suggested, the film seems to want to record "the erotic effect of the beloved," but the result is that she "always remains an object."[44]

Although Jutra wished that he had been able to get closer to Johanne in re-presenting their affair, the film questions its own tendency to objectify the female body in the context of Proust's critical attitude to the cinematic medium. Is the problem built into the codes of classical narrative cinema (as suggested by the Monroe photograph) and similar cultural practices (like the fashion industry), or is it a necessary consequence of the properties of the cinematic apparatus (as Proust suggests), which also applies to representations of men, or is it a "natural" outcome of human difference? While all these explanations remain possible, the film also implies that Claude's treatment of women as objects is the product of an insecure subjectivity shaped by an impoverished cultural environment.

Claude's attitude to Johanne begins to change after her confession, which, he comments, creates a new bond between them. The demands created by his new awareness of Johanne's subjective needs are intensified when she tells him that she is pregnant. Claude regards the foetus within her body as a "foreign element" that is at the same time a "transplantation" of himself, a projection of his desire to return to the womb. As he describes his new concern for her body, the camera pans up her legs. The erotic look is now troubled by the awareness that the body is no longer completely other. Claude cannot deal with this complication and tries to reassert the integrity of his own body. His first act after mailing the money for an abortion to Johanne is to discard his "old skin" by buying himself a new Italian sweater. The skin becomes a kind of wall that defines the boundaries of the self but also isolates the self from others.

Actual walls also function in the film to reinforce the idea of the isolated self. After their first night together, Claude drops Johanne off at her apartment and waits outside while she changes. His voice on the soundtrack comments that she is leaving him for the first time and returning to "her world behind this wall." Walls offer protection against the distractions and threats of the outside world, to both of which Claude is especially vulnerable, but they also work against his desire to possess Johanne. After they try to define themselves as a couple by cutting themselves off from the outside world in his room, Claude and Johanne are seen through a chainlink fence when they leave, and Claude comments that their "prison" goes with them.

When he breaks off their relationship, Claude celebrates his new freedom by riding his moped. He exults in "the joy of movement" that makes possible a "change of place" and describes the "prison" from which he has escaped as one "of gold and crystal but as secure as any other." He has not completely escaped, however, since superimposed shots of Johanne suggest that he cannot get her out of his mind. The sequence ends with him desperately shouting "*Non!*," and the next sequence shows him pacing up and down in his room.

If walls (like skins) provide both structure and confinement, the limits of the prison are not always visible and the freedom that Claude seeks finally results in his disappearance. This loss of physical presence is foreshadowed by lighting effects that de-realize the characters: light streaming from on-screen lamps reminds us that cinematic images are bodiless; silhouette effects turn three-dimensional bodies into two-dimensional shapes; and when Claude visits a doctor, his body appears as an x-ray image that responds to the doctor's assurance that he is in perfect health by commenting that his friends say he "looks terrible."

Physical absence can signify a godlike power, as in the case of the bank manager who speaks with authority (in English) from off-screen space, but it can also signify impotence, as with Claude's father who is both invisible and unheard. In refusing to become a father, Claude disappears and thus becomes like his own father. The instability generated by the collapse of his relationship with Johanne leads to a sequence in which they stand in front of a wall and express their mutual frustration. In voice-over, Claude laments that their love can be eroded by such "trivial assaults," and their voices (on the soundtrack only, since the figures we see do not speak) are reduced to incoherent babble while their images dissolve in and out before finally disappearing, leaving only the empty wall.

Claude cannot maintain a stable sense of identity and is easily seduced. His fascination with cinema is either the cause or the consequence of his inability to settle down. We first see him at work as a filmmaker only after his affair with Johanne is well under way, but he has already failed to remain faithful while she is away for a few days. His film is part of his search for a perfect love, which he can find only in the artificial confines of the studio. When he seduces, or is seduced by, the actress and then by the actor, it is as if the emotion generated in making the film inevitably spills over into his life.

In both cases, the seduction leads to messy complications in his private life with which Claude cannot cope, but the second experience seems to take him by surprise as he discovers his homosexual tendencies. His passion for cinema seems to create an erotic force that he is unable to resist, even to the point of crossing the gender boundaries that had previously been part of his identity. While dramatic music, a zoom in on his face, and a fade underline the traumatic effect of Claude's self-discovery, no further reference is made to it, and its effect on the breakdown of his relationship with Johanne remains undetermined. Even though Claude mutters "*Enfin!*" during the fade that discreetly ends his encounter with the actor, there is no real suggestion that Claude has finally discovered *the* truth about himself.

Alain-Napoléon Moffat, who interprets the film's play with "representational structures" in terms very similar to mine, argues that the film's style is itself evidence of a "gay sensibility." He suggests that the film breaks with "the traditional concept of the *individual*" and replaces it with that of a "*person*," open to the other and aware of the processes that go into constructing a sense of identity.[45] What emerges from the film is a vision in which "character" becomes a process of choosing among the images and roles that the cultural context provides. The seductive images offered by *Life* suggest that the choices should be easy, but Claude, as an aging adolescent in a society whose traditional values have lost their authority, is unable to play any of his roles with conviction.

The role of seducer allows him to treat bodies as objects but is undermined by the fact that he is really the one who is seduced and by the complications that even brief relationships entail. While Johanne is in her apartment after their first night together, Claude sings a song in which he asserts that "my body leaves no scar on you." Johanne later assures him in her letter that, because of her miscarriage, "your body left no scar on me." He now recognizes that this affair has not been a case of seduction that leaves both partners unchanged. They are both now "covered in scars."

The affair leaves scars in their minds if not on their bodies, and they separate amid recurring images of demolition. During a discussion in Claude's room in which he tells Johanne that their life has to change, he hears a banging noise and looks out of the window. He sees workers demolishing a nearby building, but then a crack appears in a wall as he insists that he still needs to be free and that he wants to be able to disappear for a day or two when he needs to be alone. Although Johanne agrees to his demands, she goes on to speak of the need to arrange for her divorce from her present husband and for the adoption of the child she is expecting. While she is speaking, we see shots of a bulldozer moving through the mud of the demolition site. Although Claude kisses her and says he loves her, the camera zooms in on his eye as he peers through the window, and there is a cut to a shot of a wall collapsing.

These images of demolition suggest the breaking down of barriers and a break to the new life that Claude claims to want, but his subsequent behaviour activates only the negative potential of the metaphor. When he decides that an abortion will solve his problems, he believes that a "moral edifice" will collapse in silence and that nobody will notice. When he goes to eat in a restaurant, he is humiliated by Johanne's former lover, who asks him how it feels to "demolish" a woman.

Towards a Cultural Revolution?

Claude decides that he must "think of other things." This development perhaps lends support to those critics who argue that Claude is able to consider "Quebec nationalism" once he has put the affair behind him, and he does now walk past a *"Québec libre"* sign painted on a wall. But if "revolution follows alienation," as Joan Fox suggests, the film offers little evidence that Claude will become a revolutionary.[46] He does not see the sign, although the camera lingers on it after he has walked out of the frame. The camera detaches us from Claude's perspective as if to remind us of the need for a *Québec libre* to prevent the children who now run past from being faced with the dilemmas that have prevented Claude from taking on the responsibilities of adulthood.[47]

After passing the sign, he envisages himself walking into the river and then being shot from the sky by a hunter. Claude's "suicide" allows him to escape from his body, and we last see him floating in the sky, speaking in praise of "abstraction" and the "pure delight of the spirit." He refers to Johanne as his "well-beloved prison," but his escape from the constraints that have weighed him down results in his bodily disappearance.

The final sequences hesitate between material and symbolic explanations for his absence. A jet plane flies through clouds (ironically, in view of the colonial subtext, it is a British Overseas Airways plane) accompanied by Claude's disembodied laughter. The following shot of the plantation boys freezes, suggesting that this is the end of the film, but then we see Johanne running up to Victor to ask for news of Claude. He is unable to provide any, and they separate (ironically, in view of the politics of language, the final word is *ciao*). The film ends with another freeze-frame of a plantation boy looking at the camera, an effect that implies that Claude has in some way *become* a figure created from his own fantasies but that also makes visible the colonial oppression that operates insidiously in Quebec.

Claude's hymn to abstraction places his final disembodiment under the sign of the principle that "'art' must abstract from 'life,'" which Young opposed to what he saw as the film's faithfulness to "the multivalence of an actual, untidy event." *À tout prendre* oscillates between these two impulses and thus creates an unstable relationship between (abstract) image and (untidy) reality. The same tension between abstraction and untidiness also spills over into the treatment of a subjectivity that continually tries to define itself in relation to an other that has a disturbing tendency to lose its otherness.

If ending the narrative with Claude's disappearance suggests a bleak assessment of the prospects for Quebec, the film has consistently undercut those cinematic codes that privilege the linear development of the narrative. Its playful disrespect for the dominant cinematic codes provides the basis for a new "decolonized" aesthetic that could create the supportive cultural environment that Claude so obviously lacks. Unfortunately for Jutra and the film, most reviewers in Quebec and elsewhere tended to equate Claude's perspective with that of the film, and they read the film as a simple record of personal failure rather than as a complicated call for cultural renewal.

Above: A child works on an electronic teaching machine in *Comment savoir*
(Photo Library of the National Film Board of Canada, All rights reserved)

Below: Monique (Monique Simard) in her dream sequence in *Wow*
(Photo Library of the National Film Board of Canada, All rights reserved)

USELESS BEAUTY
Wow

Despite its commercial failure and decidedly mixed critical reception, *À tout prendre* established Jutra as "one of the major hopes of Quebec cinema."[1] Nevertheless, he spent the next few years struggling to pay off the debt he had incurred, and he was unable to find backing for a new film. Until the establishment of the CFDC in 1967, there was little support for independent filmmaking in Canada and, as Jutra discovered when he approached United Artists with a project for a musical, the Hollywood studios had little interest in assisting a new national cinema in a country that they treated as part of their domestic market.[2]

Jutra did participate in minor ways in the emergence of a new Quebec cinema that took place in the late 1960s. He contributed to the screenplay of Michel Brault's *Entre la mer et l'eau douce* (*Drifting Upstream*, 1967) and acted in Gilles Carle's *Le Viol d'une jeune fille douce* (*The Rape of a Sweet Young Girl*, 1968). But his own output as a director was limited to two documentaries made for the NFB. When his new feature film, also produced by the NFB, was finally released in Montreal in March 1970, it proved to be a disconcerting hybrid of documentary and fiction cinema, and Jutra himself described it as a film "born in the midst of waiting for something else."[3]

Such a dismissive comment by the film's director at the time of its release could hardly have helped the commercial prospects of this belated follow-up to *À tout prendre*. Not surprisingly, *Wow* received only a brief run at one cinema in Montreal and has subsequently been overshadowed by the success of *Mon oncle Antoine*, which followed shortly afterwards.

The Dreams and Reality of Youth

Wow is an attempt to assess the significance for Quebec of the youth culture of the 1960s. It consists of interviews with nine teenagers, identified only as

Babette, Dave, Flis, François, Marc, Michelle, Monique, Philippe, and Pierre, on topics such as drugs, love, and family, intercut with sequences depicting their dreams. A few sequences fit into neither of these categories, and there is no commentary to orient the spectator in relation to the film's diverse materials. It certainly does not conform to the norms of classical narrative cinema, and, as Jean-Pierre Tadros pointed out in his review, its discontinuities are likely to annoy spectators not used to "this kind of fragmentation."[4]

Despite his awareness of the difficulties that it would pose for audiences, Tadros was one of the few admirers of a film that he called "one of the most beautiful visual poems that Quebec cinema has given us."[5] Virtually the only other defender of the film was Ronald Blumer who, in a brief review in *Take One*, announced that it confirmed Jutra's position as "the most original film creator in Canada."[6]

Although the disconcerting blend of documentary and fiction in *Wow* certainly limited its commercial prospects, the film also failed to appeal to those who advocated a radical political cinema in Quebec. Its break with classical narrative cinema lacked the political urgency found in the films of Gilles Groulx and Jean Pierre Lefebvre, who gained international attention when essays on their work appeared in a British book on the world's most promising new directors. As the introduction to this book put it, "the key figure" inspiring this new work was Jean-Luc Godard, whose own recent films, such as *La Chinoise* and *Weekend* (both 1967), sought a new cinematic language appropriate to the cultural crisis in France that erupted in the near-revolution of May 1968.[7] From the perspective of this kind of political cinema, *Wow* was "a film of useless beauty in our socio-cultural context."[8]

One reason for the widespread discomfort with Jutra's film was its ambivalent attitude to the youth movement. Jutra was distanced from the young people in the film because of his age but felt complicit with them because of his own persona as a "perpetual child." In the same way, the film hesitates between identification with, and critical judgment of, their attitudes and behaviour. The tension between documentary and fiction reinforces this divided perspective, and the film also questions the conventional distinction between filmmaker and subjects through its challenge to traditional notions of authorship.

The teenagers scripted their own dream sequences, but Jutra directed them, and the result is a constant uncertainty about who is responsible for the film's meanings. In its treatment of authorship (and its relation to authority), *Wow* allies itself with the collective spirit of the youth movement and with contemporary developments in critical theory and cultural practice. But the result is a disturbing film that does not fit comfortably into any of the available categories.

Although *Wow* has been described (and dismissed) as a "homage to the youth of the counterculture," Jutra insisted that he never felt "part of any of the fashionable movements of the Sixties."[9] In the mid-1960s, however, he did have the opportunity to observe the new youth-oriented counterculture in one of its strongholds when he was invited to teach at UCLA, where Colin Young, who had been so enthusiastic about *À tout prendre*, was director of the film program. On his return from California, he endorsed the movement's desire to "return to nature," which he associated with the pleasures of "surfing," and the new physical and sexual freedom that it made possible. But he criticized what he saw as the "new conformisms" emerging among young people who possessed too much "material" and "spiritual" wealth.[10]

Despite these reservations, Jutra affirmed his solidarity with youth in *Rouli-roulant* (1966, released in English as *The Devil's Toy*), a short mock-documentary on the struggle between a group of young people and the authorities who want to confiscate their skateboards. The ironic play with documentary conventions in this film, which Jutra later called "a small ode to youth, to its beauty, its grace and its vitality," sets up an implicit parallel between the skateboarders and a filmmaker challenging the institutional norms of his profession.[11]

Skateboarding offers an urban equivalent to surfing, and the film celebrates the freedom of movement of its young subjects. This freedom is communicated to the camera, which at one point turns upside-down as it follows a skateboarder demonstrating his skill. However, the soundtrack is dominated by a voice-of-God commentator who repeatedly portrays the skateboarders as a monstrous threat to the community. He claims the objectivity of a public service announcement, offering apparently neutral (and absurdly pedantic) information on how a skateboard works, but clearly sides with the authorities. His supposed neutrality is belied by a hysteria that seems more appropriate to a horror film than to a documentary, but when order is finally restored, the commentary slips into the measured cadences of "classical" French verse.

The textual authority that the commentator claims, like the social order for which he speaks, masks an underlying fear of youth. Thus the process whereby this (adult male) voice seeks to unify the film, by winning the spectator's consent to his view of the situation, implies the suppression of the "voice" of youth (and of the pleasures offered by the mobile camera). However, at the end of the film, the "official" voice of the adult male commentator gives way to the (youthful female) voice of Geneviève Bujold singing the praises of the "rouli-roulant."

Even if the traditional voice-of-God commentator is here used to ironic effect, it still works, as the direct cinema filmmakers had argued, to suppress the voices of the skateboarders themselves. A few years later, when some of the same young people appeared in *Wow*, the result was a much more troubled depiction of the cultural changes of the 1960s. The difference from the earlier film was partly that the young people were now able to speak for themselves, partly the effect of their passage from early to late adolescence, and partly the impact of events involving the counterculture that took place between the two films.

The protest movement in the United States led to unrest on many university campuses and to bloody fighting between demonstrators and police at the 1968 Democratic convention in Chicago. A student-led uprising in Paris in May 1968 almost brought about the downfall of the French government. In Quebec, where cultural institutions were still coming to terms with the effects of the Quiet Revolution, the already complex meanings of the counterculture were further complicated by the political implications of the separatist movement. The public image of a youth movement that rejected the established political system became entangled with the terrorist activities of the FLQ that began in 1963 and culminated in the October Crisis of 1970, only a few months after the release of *Wow*.

The tensions surrounding the youth movement were already apparent in a film that Jutra made for the NFB just before *Rouli-roulant. Comment savoir* (1966, released in English as *Knowing to Learn*) is a full-length documentary on new approaches to education using electronic "teaching machines." Although this was primarily an educational film, Jutra tried to destabilize its discourse by developing a tension between its "objective, neutral, detached side" (the documentation of new pedagogical methods) and its "science-fiction aspect" (a utopian vision of a future made possible by technological innovation).[12]

Rather than use a didactic voice-of-God commentator, Jutra sets up a dialogue between a male and a female voice. The male speaker is Jutra himself, and he expresses the film's overriding ideological vision, describing the success of the experiments and looking forward to the future that they will make possible. While the female voice raises questions from a humanistic perspective, the male adopts an anti-humanist position by arguing that the new approaches show that "our ideas about what it means to be human are often the result of prejudice." The image track supports this position by showing children interacting happily with the machines. Through a process of synthesis, guided by the male voice, *Comment savoir* works to bridge the gap between the real and the possible and to overcome the fear that, it implies, is a typical adult response to the new technology.

However, a new tension emerges in the final sequence and threatens to disrupt the film's project. When the male voice refers to "the rising tide of youth," we see demonstrators protesting against the Vietnam War outside the White House. This image echoes an earlier reference to the "tide of youth" illustrated by shots of surfers, whose physical skills illustrate the need to "master" rather than "drown" in "the sea of information demanded by modern life." This shift from surfers to demonstrators introduces political connotations that, as he later came to realize, were unwelcome to the film's director.

The problem for Jutra was that the demonstrators were part of a protest movement that opposed many of the technological changes that the film set out to endorse. Although Jutra insisted that he was "for civil rights ... and against the war," he thought that the "romanticism" of the demonstrators was counterproductive precisely because it prevented them from grasping the opportunities provided by the new technology. In order to reach a younger generation who shared many of the "romantic" attitudes of the demonstrators, Jutra felt that he had inscribed his own attitude into the commentary in a "too ambiguous" manner.[13]

This ending is disruptive because it brings up questions about the political and ideological uses of technology that have been ignored during the rest of the film. While the commentary makes the rising tide of youth appear to be an outgrowth of the new technology, the demonstration at the White House reminds us of the use of American power in Vietnam and thus of the cultural influence of the United States, where the new technology originated and where most of *Comment savoir* was filmed. The images of surfers and demonstrators acknowledge two aspects of the youth movement, neither of which fit comfortably with a commitment to technology and education, and the effect is to expose the instability of the film's ideological project.

Despite the unwelcome intrusion of political realities into *Comment savoir*, Jutra included another demonstration outside the White House in *Wow*. Because the young people in the film were reluctant to consider the political implications of their attitudes, he arranged a trip to Resurrection City, a camp set up outside the White House to demonstrate against poverty and racial prejudice. This strategem succeeded only in exposing the group's lack of faith in political solutions to social problems. As in *Comment savoir* (and like Claude's addiction to *Life* in *À tout prendre*), the visit to Washington mainly serves to suggest that history and reality exist "elsewhere." The Quebec teenagers seem to turn away from their own society into an imaginary world in which they enjoy the pleasurable aspects of the youth culture, namely, drugs, sex, and rock music. Nobody raises the question of Quebec's political future, even in the final interview sequence whose topic is the "future."

What we see of Resurrection City in *Wow* – a black saxophone player collapsing in the mud, members of the group wading in a pond with demonstrators, Monique holding a black child – does not seem especially political, but the accompanying comments from the interview material express a fear of commitment and feelings of impotence. Although the young people share Jutra's distrust of political rhetoric, they do not share his faith in technological change. When Philippe insists that "demonstrations are useless," Flis adds that "technology does not mean progress." There is general agreement that the future will be "violent," but Monique seems to sum up the group's pessimism when she asks, "What can I do?"

Although Jutra hoped that the visit to Washington would shake up the group and "give them a spur that would oblige them to express themselves on vital problems that concern us all," the sequence instead underlines the absence of a sense of the real in these young people's lives.[14] The film confronts us with what Tadros aptly described as the "troubling" effect of their confessions of "impotence" in the face of social injustice and suffering.[15]

For Louise Carrière this disturbance undercuts the film's project of paying homage to the counterculture so that "perhaps despite itself, and despite the filmmaker," *Wow* reveals the limitations of the social changes of the 1960s: "We denounce violence but our fantasies remain very violent, we want peace but we are intolerant, we desire love but we are deeply sexist and immersed in the most traditional imagery of the couple. We hate the system, but how well it serves us!"[16] The attitudes that Carrière describes are certainly part of the experience and meaning of the film, but so is the uncertainty about the extent to which it endorses the attitudes of the young people who participated in its production.

A desire to return to the past is a recurring motif in the dream sequences, either through a regression to childhood or to Quebec's cultural past. Babette introduces her dream (the first in the film) by relating it to stories she told herself as a lonely child; Monique calls her dream "a little girl's fantasy"; and the film ends with Pierre's dream of himself as a child when he and his parents lived in France. In her dream, Babette is a nun in a rural convent, suggesting that her fantasies are still shaped by a traditional and supposedly vanished image of Quebec; and an escape from the city to the country is a central element in the dreams of Michelle, Philippe, and Marc.

Not unexpectedly, Blumer found it strange that "half the fantasies center round a return to a simpler, more innocent form of existence."[17] Tadros also noted that the young people in the film express "a global refusal of society," implying that their outlook negates the effects of an earlier *Refus global*, the artists' manifesto published in 1948 that inspired the Quiet Revolution and insisted on the need for social commitment in art.[18]

Both Blumer and Tadros accepted the pull towards the past as part of the complex meaning of the film, but most critics felt that the film's vision was simply regressive. In an interview published in *Cahiers du cinéma* just before the events of May 1968, Jutra himself rejected a prevalent image of a "lost youth, who complain of the void while they create their own void and make a void around themselves."[19] The counterculture, in both its hippie and activist variants, also rejected this image of youth, but the young people in *Wow* do seem to exist in just such a void. They are uninterested in any form of political activity and unable to formulate any sense of collective identity. It is not surprising that, at a time of international student activism and of political crisis in Quebec, such a vision of youth should prove disturbing.

Yves Lever attributed the problem to the middle-class origins of the young people in *Wow*, suggesting that, while they might be "authentic," their "preoccupations" were "a little too romantic and bourgeois" and lamenting that they could not be counted on "to settle the social question in Quebec."[20] As in *À tout prendre*, however, Jutra questions the possibility of settling the social question without first unsettling the terms in which it is usually posed. By blurring the conventional boundaries between real and imaginary, public and private, documentary and fiction, *Wow* challenges the spectator to account for the "global refusal" that it depicts.

The "social question in Quebec" is virtually a structuring absence in the film, especially when the final dream involves a return not just to infancy but also to France. Jutra confronts the spectators with a series of fantasies of "regression" rather than with the young people's response to their immediate cultural and social problems. But the uncertain address of the film leaves open the question of its attitude to these fantasies – which is also the question of the position that it invites the spectator to adopt in relation to them.

Questions of Authorship

Wow initially presents itself as a film in which young people speak for themselves, but the question who is the "author" of its vision of contemporary youth is far from easy to answer. As we shall see, the film itself is enigmatic on this issue, and Jutra's own comments suggest that he was uncertain about its implications. On one occasion, he claimed that *Wow* is "in some ways the reverse of *À tout prendre*" and belongs to a tradition in which "the filmmaker effaces himself behind a reality that is external to him."[21] But in another interview, he insisted that *Wow* is a personal film in which he speaks of himself as much as he did in *À tout prendre*.[22] He combined these positions in a third interview in which he described himself as simply the "agent" for the group but admitted that he probably "filtered" their dreams "subtly."[23]

Not surprisingly, critics treated the question of the film's authorship in quite different ways. Even its two chief admirers disagreed. Tadros described it as "a film on young people made by young people," but Blumer insisted that "this film was not made by the kids, it was made because of them, by someone highly sensible to the vibrations of our time."[24]

Although Jutra claimed that he had no "desire to generalize" and simply wanted "to show these nine people as they were," he could not evade responsibility for the image of youth that emerged from the film.[25] Dominique Noguez asked why Jutra chose "*these* young people ... Because they are representative of a certain youth? Because they are not? And what youth?"[26] This uncertainty is built into the experience of the film and was clearly a major factor in its commercial failure and political rejection.

The tensions surrounding authorship in the film have their roots in its unusual production process. Although the NFB originally commissioned him to make an hour-long television program on drug use among teenagers, Jutra's aim from the beginning was to make a collectively authored feature film.[27] However, after the group had worked together for three months, there was no consensus on how to make "a global film involving the whole group."[28] Jutra instead decided to edit together individual dream sequences, one for each member of the group, with interviews designed to elicit opinions on social and cultural issues.

The film's fragmentation is thus an implicit acknowledgment of the group's inability to discover a "global" fiction. Since the goal of making a collective film was itself a response to the contemporary questioning of authority, the failure to achieve this goal suggests that the new attitudes will not bring about social change as easily as *Comment savoir* envisaged. In that film, Jutra argued that the electronic teaching machines were not "dehumanizing" because they encouraged "freedom." The new classroom would be one in which there is no "discipline" but also no "anarchy," because the students "participate" fully in their own education.[29] *Wow* began as an attempt to test and extend this utopian vision, but the outcome was a film whose structure verges on anarchy.

The production process also involved an attempt to work with new communications technology. Jutra wanted to explore the possibilities of video, a medium that he saw as the product of a cybernetic technology that "responds to you and ... thanks to its immediate effect, allows you to react at the precise moment when you need to."[30] The NFB eventually decided that video technology was "not sufficiently advanced" to meet its technical standards, and *Wow* was shot on sixteen-millimetre film and blown up to thirty-five millimetre for its commercial release.[31] However, although the final version contains no video images, Jutra felt that the use of video during its preparation was a "provocation" that allowed the group to gain an "apprenticeship to the camera."[32]

The film that emerged from this production process is one that does little to conceal the cultural contradictions that lie behind it. For the spectator, the narrative enigmas of classical cinema give way to questions about whose vision the film expresses and about the relationship between its documentary and fantasy sequences. According to Noguez, the film's main question involved the first of these issues: "Who is speaking? All of Quebec youth or certain young people from Montreal? These young people or Jutra? More-over: does the film present these young people themselves or the idea that Jutra has of them?" He concluded that, despite appearances to the contrary, the director still played the dominant role: the apparent "submission ... to established values exhibited by the young people is simply a response to the "situations of *passivity*" in which Jutra placed them, "sitting down to answer questions, or opening themselves up to our curiosity, offering us access to their dreams." The film thus amounted to a "gentle rape" of its participants.[33]

Even in the terms of Noguez's own analysis, the Jutra who speaks is a highly contradictory figure, since the film supposedly reveals both the "edu-cator" who lies "dormant" within him and his "refusal to grow old."[34] Tadros recognized similar contradictions but felt they had a more productive effect. He saw *Wow* as "a film about one character, a character who successively takes on nine different faces," but he did not identify this one character with Jutra.[35] For Tadros, the film was exactly what Jutra originally intended, a collective portrait of Quebec youth, albeit one that reveals "a global refusal of society."

The film draws attention to the question "who is speaking" during its opening credits sequence. In the first shot, the NFB's production credit appears over a close-up of hands tying sticks of dynamite. Despite the possi-ble revolutionary implications of this shot, the explosions that follow destroy not the institution within which the film was made but family homes in what appears to be a middle-class suburb.

This explosive opening resembles the ending of another contemporary film about youth, Michelangelo Antonioni's *Zabriskie Point* (1970), in which a house explodes in slow-motion images that dwell on the beauty of the destruction of the furniture and appliances associated with the affluent soci-ety. Noting this parallel, Noguez objected that, while Antonioni's explosion occurs only in the heroine's imagination, it nevertheless seems to be "the logical consequence of a radical opposition to established society," whereas "the recourse to this extreme solution" in *Wow* does not seem to "follow from what the young people ... say during the rest of the film."[36]

The young people appear initially as "rebels" or, especially in the Quebec context, "terrorists," but the film quickly disturbs this impression by showing them happily playing with a ball on the street as smoke drifts through the neighbourhood behind them. At the end of this sequence, a caption asserts that "the most important things in life are those that *never* happen."

Although this epigraph suggests that the explosions are fantasy images, it does not address the question of whose fantasy they represent. Jutra attributed the opening sequence not to the dreams of the group members but rather to the "simplistic" idea of youth with which he started, and he agreed that the rest of the film shows "that this first scene is very far from the reality."[37] However, there is nothing in the sequence to mark it as the director's fantasy, and it seems instead to put in place an image of the youth movement that would form part of the spectator's cultural background. The uncertain authorship of the opening "dream" thus relates the problem of representing reality to that of the film's reception by the spectator.

The credits, which reveal the film's multiple authorship, open up the question who is addressing us through the dreamlike sequence on which they are superimposed. Is this a NFB film (as the opening shot announces)? Does it express the point of view of the young people who appear in it and who are its "characters" (a term more appropriate to fiction even though the credits also inform us that they scripted their own dream sequences)? Or is it really "un film de Claude Jutra" (as the final credit asserts)?

In trying to determine who is speaking, however, the spectator also has to make connections between the fantasy and documentary aspects of the film. Jutra saw the inclusion of the dreams as a sign of a "withdrawal from *cinéma-vérité*," presumably as a result of the doubts that emerged during the production of *À tout prendre*. Instead of "filming something that was really happening," the filmmakers tried to "really make the impossible happen on the screen." Through its dream sequences, *Wow* seeks to "reach deeper levels of consciousness" than would be possible through the observational techniques of conventional documentary practice.[38]

Yet Jutra also insisted that, while "the dream level ... was essential ... it was not sufficient."[39] By juxtaposing dreams and interviews, he set out to create a film that works on "two levels, the subconscious and the conscious, which act on each other and illuminate each other."[40] Tadros agreed with Jutra that the dream sequences would be nothing without the element of speech that confers the "real dimension" on them.[41] The interplay of the two levels, however, combined with the ambiguities of authorship, means that the film does not construct clear boundaries between fantasy and reality.

Although the interviews are in black and white and the dreams in colour, this difference does not clearly establish which represents the "real dimension." According to long-established cinematic convention, colour connotes fiction as opposed to documentary, but it also suggests that the dreams capture a deeper and more intense reality. The unusual structure of the film thus provides an even more extreme response to the "crisis" of realism that lay behind the aesthetics of failure in *À tout prendre*.

During the interview sequences, scattered throughout the film, we never see the group as a whole. The camera rarely moves, but the editing presents the interviewees singly or in pairs, corresponding to already existing relationships within the group that define "couples" and "friends." No interviewer or animator is seen or heard. The interviewees sit or lounge in wooden chairs and speak in front of a neutral background, a kind of no-place, evoking the conventions of the studio interview that Jutra rejected in *Fred Barry comédien* and *Félix Leclerc troubadour*.

In those earlier films, the placement of the subjects in the environments that shaped their artistic personae implied the existence of a cultural context within which the artist reacts to familiar landscapes and institutions. The comparison of *Félix Leclerc troubadour* with *Wow* is especially pertinent because the shift into the fantasy world of Leclerc's songs in that film also involves the use of dream imagery to reach "deeper levels of consciousness." Yet Leclerc's flights of fantasy emerge from the detailed depiction of his domestic life, while the homes of the teenagers in *Wow* appear only briefly before being blown up in the credits sequence. After this imaginary act of rebellion, the dreams come to seem like a quest for a real dimension in the context of a cultural void signified by the no-space of the interview sequences. In the absence of a clearly defined authorial position, however, the film's fragmented structure and instability create a textual counterpart to the social issues of freedom and authority with which it deals.

In the first sequence after the credits, Jutra briefly inserts himself into the film in a way that highlights his problematic situation as its director. At the end of the credits sequence, the camera pulls back from the young rebels at play, as if asserting its independence from them. Jutra then appears as a schoolteacher who lectures on the need to relate the parts to the whole if there is to be a "system." While he speaks, his authority is contested both by the students, who smoke pot at their desks, and by the camera, which begins in the position of a pupil but then offers a series of close-ups of the uninterested class as the teacher's voice fades to inaudibility. Jutra's plea for order gives way to disconnected words and phrases muttered by the spaced-out students, including the quintessential psychedelic expression that gives the film its title.

The camera then demonstrates its ability to enter "inner space" as we see what appears to be a representation of a "bad trip" in which a youth runs through an underground parking lot shouting loudly with his hands over his ears. At the end of the sequence, we return to the classroom where Jutra ends his lecture by declaring, "Let's see what really happens." The traditional teacher/student relationship, quite different from the "progressive" classrooms seen in *Comment savoir*, suggests that the film grows out of a tension in which the director stands for structure and system while his young collaborators introduce a capacity for fantasy and anarchy. Jutra's final words, however, make clear that his authority is tempered by curiosity, and the wandering camera indicates that the cinematic apparatus is at least partially complicit with the challenge to authority.

The appearance of the director in the film, discussing part/whole relationships within a system, confronts the spectator with the problems of form and structure that emerged during the production process. By stressing the need for "system," Jutra also invokes contemporary developments in systems theory and cybernetics. From this perspective, a system (social, psychic, cinematic) exists in a dynamic relationship with its environment and works to reduce the complexity of that environment. Yet the field of tensions and contradictions in *Wow* undermines the confidence of the technological discourse found in films like *Comment savoir* and suggests the possibility that, in Quebec at the end of the 1960s, the distinction between system and environment may no longer hold.

As we have seen, the film's own system involves the alternation of interview and fantasy in an effort to reveal aspects of the youth culture that would not be accessible if either approach were used separately. This strategy emerges only gradually and is never consistently established. The opening sequences are highly enigmatic substitutes for the explanatory commentary or captions that conventionally orient spectators at the beginning of documentaries. Although the next segment, an interview sequence introduced by a caption that identifies its topic as drugs, seems to set the basic alternation in motion, it is followed by another sequence whose status is uncertain.

Labelled simply "A memory," the sequence begins with three youths (Flis, François, and Pierre) smoking pot in the courtyard of an apartment building.

At first, this seems to be a flashback illustrating the topic of the preceding interviews, but it shades into fantasy as the camera follows the joint passing from hand to hand until it reaches a black youth who is clearly not present in the "real" space of the sequence. When the joint reaches an oriental youth, the fantasy becomes a utopian representation of the drug culture as a means of building a "global village." But it takes on more disturbing connotations when a baby begins to cry, the walls start spinning, and the three youths rush into the street where they tear down posters of Marx, Freud, Kennedy, and Laurel and Hardy. The sequence ends with Flis hiding in a tree from a policeman on a motorcycle.

It is not clear whose memory this sequence represents, although the final image may retroactively attribute it to Flis. While it does conform to the ambivalent view of drugs, developed verbally in the previous sequence, as a means of escape from social constraints and as potentially self-destructive, the meaning of the act of tearing down the oddly juxtaposed posters remains elusive. It involves the desecration of the images of figures highly regarded by different elements within the counterculture, but, as in the first two sequences, it is uncertain whether the fantasy originates from inside or outside that culture.

When this sequence is followed by another series of interviews on youth and then by the first of the dream sequences, the pattern of alternation seems finally to be in place. However, the visit to Resurrection City again breaks the pattern when it is inserted into the middle of the film with no explanation of the circumstances behind it. As noted earlier, the introduction of the White House as the site of political struggle creates tensions similar to those found in the ending of *Comment savoir*, but the effect in *Wow* is to complicate still further the distinction between reality and fantasy. Even though the sequence is in colour (like the dreams), Washington becomes the only "real" space in a film that otherwise consists of the "imaginary" spaces of the dream sequences and the no-place of the interviews.

It is in the dream sequences that the question of the film's orientation towards the group becomes most urgent. Was Jutra simply the agent of the young people who used his technical skills to visualize their dreams, or did he filter the dreams, all of which bear the marks of his authorship? The dream sequences become sites of tension between two discourses that exist in a relationship that combines complicity and criticism.

The filmmaker is presumably responsible at least for the order in which the diverse materials appear in the finished film, but even here the boundary between the two discourses remains unstable. Although the film offers no explanation for the ordering of the sequences, Jutra took responsibility for the film's structure in an interview given at the time of its release. He suggested that the order in which the dreams appear "clearly indicates my personal development in relation to them" because "they go further and further into the intimate life of the characters." He added that "the degree of personal engagement progresses in the course of the film."[42] But whether this "personal engagement" is Jutra's own or that displayed by each member of the group in relation to his or her dream sequence remains ambiguous.

The first dream is Babette's fantasy in which she pictures herself as a nun in rural Quebec. This is followed by Flis's realization of his desire to run naked through the city streets. An interview sequence on the topic of love then leads into two more dream sequences that affirm the love of Michelle and Dave. Whereas the dreams of Babette and Flis do not acknowledge their status as a couple outside the dreams, those of Michelle and Dave end with celebrations of romantic love. The frankness of the group in the interviews reflects the new sexual freedom associated with the counterculture, but the dream sequences either ignore sexuality or deal with it in ways that reveal the residual power of supposedly outmoded cultural forms.

In one of the interviews, Dave expresses the attitude most typically associated with the counterculture when he declares that his motto is "Make love as often as possible." Some of the others question this equation of love and sex, and Philippe argues that making love before marriage is "only fucking." The sequence on love ends by focusing on Michelle and Dave as a couple, in a way that brings out the uncertainty underlying the regressive tendencies within the group. Although Michelle affirms her confidence in Dave's love, he ends the sequence with a question: "Why can't we find it?" Since Dave's two contributions to this sequence are in English, clearly his first language although he normally speaks French, the effect is to link the ostensible topic of youth culture to the broader issues of cultural tensions in Quebec.

Philippe's dream follows an interview sequence on parents and involves a rebellion against figures of authority. Dressed in a white sheet, he sits beside a river and shrinks away from four male figures – a priest, a policeman, a businessman, and a soldier – who seem to represent the masculine role models that society offers him, although their power is undercut by the fact that they are played by other members of the group. An older woman – seemingly a prostitute – embodies the threat of adult sexuality, but when Philippe catches sight of a young woman also dressed in a white sheet (played, apparently, by his real-life girlfriend who is not one of the interviewees), he throws all these threatening figures into the river, after being magically transformed into a judo expert.

The ritualistic aspect of this fantasy is underlined by the organ music that carries connotations of the past both of Quebec (religious) and of cinema (silent film). These associations with the past foreshadow the replacement of the dream of rebellion by regressive imagery familiar from the earlier dreams. Philippe and the young woman, now dressed in modern clothes, run from the urban docklands into the country and reappear as an eighteenth-century couple living in a farmhouse. The dream ends with the young woman waiting for Philippe to come to bed, while he sits downstairs writing the word love with a blue feather pen.

Philippe's situation at the end of his dream recalls his earlier comment on sex before marriage, but his rebellion against the castrating force of the modern adult world leads only to self-imposed impotence expressed through an image from the past. This image implies a self-critical impulse in the dream, but it may also suggest Jutra's detachment from the dream that he is supposedly realizing. In any case, Jutra's discourse, as the film's structuring agent, does make itself felt at this point. There is a sudden cut from Philippe in his eighteenth-century costume to a shot labelled "Resurrection City. Washington, DC (USA). 1968." A specific present (or at least recent) reality, labelled with an ironic attention to detail, intrudes abruptly into the fantasy of the past, to be followed a few moments later by Flis's prophecy of a violent future.

The film thus juxtaposes the retreat to an imaginary past, the inability of the group to relate to symbolic political activity in the present, and the fear of real violence in the future. It is hardly surprising that the discussion of the visit to Washington ends with general consent to Monique's expression of impotence: "What can I do?" This question immediately provokes another retreat, this time into what Monique calls her "little girl's fantasy."

Monique's dream raises disturbing questions about the filmmaker's and the spectator's investment in the process of investigating the social and fantasy lives of these young people. It begins with Monique riding with children on a carousel, but within the dream she drifts into a fantasy in which she first rides alone on the carousel and then bounces ecstatically on an (unseen) trampoline, moving in and out of the frame while colourful optical effects create patterns on her body.

The traces left by the use of video in preparing the film are most apparent in this sequence. Jutra related it to his early background in animation and saw it as an expression of his love of "playing with the instrument" in order to "extend its possibilities."[43] However, the sequence also plays with the spectator's response to Monique's body. Although the superimpositions and silhouette effects prevent clear vision, she appears to be naked towards the end of the sequence, and there is a shift from negative stock to positive images that finally and briefly allow full vision of her naked body.

The erotic effect of Monique's dream again underlines the complex implications of the film's disruption of familiar patterns of authorship and spectatorship. Do the tantalizing glimpses of the naked body, followed by its full (but quickly withdrawn) revelation, express Monique's fantasy of freedom and pleasure in her body? Or does the sequence reflect Jutra's objectification of her body for his own aesthetic or erotic purposes? And is the spectator invited to identify with the fantasy or to become a voyeur? If the latter is the case, does the sequence simply make explicit the voyeurism underlying the entire enterprise not just of this film but of cinema itself? The use of an image from this dream in the film's publicity certainly suggests that its producers or distributors felt that it was vital to any commercial prospects that the film might have.

Monique's dream may expose the voyeurism involved in the film's project, but a resistance to its claims to represent the subjectivity of its characters emerges when a caption announces that "François doesn't dream." Instead of a dream sequence, the camera follows him through the city as the other members of the group discuss his attitudes. Monique, who describes herself as his ex-girlfriend, sees him as a "conservative." François himself claims that he believes in the value of doubt and that his dream is to be a spectator within the film, presumably because he has no dreams of his own. The cinematic apparatus seems to have the last laugh because, even in this non-dream sequence, François becomes the object of the camera's gaze. Even his claim not to dream is belied by the final zoom in on him as he stands with arms outspread on top of a cathedral next to a statue of the militant Christ. We are again left asking whether this represents his own fantasy or Jutra's ironic comment on his claim to modest self-effacement.

According to Jutra's account of the film's structure, the final dreams should come closest to expressing his preoccupations. Since these dreams reinforce the regressive tendencies in the earlier dreams, the film's voice finally seems to blend with the voices of the dreamers. Marc's dream takes him away from the city to the country where he lives in harmony with nature, makes clay pots, and meets an old (English-speaking) tramp. Although the tramp has also gone "back to nature," he urges Marc to sell his pottery in the city. When Marc refuses to make the kind of pottery that people will want to buy and defends the pleasure that he finds in playing with the glaze, he articulates Jutra's approach to filmmaking.

At the end of the following, and final, interview sequence on the future, Pierre expresses his hope that things will stay as simple as they are now. His wish sums up the outlook of the entire group who insist on the need to experience life to the full in the present, despite the regressive imagery of their dreams. At the beginning of the dream that follows, Pierre is in the present, as represented by a small apartment in which he plays his guitar and shares a joint with a friend. The dream interweaves this space with visions, presumably drug induced, of two alternative spaces: a much larger apartment, in which Pierre plays a sitar and pats an Afghan hound, and his childhood home in France.

In the latter space, the converted barn of an old monastery, a young boy crawls on a wooden floor and plays with a pet porcupine, while his mother watches over him and his father plays the piano. The parents are dominant, mythic figures seen from the point of view of the child who innocently examines a small turd left by the porcupine. He is confronted with the complications of the adult world when his mother asks what they will do with this unusual pet when they leave. The child's disregard for the boundaries between nature and culture suggests that this is a wish-fulfilment dream that seeks to overcome the cultural divisions of the adult world.

Although Jutra claimed that the final dream sequence is "stuffed with all sorts of my own preoccupations," Pierre's dream encapsulates the "global refusal" of modern urban life in all the other dreams.[44] With the final image of his dream, a return to the dreamer smoking in the present, the film comes to an abrupt end. While Jutra justified this enigmatic ending by insisting that there was "nothing more to say" after the last dream, it leaves the spectator with the impression that something else needs to be said.[45]

Pierre's dream laments the loss of childhood innocence from the perspective of an adolescent who resists becoming part of an inadequate adult society. The sudden ending confronts the spectator with the question whether the difficult transition from childhood to adulthood is a state of affairs endemic to all human experience, the consequence of the situation in the 1960s, or a sign of the colonial status of Quebec culture.

Technology and Social Change

While the film leaves the spectator struggling to cope with its representation of the youth culture, its structure and strategies also owe a great deal to contemporary discourses on technology and society. Jutra's own views on the new "technology of communication" that he first encountered in California were close to the controversial ideas recently expressed by Marshall McLuhan in *Understanding Media* (1964). From his perspective as a filmmaker, Jutra stressed that "kids today are absorbed in television and all sorts of other technological means of communication," with the result that film had lost its former "magic" and must find ways to respond to this "revolutionary" new "way of perceiving" and its "psychological consequences."[46] His attempt to explore the potential of video in making *Wow* was one way of responding to this challenge.

Blumer described the young people in *Wow* as "children of McLuhan and Coca Cola," adapting a phrase from Godard's *Masculin Féminin* (1965) in which a caption refers to its characters as "the children of Marx and Coca Cola."[47] The substitution of McLuhan for Marx implies that these "children" belong to an emerging culture that envisages social change as the result not of revolutionary political activity but of technological developments. According to McLuhan, the most significant of these developments was the replacement of media such as print and film, which require linear "reading," by electronic media that encourage a more active response from audiences and that spill over national boundaries to create a new "global village."[48]

The question of *Wow*'s involvement in this kind of discourse is not a simple one. Given the topic and Jutra's reputation as a perpetual child, *Wow* provided an opportunity to explore the cultural effects of the electronic media, including what Joshua Meyrowitz has called the "overall homogenization, or merging, of childhood and adulthood."[49] To some extent, the film does move in this direction. Its structure – which resembles the discontinuous flow of television programming more than the linear continuity of classical narrative cinema – blurs conventional boundaries, such as that between fantasy and documentary; and the playful quality of much of its imagery confirms the need for a childlike vision, which Jutra had celebrated in *Comment savoir* and *Rouli-roulant*. Nonetheless, despite the fantasy of a joint uniting the races in the "memory" sequence, the film's vision is a more disturbing one in which the global village of electronic communications is less apparent than a global refusal of social concerns.

Rather surprisingly, television does not figure in any of the interview or fantasy sequences in *Wow*. Instead, there are frequent allusions to other films that point to *Wow*'s immersion in what would seem to be an old-fashioned cinematic culture. For example, the freeze-frame technique that Michelle uses to realize her dream of stopping the world derives from René Clair's classic science-fiction film *Paris qui dort* (*The Crazy Ray*, 1923). Allusions to Luis Buñuel's *Un Chien Andalou* (1928) occur in Philippe's and Marc's dreams: in the former, an insert shot of a cloud slicing across the disc of the sun echoes a similar shot (with moon rather than sun) that precedes the infamous slicing of the eye at the beginning of Buñuel's film; in the latter, Marc closes a door on the city and opens another on the country in the same way that Buñuel's heroine steps straight from her house on to a beach.

The effect of these borrowings from the cinematic past is to draw attention to the director's role in constructing the dreamscapes. There are also a number of allusions to more recent films whose presence is less clearly attributable to Jutra's influence. The intrusion of war into the idyllic landscape of Babette's dream may suggest an underlying fear of the political tensions in contemporary Quebec, but there is also a clear visual echo of *Shame* (1968), Ingmar Bergman's film about a couple caught up in the nightmare of civil war. When Dave smashes his guitar in his dream, he seems to be drawing on a similar incident in Antonioni's *Blow Up* (1966), and we have already seen that the opening sequence virtually quotes the ending of the same director's *Zabriskie Point.*

Apart from these allusions (some more obvious than others) to images from earlier films, there are two references to other films that relate even more directly to *Wow*'s play with the issue of authorship. During Flis's run down rue Sainte-Catherine, he passes a cinema marquee advertising Brault's *Entre la mer et l'eau douce,* a new Quebec film made while Jutra was "waiting for something else" (that the cinema is the "Parisien" adds an ironic touch). Did the cinema happen to be showing this film or did Jutra arrange the allusion, with or without Flis's support? Whoever was responsible, the allusion adds a layer to the regressive texture of the dream sequences since, as Peter Morris puts it, Brault's film depicts "the city as a place of material success but emotional loss" and evokes "nostalgia for a once-upon-a-time harmony with nature."[50]

The second such reference occurs during Michelle's dream in which she uses the power she has temporarily acquired to address questions to the other members of the group. When she asks Marc to name his favourite film, he unhesitatingly chooses Godard's *La Chinoise.* His answer disturbs any confidence that Jutra was solely responsible for the cinematic allusions; but as an allusion, it also serves to underline the political reticence of the group and the filmmaker. The Maoist militants in Godard's film may be politically inept, but they are certainly much more committed than Jutra's group, while the fragmented and disruptive style of Godard's political cinema serves didactic purposes quite alien from those of the similar strategies in *Wow.*

The issues of technology and authorship come together in Jutra's use of the medium to realize the characters' dream scenarios. I have already discussed the effects of his "playing with the instrument" in Monique's dream, and a similar tension occurs when the film employs sophisticated split-screen effects to represent Marc's discovery of the simplicity of the natural life. The intervention of the filmmaker is perhaps most evident in Michelle's dream in which she acquires the power to "stop time," to "take life away and give it back again." After using her power to stop the action at a fairground and to manipulate the other members of the group, Michelle ends her dream by retiring to the country to make love with Dave. Jutra then takes back the power of the cinematic apparatus to underline the conventional romantic ending with a freeze-frame of the couple kissing.

The film is thus simultaneously immersed in cinematic culture and disruptive of conventional forms of film spectatorship. It celebrates the liberating potential of the new communications media, as described by McLuhan and by Jutra in *Comment savoir* and in interviews, while also stressing the disorienting effect of the breakdown of traditional cultural boundaries. The very form of the film testifies to this ambivalence, and its divided authorship is the sign of a "failed" attempt to develop a new cultural order.

The Death of the Author

Questions about authorship were very much in the air at the end of the 1960s. In 1967 the NFB launched the Challenge for Change/Société Nouvelle program, which, according to Boyce Richardson, one of the filmmakers involved with the program, "turned on its head the usual exploitative and predatory relationship between media technician and subject and handed over editing authority to the people in the film."[51] The aim was to allow the people affected to speak directly about social problems and conditions, and the program soon took advantage of the flexibility offered by video equipment. By inverting the conventional hierarchies of documentary cinema, the program linked a concern to change social institutions with a challenge to the authority of the NFB's technical standards (which prevented the use of video images in *Wow*) and of the filmmakers who mediated between the institutions and the film's subjects.

The relationship between authority and authorship in the Challenge for Change films led to lively debates inside and outside the NFB. *Wow* engages with the issues involved in these debates and, in so doing, also reflects recent developments in film theory. After the celebration of the authorial voice in the *auteur* theory developed at *Cahiers du cinéma* in the 1950s, the influence of structuralism led to a questioning of "humanist" notions of individuality and authorship. It was Roland Barthes who proclaimed the new attitude with most authority in his famous essay on "The Death of the Author," first published in 1968.

Barthes argued that the author in a traditional text functions, much like a teacher in a traditional classroom, as the source of "authorized" meanings that the reader (student) must come to understand and accept. When this authority breaks down, the text becomes an interweaving of "multiple writings, drawn from many cultures and entering into mutual relations of dialogue, parody, contestation." Since all the "traces" that make up the text attain unity only through the activity of the reader, the "death of the Author" implies the "birth of the reader."[52]

If *Wow* is read as a Barthesian text, its fragmented structure exposes the way the film, like the culture with which it engages, is made up of "multiple writings" that are not unified by a consistent and identifiable authorial voice. The meaning(s) of the relationships between the film's diverse materials must be supplied by the spectator, as in Barthes's unauthored text.

While the film may have set out, in the spirit of Challenge for Change, to allow its subjects to speak for themselves, the actual effect is to call into question the possibility of such transparent communication. The resulting instability points to the ideological problems underlying the apparent abdication of authority and links the film to the "playful" aesthetic that underpins the version of the "Death of the Author" put forward by Barthes. The extent to which the shift of power from author to spectator is actual rather than apparent remains uncertain, but this only adds to the instability of the spectator's experience of the film.

As in the case of *À tout prendre*, however, the main effect is to set the global refusal, revealed in the progression of interviews and dreams, against a utopian potential grounded in the spectator's interaction with the play of the text. Like the contemporary writings of Jürgen Habermas that called for "a critical dimension" in systems theory, *Wow* seeks to "take into account the ideological distortions of the present and the utopian aspirations of the future."[53] Although Jutra explicitly invokes systems theory during his appearance as a schoolteacher, only a few critics recognized the play with systems in Jutra's challenging film. As a result, *Wow* failed to satisfy the prevailing expectations of commercial or radical, fiction or documentary cinema. It was a film both of and against its time and place.

Above: Benoît (Jacques Gagnon) watches his uncle (Jean Duceppe)
eating after their journey to the Poulin farm
(Photo Library of the National Film Board of Canada, All rights reserved)

Below: The explosive arrival of Alexandrine (Monique Mercure) at the village store
(Photo Library of the National Film Board of Canada, All rights reserved)

BETWEEN YESTERDAY AND TOMORROW
Mon oncle Antoine

On 6 June 1970 an article by Jean-Pierre Tadros appeared in *Le Devoir* describing a reception given by the NFB for the people of Thetford Mines to mark the completion of shooting for Jutra's new feature film. Many of the guests had appeared in the film, and Tadros described a community united by "enthusiasm" and "euphoria" after having experienced "something marvellous and mysterious." The impact of the film on the community anticipated its effect on its eventual spectators. Tadros, however, also referred to darker undercurrents that threatened this sense of community and influenced the film's depiction of small-town life during the Duplessis years.[1]

The community's memory of its tragic past, when it was ravaged by the effects of asbestosis, led to an initial distrust of the filmmakers. A few years earlier, Arthur Lamothe's *Poussière sur la ville* (*Dust over the City*, 1965) had stressed the bleakness of life in the shadow of the mines through its depiction of a couple whose marriage breaks up when they move to the area. The production of *Mon oncle Antoine* thus helped to restore a sense of community despite the suspicious eye of people who were tired of being cast in the role of victims.

After winning the trust of the citizens of Thetford Mines, Jutra's next problem was to find an audience for his film. His experiences with *À tout prendre* and *Wow* did not inspire confidence, and *Mon oncle Antoine* ran into difficulties soon after the reception. At the end of his article, Tadros reported that the film would be completed within six months, in time for a December release, appropriately enough since most of the action takes place on Christmas Eve. In fact, it was not until almost a year later, in November 1971, that the film was finally shown in Montreal. According to Gary Evans, the delay occurred because Sidney Newman, who became commissioner of the NFB in August 1970, requested the reshooting of two sequences for technical reasons.[2] Martin Knelman, however, claimed that the NFB had little faith in the film, especially after it was rejected by the Cannes Film Festival, and only released it at all because of its success at the Canadian Film Awards in September 1971.[3]

Whatever the reasons for the delay, *Mon oncle Antoine* received highly enthusiastic reviews in Quebec and throughout Canada. It was clearly more accessible than Jutra's previous films, more like European art cinema (comparisons with Truffaut abounded), and it quickly established its director as one of Canada's major filmmakers, a true Canadian *auteur*. But while the film that finally established Jutra's reputation was autobiographical (like *À tout prendre*), it drew on the childhood memories not of the director but of its screenwriter.

Double Vision

Clément Perron based his original screenplay on his personal experiences in a community near Thetford Mines. He had previously directed a number of short films for the NFB, most notably *Jour après jour* (*Day after Day*, 1962), a poetic documentary on workers in a paper mill, but had now decided to concentrate on screenwriting. After *Mon oncle Antoine*, he returned occasionally to directing, and this film became, in effect, the second in a trilogy devoted to Quebec's recent history as reflected in small-town life; the other films were *Taureau* (1973), set in the present, and *Partis pour la gloire* (*Going for Glory*, 1975), set during the conscription crisis in World War II.

The collaboration between Perron and Jutra, who helped to revise the screenplay, seems to have gone smoothly, but the presence of two authors is the first indication of a kind of "double vision" that recurs in many aspects of *Mon oncle Antoine*. The film also has two titles. When Tadros wrote his article, the working title was *Silent Night* (in English), and these words appear as a subtitle in the opening credits of some English-language prints. Jutra explained that Perron chose the title for several reasons: "First, *Silent Night* is Christmas Eve; second, it is an English title because, in this francophone community, English words slip in very easily and, third, more than Christmas Eve, the English title would suggest the Quebec night which had been so long." Although Jutra himself preferred *Silent Night* as a title, it was eventually dropped because it had become something of a mannerism to give English titles to works in French, and the filmmakers eventually agreed on a new title that would encourage the "phenomenon of spectator identification."[4]

As *Mon oncle Antoine*, the film achieved a greater popular success than any previous Canadian film and created an experience of solidarity for many of its audiences.[5] But the other title lingered as a reminder of its darker implications. David Beard identified the film's dual personality when he argued that, as *Mon oncle Antoine*, "it is a heart-warming film," but as *Silent Night*, "it is a vibrant and subtle political statement by a mature film maker."[6]

More recently, Jacqueline Viswanathan has made a similar point about the two titles: "On the one hand, *Mon oncle Antoine* is a light comedy, a 'Christmas film' suitable for the entire family. But on the other, it is also a film noir, an 'anti-celebration' with an 'anti-Father Christmas.'" She goes on to suggest that "*Silent Night*, better than the inoffensive joviality of *Mon oncle Antoine*, evokes the double face of this work."[7] Although Tadros stressed the creation of a sense of community during the filmmaking process and later argued that the film's "simplicity ... attracts our adhesion," it is the tension involved in the film's "double face" that creates a powerful combination of identification and critical distance.[8]

This tension proved to be more acceptable than the similar disturbances in Jutra's earlier (and later) films, but a few critics, mainly in Quebec, argued that, like *Wow*, *Mon oncle Antoine* failed to engage with the disturbing political realities of the day. As Knelman suggested, there was probably some resentment that Jutra was becoming "English Canada's favourite French Canadian," but Knelman himself perhaps added fuel to the fire when he argued that the success of *Mon oncle Antoine* at the Canadian Film Awards disproved charges that the competition was rigged so that "no true Quebec movie would stand a chance."[9]

Predictably, the film's opponents insisted that it was not a "true Quebec movie." There were two major grounds for this claim: first, it abandoned the direct cinema tradition that made Quebec cinema distinctive; and second, it retreated into the past and thus failed to engage with the issues facing Quebec in the present. Although the film's success swept these objections aside, they do point to the key aspects of the film's construction of its double face, and I will address each of them in turn as I develop my own account of the film.

Classical Form

At the end of his book of essays on Quebec cinema, published in 1970, when Jutra was already working on *Mon oncle Antoine*, Dominique Noguez identified a trend away from direct cinema towards what he called a "cinema of fable."[10] Noguez did not make clear exactly what this change involved, but Peter Harcourt suggested, a few years later, that Canadian cinema as a whole tended to work in "a mode ... that touches upon fable." This is an essentially indirect mode "that *implies* more than it says" and "that does not spell out with great psychological authority a specific social problem."[11] I would add that it is a mode in which the connotations of the images and the narrative develop a rich pattern of potentially allegorical, but fundamentally ambiguous, meanings.

I will argue that *Mon oncle Antoine* was a key film in the development of this mode but that it involved a shift in emphasis rather than a complete break with Jutra's earlier practice. As we have seen, he had already confronted the possibilities and limits of fable through his work with Norman McLaren on *A Chairy Tale*. Under the influence of Jean Rouch, he had combined this awareness with the observational thrust of direct cinema with results that often blurred the traditional boundaries between documentary and fiction. To many observers, *Mon oncle Antoine* abandoned the direct cinema tradition, but there was some disagreement about whether it represented a new direction for Quebec cinema.

Even before it was released, a reporter in *La Presse* noted that Jutra's new film promised a return to "a more classical form of cinema."[12] Jutra himself acknowledged there had been a change but claimed that the "simplicity" of *Mon oncle Antoine* was dictated by the subject matter.[13] In other words, the form was appropriate to the depiction of an apparently simpler past viewed through the eyes of an adolescent on the verge of becoming an adult. As we shall see, the film's perspective is not entirely limited to Benoît's critical look at his uncle and his small-town community, but that look is vital to the development of a fable that often defies the norms of classical narrative. It is also a rather deceptive simplicity since the pressures on the adolescent viewer in the film are conveyed through its form to the spectator viewing the film.

While some critics welcomed the film's apparently simple style, others accused Jutra of betraying the documentary roots of Quebec cinema. A US critic, Herman Weinberg, argued that his betrayal was evident in the film's narrative structure: "For two-thirds of its way it shows scenes of French-Canadian (Quebec) provincial life during a long cold winter, without stressing any particular theme, when suddenly it tells a harrowing anecdote of that winter." Although Weinberg admired the film, he regretted "the implementation of an imposed 'story'" and thought that it would have worked even better as a "straight documentary on the Québécois."[14]

On the other hand, an English-Canadian critic, Bruce Elder, insisted that *Mon oncle Antoine* owed little to the documentary tradition and stressed "the importance of narrative in the film."[15] Even those who admired the film, however, often expressed unease at the way its narrative is structured. Tadros, for example, felt that the plot was not always developed efficiently and economically, but he also argued that it would be wrong "to judge the film solely in terms of its dramatic structure."[16]

Some Quebec critics were far more harsh in their judgments of the film's alleged narrative failings. Jean Leduc published a ferocious attack in which he, like Weinberg, objected to the "sudden change of tone" and condemned "the extreme architectural weakness" of the entire screenplay.[17] Although the film has certainly outlasted Leduc's prophecy that it would be forgotten within five years, similar complaints about the construction of the narrative continue to appear in discussions of *Mon oncle Antoine*.[18]

What these complaints amount to is the somewhat contradictory claim that Jutra had betrayed Quebec's cultural identity by reverting to the norms of classical narrative cinema, and that the film does not work *because* it violates these same norms. The critics thus imposed an aesthetics of failure on the film by refusing even to consider the possibility that it might deviate from classical norms because its simplicity is not quite what it seems. The film's narrative disruptions derive from the underlying tensions that make *Mon oncle Antoine* something more than a charming story, set in Quebec's recent past, of a boy's coming of age.

Although Tadros insisted that these criticisms were beside the point, he expressed regret that the film lured the spectator down a number of "false trails."[19] But there is really only one false trail of any significance (the only one that Tadros mentioned and that many critics noted). The problem has to do with the "Benoît perspective" that comes to dominate the film but is not established in the opening sequences. Instead, four of the first five sequences deal with the events leading to the decision of a middle-aged man, Jos Poulin, to leave his job at an asbestos mine and to depart in search of work in a logging camp.

These opening sequences do not act as a conventional introduction to the main narrative line, but they do provide a context that helps us to understand the implications of Benoît's experiences. Our introduction to the world of the film comes through an argument between Poulin and a foreman in the wasteland around the asbestos mines. Jos speaks colloquial Québécois French when he swears at his broken-down truck, while the foreman uses English as the language of authority, even though he insists that the truck does not belong to him and that he is merely protecting the company's property.

Benoît does appear in the second sequence, in which he assists his uncle Antoine and Fernand (played by Jutra) in their role as undertakers at a communal wake, but the next three sequences return to Jos who expresses his frustrations to a group of men in a tavern, says farewell to his wife in the barn on their farm, and leaves home with his axe. At this point, the narrative focus shifts permanently to Benoît. Jos becomes a minor character, with only a few brief sequences devoted to him before he returns at the end of the film.

As this account suggests, the initial focus on the Poulins seems like a distraction from the film's central concern with Benoît's subjective experience.[20] Even in purely narrative terms, though, the introduction of the Poulin family has an important function. It is the death on Christmas Eve of Marcel Poulin, a youth of about Benoît's age, that sets in motion the events that lead to the film's dénouement. The opening sequences also help to build up a sense of the community in which Benoît lives, and they contain some specific anticipations of later developments. The case of beans that falls from a horse-drawn sleigh in the background as Jos says goodbye to his children may seem like a distraction within the sequence, but it is a macabre foreshadowing of a major event later in the film when Marcel's coffin falls from the sleigh on which Benoît and Antoine are taking it to town.

On a deeper level, as Jacqueline Viswanathan has pointed out, there are clear thematic links between "two plots" that centre on "the death of one young boy and the maturing of another."[21] So the issue seems to be less the irrelevance of the Poulin material than the way it disrupts the patterns of identification on which classical narrative cinema supposedly depends. In other words, we are first asked to identify with Jos but must then shift the focus of our attention to Benoît. Although much less violent, this process is not unlike the way Alfred Hitchcock invites us to identify with Marion in *Psycho* (1960) but then kills her off part way through the film. The difference is perhaps that Jos is still alive and thus available as a focus of identification, but, allowing for the major differences between the two films and their directors, the effects are quite similar.

Elder suggests some of the implications of this transfer of identification from one character to another when he argues that, "for Jos Poulin, reality is too oppressive to be overcome," while by the end of the film, Benoît has "seen the weakness of those who hold power and the stage is set for him to take revolutionary action."[22] The ending hardly points unequivocally towards revolution, as we shall see, but Elder's interpretation does suggest the way the film's structure offers Benoît as a younger version of Jos. In other words, Jos represents what Benoît may become. The shift of focus from Jos to Benoît thus functions as a kind of flashback to an earlier stage of the process by which (male) identity is constructed in this culture.

A third male figure also looms large in the film: the uncle to whom the film's title draws our attention. Antoine is a patriarchal figure who belongs to an older generation and acts as a substitute for Benoît's absent (and unmentioned) father. He gradually becomes the object of Benoît's increasingly critical gaze, and the film never offers him as an identification figure. Even though his store and his undertaking business place him at the centre of community affairs, he is finally revealed as a fearful and impotent man whose desires no longer have any place in his conscious life. The spectator's engagement with the consciousness first of Jos and then of Benoît implies that, unlike Antoine, these males are still looking and searching.

The opening sequences also employ stylistic devices that Leduc condemned as "obvious weaknesses in the direction" because they violate the dictum of classical cinema that style should not call attention to itself.[23] At the end of the quarrel between Jos and the foreman, the camera zooms in on the mountain of waste from the mine, and there is a sudden cut to a body in a coffin. A few moments later, a cut juxtaposes the coffin with bottles of beer on a table in a tavern. After Jos has declared his intention of quitting his job at the mine, another zoom brings the parish church into focus through the tavern window. This effect, obtrusive in itself, is even more strange because it does not introduce a sequence in the church. Instead the narrative takes us to the Poulins' farm, and only after Jos's departure do we see Benoît assisting the priest at morning mass, a sequence introduced by yet another zoom and a montage effect that this time juxtaposes the church with the mine.

These obtrusive editing and camera effects draw attention to the unusual narrative structure of the opening sequences, but they also establish a number of connections: between the oppression of Jos at the mine and the old man's death; between the fact of death and the drinking at the tavern; and between the tavern and the church as twin focal points of community life. In drawing attention to its own activities, the film reminds us of the processes of looking and making connections basic to all cinematic production and spectatorship and, at the same time, distances itself from those styles that depend on the concealment of such processes. While we are soon invited to identify with Benoît as he looks at and judges his surroundings, the opening sets up a distance that allows an ongoing awareness that we are also looking both with and at Benoît.

Coming between the sequences showing Jos at the mine and in the tavern, the funeral reception places the entire opening under the sign of death. Benoît's observation of the corpse and its treatment anticipates his confrontation with another dead body at the end of the film. If Jos and Antoine represent what awaits Benoît as an adult male in this culture, the old man in the coffin is a reminder of the final outcome of this process. Death is a natural event incorporated into communal life through religious and social rituals that grow out of the closeness to nature of traditional peasant culture. But the film also links death to the effects of asbestosis, hence to the exploitation of workers like Jos, and to the death-in-life existence that is all Quebec has to offer during the Duplessis era. In the tavern, Jos speaks of not wanting to end up like Euclid, the dead man; he then finishes a beer and remarks, "That's another one the English won't get."

Death as a biological and cultural event becomes entwined with a similar complex of meanings surrounding sexuality. When Jos and his wife make love among the animals in the barn, the sexual act is an affirmation of life in the face of a social and cultural reality that drives them apart. From Benoît's perspective, however, sexuality is associated with death rather than life. He watches Antoine and Fernand strip the dead man's body, removing a formal suit that is just a façade that conceals the man's social class and his naked flesh.

The suit looks exactly like the ones worn by the living men, and this glimpse of the flesh hidden under the pretences of social decorum introduces Benoît's fascination with, and fear of, the sexuality and mortality of the human body. Our gradual involvement with Benoît's look develops under the influence of pressures that combine attraction with rejection. At first, he seems to take a childlike pleasure in witnessing the weaknesses of his elders. When he catches the priest secretly drinking the sacramental wine, as Benoît himself had done before the mass, the effect is to blur the distinctions between childhood and adulthood and between church and tavern. He also smiles when he sees his aunt and uncle drinking gin in the morning and when Antoine starts to tell a joke to an admiring audience of customers.

As Benoît observes the activities in the store, we discover both the attraction and the constraints of a community based on tradition. The store functions as a kind of community centre, occupying a space midway between the tavern and the church, at least metaphorically, since the geographical layout of the village is never clearly defined. Although Fernand tries to persuade a man to buy a pair of pants that are obviously too large for him, the store belongs to a time before the development of modern practices of marketing and consumption. The highpoint of Christmas Eve is the annual unveiling of the manger scene in the store window, followed by the impromptu celebration of the engagement of a young couple.

Yet there are already hints that something is wrong with this traditional way of life: the Jesus figure is broken, the curtain collapses during the unveiling, and a large Father Christmas looms incongruously over the manger. The public celebration that results from an embarrassed young woman's whispered request for a bridal veil suggests the lack of privacy in a small community, although this may be the couple's modest way of announcing their engagement.

Just as the rituals of religious and social life seem to be wearing a little thin, so the tensions within his own family undermine Antoine's patriarchal status in the community. He is married to Cécile but has no children of his own, and he later blames his alcoholism on the lack of children and his wife's refusal to move with him to the United States. Antoine is Benoît's uncle, but there is no mention of the boy's parents or of how he came to be living at the store. The father of Carmen, an adolescent girl who also lives at the store, does appear but only to pick up her wages, and Fernand questions the reluctance of Antoine and Cécile to adopt her.

Fernand is the other member of Antoine's family, although he does not seem to be related to any of the others. Jutra explained his decision to cast himself in this role by claiming that Fernand is a "director" within the film:

"He is a character who effaces himself behind other more active and more important characters but who, in a sense, manipulates and directs them."[24] While it is Fernand who really runs the store and who eventually displaces Antoine in Cécile's bed, the film stresses his effacement rather than his directorial skills. He exists outside the family unit and outside the generational sequence of males represented by Benoît, Jos, and Antoine. Just as Claude drifts into his affairs in À tout prendre, Fernand's affair with Cécile seems to develop out of their proximity, apparently sparked by the sight of the older woman coming downstairs in her nightgown. At the end, Cécile tells him that he is not yet ready to fill Antoine's boots.

These "family" relationships emerge from the activities leading up to the Christmas celebrations. We are not limited to Benoît's perspective during these sequences: for instance, the unveiling of the manger is viewed from outside when Benoît is in the window. There are also brief inserts showing the events at the Poulin farm when the eldest son suddenly becomes ill. However, our increasing engagement with Benoît's look encourages us to relate everything to his scrutiny of the world around him.

His increasingly critical perspective on the community develops alongside his sexual awakening. First, he engages in an erotic scuffle with Carmen after watching her try on a bridal veil, which she has been sent to fetch from the attic, and the ensuing chase among empty coffins again leads to the association of sexuality with death. Then he spies on Alexandrine, the glamorous wife of the notary, as she tries on her new girdle, her nudity a contrast to, but an uneasy reminder of, that of the dead man at the funeral reception.

The film uses point-of-view shots to implicate the spectator in this act of voyeurism, which Benoît shares with Maurice, another boy who works in the store. Although the male look at the woman seems to accord with the gender dynamics of classical narrative cinema, as described by Laura Mulvey and others, Alexandrine's arrival at the store has already disturbed the expected pattern. Her entrance occurs at the same time as the regular daily explosion at the mine, and she is very much in control as everyone in the store turns to look at her. When Carmen catches the two boys spying, she denounces them as "pigs," but Denyse Therrien has described this episode more charitably as "a moment of healthy curiosity."[25] These two interpretations of the boys' looking are both quite convincing, but in view of Benoît's usual inability to separate sexuality and death, the excitement he shares with Maurice does seem decidedly "healthy."

The erotic power of this sequence seems to spill over into the one act of political defiance in the film. As the mine owner drives his sleigh through the village, solemnly throwing trinkets to the children of the workers he exploits on every other day of the year, Benoît and Maurice pelt his horse with snowballs, causing it to bolt and the owner to beat an ignominious retreat. While the people seem to enjoy this spectacle, they fearfully close their doors to avoid being associated with the perpetrators. Only Carmen looks directly at them and smiles her approval. Since she has just been shocked by Benoît's sexual attentions and annoyed by their spying on Alexandrine, Carmen's smile seems to combine approval with forgiveness, implying the possibility of a new sexual and political freedom.

But the snowball attack remains an isolated incident. The warmth of communal life in the store seems to depend on an acceptance of existing social conditions. That the narrative hardly progresses during these sequences accentuates the sense of inertia, while annoying critics who nevertheless accused the film of viewing the past nostalgically. Jutra does maintain interest during the episodic sequences in the store through a running gag, but this also highlights the impact of inertia and conditioned responses.

In the first sequence at the store, Cécile comes downstairs to fetch some tea for her breakfast and notices a barrel of nails at the foot of the stairs. She tells Fernand to move it, but when Benoît arrives, he orders the boy to take it upstairs. Benoît is unable to lift it because his arm is in a cast (the origin of the cast is never explained but it suggests the impotence of the adolescent male), and the barrel repeatedly gets in the way of staff and customers. Eventually, Fernand picks up the barrel and hands it to Maurice, just as Alexandrine makes her dramatic entrance, silhouetted in the doorway. Like everyone else, Maurice cannot take his eyes off this spectacle, and he carefully steps over the empty space where the barrel had been standing. After carrying it to the attic, he puts the barrel down to spy on Alexandrine, and Carmen sprawls over it when she bursts in on the voyeurs.

Although the gags involving the barrel encourage an ironic detachment from the communal life centred on the store, there is now also an increasing number of shots of Benoît watching and judging the behaviour of his elders.

Our involvement with Benoît's look reaches a higher degree of intensity when he and Antoine travel to the Poulin house to collect the body of the son who has suddenly died on Christmas Eve. This is the first time that Benoît has accompanied his uncle on such an errand, and his eyes are drawn irresistibly, as represented by another zoom shot, to the half-open door of the dead boy's room. His anxiety emerges most vividly, however, through his evident disgust at the sight of Antoine eating the food that the grieving mother has provided.

Bruce Elder describes these shots of Antoine eating as the climax of a series of images in which he is depicted as "greedy and exploitive." According to Elder, he fails to offer Mme Poulin "the comfort which in the absence of her husband she so desperately needs" and instead "proceeds to gorge himself on pork and swill his gin, leaving the corpse of the young man unattended." Although Elder does go on to acknowledge that the key shot in the sequence is "from the boy's point of view" and shows "his perception of Antoine as disgustingly piggish," he equates Benoît's perception with that of the film/spectator.[26]

The (appropriate) use of the term "piggish" to describe how this shot presents Antoine's gluttony links Benoît's experience to Carmen's denunciation of the boys as "pigs" when she finds them spying on Alexandrine. But since the "piggish" effect is the product of a fish-eye lens that distorts Antoine's appearance, there is clearly a process of double vision involved here. When viewed "normally," Antoine's behaviour does not seem so inappropriate. He hugs the wife when he arrives and tells her that he has tried to contact her husband. Her provision of food and his acceptance of it, after a long and cold journey, are expected behaviour in a traditional peasant culture in which mourning for the dead does not exclude a practical concern with the needs of the living. If this is the case, the distortion reflects Benoît's alienation from this culture as he grapples with his own fears and desires.

Even if Benoît's perception is here shown to be "abnormal," the traditional order does involve constraints that make it seem less than ideal. These emerge more from the treatment of gender roles than as a result of Antoine's behaviour. After the mother has taken Antoine's coat, the daughter comes forward to take Benoît's, as if trying out her future role as wife and mother under the benevolent gaze of the Virgin Mary looking down on them from a calendar on the wall. She represents one possibility for resolving Benoît's sexual anxieties, by conforming to the norms of the patriarchal family, but this option is again tainted by the proximity of death.

It is Antoine's drinking, rather than his eating, that reveals his inability to live up to the patriarchal image. Before he leaves the store, both Cécile and Fernand, secretly and separately, give him bottles of gin to keep out the cold, with the result that he gets even more drunk than usual and falls asleep on the return journey. The coffin falls from the sleigh, however, only because Benoît takes a swig of gin and whips the horse into a gallop rather than simply allowing the horse to find its own way home. As Benoît tries to rouse his uncle from his drunken stupor to help with the coffin, Antoine abjectly confesses to his fear of corpses and pours out the resentments that he normally hides behind the patriarchal mask.

On returning to the store, Benoît finds Fernand and Cécile together in the bedroom. Two identical close-ups of his silent reproachful look, first at Fernand and then at Cécile, emphasize his disgust as they both try to come up with a plausible explanation of what he has seen. While Fernand and Cécile drag Antoine to his bed, Benoît falls asleep on a counter in the store and has a dream in which his recent experiences of sexuality and death are condensed into disturbing surrealistic images.

The visualization of this dream has been foreshadowed by the subjectivity of the distorted shot of Antoine eating, and it is the climax of the process by which we gradually come to share in Benoît's acts of spectatorship. In the dream he sees himself, dressed in the costume he wore when assisting at mass, lying in a field with his hand on his crotch, echoing the position of the dead youth in the coffin. He gets up, and there is a dissolve to a close-up of hands that remove the suit from a body in a coffin, as in the film's second sequence. The dream substitutes Alexandrine's body for that of the old man, and she then also rises from the dead and bounces in her girdle in front of an ecstatic Benoît.

This dream looks very much like Monique's fantasy in *Wow*, an association enhanced by the flowery backgrounds apparently suggested by fabrics displayed in the store. However, whereas Monique was the dreamer, Alexandrine's performance is part of Benoît's dream and expresses his growing awareness of his own sexuality and mortality. Both the dream and the performance end abruptly when the hands of Fernand/Jutra shake Benoît and draw him back into the real world so that he can act as a guide in an attempt to retrieve the corpse.

Having failed to find the coffin, Fernand and Benoît arrive at the Poulin house, and the film ends with an effect that both underlines our complicity with Benoît's look and invites us to consider the implications of what he sees. A long shot shows him following Fernand towards the house, and there is a cut to a shot in which the camera, apparently hand-held, moves unsteadily forward. The instability of the moving camera and the sound of drumbeats on the soundtrack evoke the pressures weighing on Benoît, whose point of view the shot clearly represents, as he approaches the front window of the house. Three shots from inside, showing Benoît peering through the window, alternate with two shots of what he sees: the Poulin family gathered around the open coffin. The final shot of Benoît's face at the window freezes and forms a background for the unrolling of the credits.

A French critic described a version of the film that apparently showed Jos finding the coffin on his return from the logging camp and, mistaking it for a box like the one that fell from a sleigh just before his departure, taking it home to his family as a gift.[27] If, as seems likely, this grotesque image was a figment of the critic's imagination, his mistake underscores the effect of the omission of the discovery of the body. There has been a considerable shift in perspective since the opening sequences in which Jos's experiences introduced us to the world of the film. While we have seen Jos making his decision to return home from the logging camp for Christmas, abandoning his job yet again, and travelling home by train, the omission of a key event in the plot confirms that our involvement in the film is now completely bound up with Benoît.

The freeze-frame ending, like the famous freeze-frame on Antoine's face as he turns back from the sea at the end of Truffaut's *Les Quatre Cent Coups*, functions as a challenge to the spectator to respond to the questions that have troubled the adolescent throughout the film. In both cases, the effect of the final image is difficult to decipher because of the virtual silence of the protagonist during the last part of the film. Benoît never speaks of his fears and desires, which emerge mainly through his observation of his community and our observation of his behaviour. What is read into the final image will thus be largely a projection of the spectator's response to the entire film.

One spectator on whom the final image had a powerful impact was Margaret Atwood, who used it as evidence for a sweeping claim about Canadian culture: "If the central European experience is sex and the central mystery 'what happens in the bedroom,' and if the central American experience is killing and the central mystery is 'what goes on in the forest' (or in the slum streets), surely the central Canadian experience is death and the central mystery is 'what goes on in the coffin.'" Atwood's conclusion is that "the knowledge that is important" in Canada is "not your first woman or your first murder but your first dead person."[28]

Atwood argues that the depiction of Benoît's initiation into adulthood is an archetypal representation of a biological process shaped by broad cultural forces. The ending can sustain this kind of reading, although it is not really Benoît's "first dead person" and Atwood does not point out that the film itself gives Benoît's vision of the mourning family overtones of sexual voyeurism. The question "what happens in the bedroom" has just been raised by his intrusion on Fernand and Cécile, and its effect, heightened by Benoît's dream, hovers over the final sequence.

The camera (Benoît, the spectator) is drawn irresistibly towards the window, evoking the mixture of fear and fascination with which Benoît has approached both death and sexuality throughout the film, and the look frozen in the final shot may not be entirely innocent of erotic desire. In the previous shot, the camera has moved across the faces of the family group and come to rest on the daughter who showed an interest in Benoît during his earlier visit. While the previous shots of Benoît at the window show him in the centre and looking straight forward, his face is off-centre in the final shot and the direction of his eyes suggests that he may be looking at the young woman. The ending thus echoes the tension in the dream sequence in which Benoît, who identifies himself with the dead Poulin son, is revived by Alexandrine's erotic attractions, and the freeze-frame may be the equivalent to the hand of Fernand/Jutra waking up Benoît/the spectator.

Atwood also fails to mention the specific cultural associations of the "dead body" that Benoît witnesses. He is confronted with what amounts to an anti-nativity scene: the son, crammed into a coffin that is too small for his body, is equivalent to the broken Jesus in the display in the store window. This blatant allusion to an image from Quebec's Catholic tradition makes the ending into a cultural as well as a personal revelation. Thus, Heinz Weinmann claims that "Benoît sees with horror what Quebec glimpsed when it allowed itself to look into the depths of its own experience: the spectre of its own 'disappearance,' of its death." The ending becomes an allegory in which "Quebec, hallucinated, sees ... its own possible death."[29] It is not clear whether this confrontation results in despair or, as Elder suggests, in an awareness of the need for "revolutionary action," but a full assessment of the film's possible cultural and political meanings must deal with the question of its historical setting.

History and Fable

The critics who claimed that *Mon oncle Antoine* was regressive complained not only about its alleged formal deficiencies but also about its apparently nostalgic view of the past. As we have seen, the frequent allusions to the past in *Wow* had disturbed a number of critics, and *Mon oncle Antoine* seemed to confirm Jutra's reputation as a filmmaker who refused to confront the problems of modern urban society and the urgent political issues in Quebec. Leduc, for example, condemned what he saw as its "folklore" image of Quebec's past and diagnosed the film's popularity as a symptom of a viral infection called "Québécitude."[30]

Jutra responded to his critics by insisting that the only way to escape from folklore in contemporary Quebec was to make films like those produced by Cinépix, a production company that specialized in sex comedies and other genre films made with the international market in mind. He insisted that he had simply remained faithful to his own "sociological and cultural reality."[31] In returning to the recent past, he felt that he was in fact dealing with issues that still affected the contemporary situation in Quebec, and he argued that, "for people of my generation, faced with current events, we can judge the present only in relation to a certain past which we have known." He claimed to be "playing ... the role of intermediary between yesterday and tomorrow," implying that Quebec had lost touch with its past and was thus vulnerable to the homogenizing influence of multinational capitalism.[32] Jutra saw his film as working against the forces that were reducing Quebec culture to the status of folklore.

There is no doubt that some spectators did respond to the film's treatment of the past as "nostalgic." Léo Bonneville, for example, attributed its "charm" to a sense of "authenticity," but this was defined not in terms of historical accuracy but as fidelity to the traditional image of Quebec life presented in the paintings of Cornelius Krieghoff and Clarence Gagnon.[33] As I have already suggested, however, the film's depiction of the past carries with it a dark undertow that works against the comfortable warmth expected of a nostalgia film. Heinz Weinmann even argued that "this Christmas Eve is a veritable 'twilight of the Gods' … for Benoît."[34] These extremely different responses suggest that the film's treatment of history is also subject to its characteristic double vision.

The ambiguity generated by this doubleness extends to an uncertainty about exactly which past the film depicts. A caption at the beginning identifies the period as "not so long ago," but this imprecise dating led to a wide variety of interpretations. Weinberg simply ignored the caption and treated the film as a virtual "documentary" on present-day "French-Canadian (Quebec) provincial life."[35] Weinmann, on the other hand, took the caption literally and assumed that the action takes place just a few years before the film's production, during the "process of desacralization … at the end of the 1960s."[36]

Since the name Maurice Duplessis appears among the sexual graffiti in the tavern washroom, the period would seem to be somewhat further back in Quebec's past, unless we assume that the graffiti are themselves relics of the past. In an interview, Jutra confirmed that the historical period was intended to be the 1940s, and he underlined the political significance of locating the action in "the asbestos country, one of the first hotbeds of the political agitation and labour unrest" that set the stage for the Quiet Revolution.[37]

The question remains why Jutra could be so precise in this interview and yet choose to be so vague in the opening caption. In order to answer this question, we need to examine the film in relation to two interrelated questions that any historical fiction provokes, and that will also be relevant to my discussion of Kamouraska and La Dame en couleurs. What "signs of the past" does the film deploy? What relationship between past and present does it imply?

One familiar approach to the historical film, adopted by most classical Hollywood films set in the past, is to take advantage of the controlled environment of the studio to construct a replica, mainly through sets and costumes, of what the past is assumed to have looked like. With the emergence of more realist styles of filmmaking in the wake of Italian neorealism, however, such versions of the past came to seem artificial. All (re)constructions of the past are inevitably artificial, but in order to make the past seem more immediate, many filmmakers (notably in Europe) used actual locations in their historical films. They could either make use of historical sites preserved under museum conditions or allocate a portion of the budget to the removal of signs of the present from the view of the camera.

In both kinds of historical film, the impression of the past diminishes when images of the natural world appear, as during interludes in the countryside or when characters shed their costumes, and such (usually brief) passages are often used to connote an escape from "cultural" constraints. In *Mon oncle Antoine*, there is hardly any sense of escape from these constraints, but there is a constant tension between the historical fiction and an awareness that the film was shot on location, testifying to the "present" existence of what the camera shows and providing the basis for Weinberg's "documentary" reading. The signs of the past are sufficient to place the action, for those familiar with Quebec history, at a specific and significant juncture in the recent past, but they are relatively sparse so that, even for spectators aware of that past, the experience of viewing the film involves a constant oscillation between impressions of past and present.

This tension emerges in the opening credits sequence. After a distant shot of people milling around on a school playing field, the camera slowly pans across a misty landscape, the green trees giving way to what appears to be a snow-covered hill. The idyllic effect is reinforced by background music featuring a female voice humming to a guitar accompaniment. When the moving camera reaches a stream of dust spewing out on top of the hill, we realize that it is a mound of waste from a mine, a product not of nature but of industry. The caption, which is then superimposed on the shot, reveals that this is "the asbestos country" and that these images belong to the recent past.

Do we believe what we see or what we read? The uncertain temporality indicated by the caption struggles against an awareness that the school, the landscape, and the mine must have been filmed in the present. While such a tension is endemic to all historical films, it becomes a structuring principle in *Mon oncle Antoine*. The blurring of past and present is perhaps most evident in the appearance of the inhabitants of the region in a number of sequences. As they stand outside the store, waiting for the unveiling of the manger scene in the window, the eager spectators do not wear costumes referring to a specific past but rather what appear to be their everyday clothes. There are no obvious anachronisms but there is also very little attempt to historicize the image. It seems to be timeless even as it testifies to the myths and rituals that shaped a particular period in Quebec history.

Martin Knelman effectively conveyed the implications of the fluid treatment of time in *Mon oncle Antoine* when, after correctly identifying the period as "the late forties" just before "the so-called Quiet Revolution," he added that "the persuasively detailed milieu feels much more than thirty years in the past: the way of life it represents hardly seems to belong to the twentieth century." The film thus reaches back beyond the 1940s to a more remote past, but, as Knelman also suggested, it looks forward to "the explosive public debates of the sixties" by catching "the way that grievances, not yet openly articulated, were expressed in private grumbling."[38]

What this suggests is that the film is both a convincing depiction of a period when discontent was confined to "private grumbling" and a representation of cultural forces in Quebec that still have a powerful resonance in the present. While one critic (Weinberg) could ignore and another (Weinmann) play down the film's historical dimensions to stress its relevance to the immediate realities of life in Quebec, yet another (Leduc) could see it as a flight from the present into a mythical past. It was also possible to read the film as an expression of Jutra's own sense of himself as an "intermediary," as a "provocation" bringing home "the urgency of building our own future." From this perspective, the film's mixture of tenses invites the people of Quebec "to assume our past, in order to better understand our present, the only guarantee of a possible future."[39]

Mon oncle Antoine thus develops a fluid and dreamlike time scheme that allows it to function as an example of Noguez's "cinema of fable." The meaning of Jutra's fable is highly unstable and depends on how the spectator reads the implied relationship between past and present. Jutra produced his own optimistic reading by stressing the difference between then and now, insisting that a new "cultural awareness" had eliminated the forces that blocked Benoît's development.[40] According to Tadros, however, the actors did not share the director's view but rather felt that "this reality which is set in the past is not as old as all that and is still very much with us."[41]

In responding to an interviewer who thought that "at first sight … the story could take place today," Jutra could only define the signs of the past negatively by referring to the absence of modern technological devices such as cars and television.[42] Implicitly, the depiction of village life offered a striking contrast to the increasingly urban culture of modern Quebec. A nostalgic reading of *Mon oncle Antoine* might blame the spread of television for the decline of the communal life found in Antoine's store, but the narrative certainly also demonstrates the hardships caused by the lack of modern communications and technology.

The absence of cars and the corresponding presence of horse-drawn vehicles creates the impression of a preindustrial society that, as Knelman points out, seems to date back well beyond the 1940s. The first sequence after the opening credits features two trucks operating in the wasteland surrounding the mine. While these battered and broken-down vehicles seem to belong to the past, they could conceivably be relics of the 1940s still, more or less, functioning in the present. In abandoning his job at the mine and leaving home to work as a lumberjack, Jos rejects his English-speaking bosses but also withdraws from Quebec's industrial future. His new, more traditional job, in an industry that had long exploited Quebec's natural resources and French-Canadian manpower, proves no more satisfying. In its treatment of Jos, the film implies the difficulty of either simply endorsing or rejecting the historical forces that have shaped modern Quebec society.

If the mine suggests that modern production methods do not necessarily entail a break with the oppressive ideological structures of the past, the depiction of the store seems to put the past in a more nostalgic light. It belongs to a time preceding the coming of modern consumer society to Quebec, although a Coca-Cola sign is visible in several long shots of the main street. Jutra pointed out that such stores had been replaced by supermarkets, and he felt lucky to have found "a real general store of the period, perfectly preserved, which belonged to two old women."[43]

As noted earlier, the store is as much a community centre as a place of business and, unlike the mine, it is clearly not a capitalist enterprise. Yet if the introduction of modern industrial relations hardly seems a blessing, the archaic past is by no means idealized, and both Tadros and Jutra claimed that industrial and cultural development had brought about improvements so that most of the abuses associated with the mine no longer existed in the present.

It is true that the film itself does not simply endorse the "progressive" view enunciated by Tadros and Jutra. The need for a political reading is to some extent masked by the focus on Benoît's passage from adolescence to adulthood, a psychological process that seems to record a universal human experience. Yet the film's mode is not that of psychological realism, and the specific forms in which Benoît's experience manifests itself clearly demonstrate the inadequacies of the cultural context in which he lives. While most critics were prepared to see Benoît's story as emblematic of certain cultural developments, there was widespread disagreement about the ultimate meaning of the film's treatment of these developments.

The debate largely centred on the ambiguity of the final image. It is here that the film's double vision reaches its climax, as suggested by two different interpretations of the ending given by the director himself. In one interview, Jutra argued that "in the context of the period," Benoît's future seems "hopeless" because there is "no opening available to him."[44] As shown, "the context of the period" is very unstable in the film, and in another interview Jutra envisaged Benoît's future as one in which he will be able to "exorcise" his past and "learn to live ... collectively."[45]

Mon oncle Antoine thus looks back on a communal life that may have existed in the past, no longer exists in the present, but may return in a "collectively" oriented future society. If the present lacks a sense of community, it has progressed beyond the repressive morality that provided the stability of the past culture. The movement from the "not so long ago" of the opening caption to the freeze-frame on Benoît's face at the window suggests that the past lives on in the present, despite obvious changes and differences, and that the film functions as a documentary/fantasy about the past/present. As a fable, the film invites the spectator to adopt both perspectives and to be prepared to move between them. Past and present, the real and the possible, "earthy realism" and "theatre of the absurd" (Leduc), *Silent Night* and *Mon oncle Antoine*, all come into a critical and unstable relationship in the experience of watching the film.

Above: The young Elisabeth (Geneviève Bujold) with her aunts (Janine Sutto, Olivette Thibault, Marie Fresnières) (Pierre Lamy)

Below: Elisabeth takes a ride with her first husband (Philippe Léotard) (Pierre Lamy)

MAD LOVE, LETHAL LOVE
Kamouraska

The commercial success and critical recognition of *Mon oncle Antoine*, along with the earlier success of Don Shebib's *Goin' Down the Road* (1970), suggested a promising future for Canadian cinema in both official languages. This promise has remained largely unfulfilled, at least partly because of the persistent problems of distribution and exhibition. Most of the growing number of films produced in Canada received little, if any, exposure in Canadian cinemas. The result was a strong tendency at the CFDC in the 1970s to support films supposedly aimed at the "international" market. Among other things, this meant films that adhered to the norms of classical narrative cinema and drew on the popular Hollywood genres rather than films that belonged to the distinctively Canadian direct cinema tradition.

Some Canadian genre films, like Shebib's *Between Friends* and Peter Pearson's *Paperback Hero* (both 1973), did develop distinctive inflections of their Hollywood models by exploring the tension between American dreams and Canadian reality.[1] Yet the general trend was towards films that downplayed or concealed their Canadian origins. Most of these films were simply inferior versions of what Hollywood did well, and few were commercially successful, although the box-office returns on Ivan Reitman's *Meatballs* (1979) and Bob Clark's *Porky's* (1981) gave a major boost to the proponents of the Hollywood Canada approach.

The imitation of Hollywood genres is usually seen as a feature of English-language production in Canada, but similar tendencies were apparent in French-language production in the 1970s. Gangster films like Denys Arcand's *La maudite galette* (*The Damned Dough*, 1972), Jean Pierre Lefebvre's *On n'engraisse pas les cochons à l'eau claire* (*Pigs Are Seldom Clean*, 1973), and Jacques Godbout's *La Gammick* (*The Racket*, 1974) reflected the tensions in Quebec society after the October Crisis of 1970. However, as Jutra noted in 1978, the strategy of producing films for the international market also resulted in increased pressures to make films in English.[2] Low-budget genre films like *Born for Hell* (Denis Héroux, 1975) and *Visiting Hours* (Jean-Claude Lord, 1981) sought commercial success by abandoning the language that was so important to Quebec's cultural identity.

Ironically, at the same time that Canadian cinema was moving in this direction, Australia established a system of state film boards modelled on the NFB and developed an internationally successful national cinema. Films like *Picnic at Hanging Rock* (Peter Weir, 1975), *The Chant of Jimmie Blacksmith* (Fred Schepisi, 1978), *My Brilliant Career* (Gillian Armstrong, 1979), and *Breaker Morant* (Bruce Beresford, 1981), received much critical praise and wide distribution on the "art house" circuits. Australian cinema produced a wide variety of films but became especially associated with historical films based on literary sources. Noting this trend, Graeme Turner has argued that Australian filmmakers tried to establish a distinctive national cinema by rejecting the Hollywood genres and by "selecting stories proved in other narrative media – novels, history – rather than writing original screenplays."[3]

In marked contrast to the Australian model, historical films and literary adaptations were quite rare in Canadian cinema in the 1970s. The influence of the documentary tradition was partially responsible for this apparent lack of interest in the past and in Canadian literature, although the NFB had produced a number of docudramas on historical subjects. The direct cinema approach was itself coming under pressure at this time, but clearly Canadian cinema did not share the Australian concern, as described by Turner, to demonstrate the existence of a national culture by showing "that the nation had a past."[4]

Jutra's decision to work on an adaptation of Anne Hébert's historical novel *Kamouraska* – which had been published to great acclaim in 1970 – preceded the success of the Australian films but involved the adoption of similar strategies. However, when the film was released in 1973, in a heavily cut version at the insistence of its producers, it was a commercial failure and contributed to a growing crisis in Canadian cinema. After the (mainly) glowing reviews accorded to *Mon oncle Antoine*, many critics attacked *Kamouraska* as a failed response to the commercial and cultural pressures on the Quebec film industry.

The main complaints had to do with the economic implications of producing a historical film and with the aesthetics of literary adaptation. In order to explore these objections, I need first to specify the text I will be discussing. Jutra's contract did not give him the right to the final cut, and the producers rejected his first version, which was two hundred minutes long.[5] Pierre Lamy, who was one of the producers, insisted that the long version was "boring," but Jutra maintained that it "was a better film when it ran to three hours."[6] In 1983 the growing need for Canadian content on pay-television gave him the opportunity to return to the original negative to prepare a new 173-minute video version.[7]

Films based on novels often face difficulties in conforming to the conventional limit of a two-hour running time. The most notorious example is Erich von Stroheim's *Greed* (1923), which was cut to one-quarter of its original length. David Selznick successfully defied this restriction in 1939 when he released *Gone with the Wind* in a four-hour version with an intermission, but the producers of *Kamouraska* evidently felt that this approach would be too risky. A few years later, in films like Gilles Carle's *Les Plouffe* (*The Plouffe Family*, 1981) and Claude Fournier's *Bonheur d'occasion* (*The Tin Flute*, 1983), the problem was tackled by producing two versions, a shorter version for release in cinemas and a longer one for presentation as a television mini-series.

The option of making different versions for film and television was not available in 1973, and given the dubious results of most examples of this practice, it is doubtful whether it would have helped *Kamouraska*. There is also no way of knowing whether the release of the complete film in 1973 would significantly have altered its reception. Although the long version did win a brief notice in *Cinema Canada*, which reported that the restored parts of the film "add clarity and beauty," it has received little critical attention.[8] Almost every sequence gains through added detail and more fluent editing, creating a richness of effect and a rhythmic assurance that make the film seem shorter rather than longer. My analysis of the film is based on this version, which exists only in video format, although the critics whom I quote, of course, refer to the shorter version.

History, Myth, and Fable

Kamouraska is based on an actual event, a bloody murder committed in 1839, shortly after the British authorities had ruthlessly suppressed a rebellion in the colonies of Upper and Lower Canada. In embarking on a historical film and an adaptation – as we have seen, a rare venture in the Canadian context – Jutra might have been trying to disprove the notorious judgment of Lord Durham, written shortly after the 1837 rebellion, that "the descendants of the French in Lower Canada ... are a people with no history and no literature."[9]

The attempt to demonstrate that "the nation had a past" was somewhat problematic in Quebec, not just because of Lord Durham's imperialist denial of French-Canadian history and culture but also because of the reactionary use to which the appeal to the past had been put during the Duplessis era. Unfortunately, to many critics in Quebec, Jutra's film failed to confront these issues and became complicit with Lord Durham's judgment, because it excluded all reference to the political events of the period.

The novel also largely confines itself to the events surrounding the murder and draws heavily on contemporary newspaper reports, although the names of the people involved have been changed. At the centre of the novel is Elisabeth d'Aulnières who conspires with her lover, George Nelson, to murder her husband, Antoine Tassy, the squire of Kamouraska. Although the political context is not represented in detail, Hébert does provide enough information to establish the chronology of the events, and there is a single reference to the 1837 rebellion. As Elisabeth thinks back to her trial, she exclaims that the court should spare her lover and punish the "patriots" who fought at "Saint Denis and Saint Eustache" instead.[10]

The novel here draws attention to Elisabeth's preference for the personal over the political and to that of its own narrative, which emerges from her consciousness. But even this acknowledgment of the political and historical context is absent from the film, in which no dates are provided, and the only way of dating the action is visual, through the information provided by costumes and setting. Just as Hébert grounded her subjective narrative in objective research into the historical incident, so Jutra and his cinematographer, Michel Brault, undertook extensive research to create an authentic visual style in a historical film that excludes all reference to major historical events.

Jutra justified the omission of these events by insisting that it was "a completely apolitical subject" in which everything happens "on a personal level." A sense of history, as defined by dates and public events, gives way to the construction of a visual simulacrum of the period. The treatment of the past is thus quite different from the strategies adopted in *Mon oncle Antoine* in which the signs of the past are deliberately sparse and imprecise. Jutra declared that the earlier film is really "a film on the present," whereas *Kamouraska* is "a historical film," but one in which the history is "very personal, very distant from the socio-political context in which people lived."[11]

Such an approach to history could not deflect attention from the film's relation to its own sociopolitical context. From an English-Canadian perspective, John Hofsess agreed with Jutra that *Kamouraska* is "apolitical," but he added that the film "couldn't be made anywhere in Canada except Quebec" and that it has "psychic roots."[12] In Quebec itself, the film was attacked for not being "sufficiently rooted in a historical space" and for lacking "psychological plausibility."[13] Some critics argued that its focus on the private life of a woman from a wealthy family revealed the social origins of the authors, Hébert as well as Jutra, who belonged to a privileged social class. Robert Guy Scully thus saw the novel and the film as texts of the "*grande bourgeoisie*," while Luc Perreault asked whether the film's "middle-class universe" could be regarded as "representative."[14]

Perreault clearly assumed that his question must be answered in the negative and that *Kamouraska* had little to say about contemporary life in Quebec. However, the assumptions about the social and political meanings of works of art on which these judgments were based came under attack from an unexpected quarter. Pierre Vallières, a political activist whose own social background, as described in his *White Niggers of America* (1971), was quite different from Jutra's or Hébert's, protested against the treatment of *Kamouraska* in the Quebec media. He described how he had been deeply moved when he first read the novel in prison during the October Crisis. Turning to the film, he condemned reviewers like Scully who, instead of providing "critical analyses of the film," produced only "a mass of political, social and literary considerations that have nothing to do … with the object of the criticism."[15]

In calling for a critical approach that would find political meanings not in stock responses to the subject-matter but in the dynamics of the text, Vallières cited the Marxist critic Georg Lukács and insisted that the historical fiction in *Kamouraska* was highly relevant to the contemporary situation in Quebec. He noted the tension, which he evidently found productive, involved in the choices made by the filmmakers with regard to historical representation. While recognizing that "the period in which Elisabeth's drama is set is ultimately of little importance," he nevertheless praised the "consistency … intensity and … beauty" with which the past world is represented.

As this argument recognizes, Jutra's claim that *Kamouraska* is a "historical film" refers to the visual density and consistency of its signs of the past. But the process by which these signs were constructed involved problems that complicated the film's sense of Quebec's history. It was shot in locations that were, as far as possible, made to look as they would have done at the time of the action. The filmmakers "wanted things to be like they were."[16] Yet, as we shall see in discussing the production process, many locations were contaminated by intrusive signs of the present, and Jutra was driven to complain that Quebec was not caring for its "heritage."[17]

Jutra's lament implies a view of history that links *Kamouraska* to the heritage films that would become a fully fledged genre and bring international success to British cinema in the 1980s. Like the Australian films of the 1970s, which they resemble and which were themselves indebted to British television serials of the 1960s, these films focus on the dilemmas and aspirations of private life in a cultural context more stable and attractive than the complicated modern world. In the heritage film, according to Andrew Higson, "period authenticity" is a sign of "the desire for perfection, for the past as unimpaired paradigm, for a packaging of the past that is designed to please, not disturb."[18]

In the case of the Australian films, the style and manners of a more elegant past come into conflict with the elemental forces of the outback. A similar conflict is also apparent in *Kamouraska* in the contrast between the genteel domestic spaces inhabited by Elisabeth's family and the snow-covered wilderness around Kamouraska. The careful reconstruction of the costumes and settings provides a background against which Jutra brings out what he called the film's "mythological" dimension. He claimed that it does not deal with historical issues but with "eternal themes" such as "possession, complicity between lovers, the desire to kill, rebellion against society, living one's life in spite of all social imperatives, mad love, lethal love."[19]

Insofar as *Kamouraska* is a heritage film, it underlines the fragility of a social order that tries to control the natural world but encounters resistance both from within (passion) and from without (the Canadian climate). In Jutra's version of nineteenth-century Quebec, in sharp contrast to the British situation, isolated communities impose social imperatives in an environment in which the "primitive" is still very close. On this level, the film does suggest the absence of a historical dimension in Quebec: "For us," said Jutra, "a hundred years ago is prehistory, it is before everything."[20]

As Jutra was well aware, the return to "prehistory" in search of eternal themes placed the emphasis on myth rather than history and defied the trend towards demystification in contemporary cultural theory. According to Roland Barthes, myth is a conservative force because it "transforms history into nature" so that cultural values will seem to be part of a natural order of things.[21] In similar terms, Susan Buck-Morss argues that "myth and history are incompatible." Whereas myth "dictates that because human beings are powerless to interfere in the workings of fate, nothing truly new can happen … the concept of history implies the possibility of human influence upon events, and with it, the moral and political responsibility of people as conscious agents to shape their own destiny."[22]

This kind of argument was taken up in the 1960s and 1970s by the supporters of separatism who wanted to create conditions in which the people of Quebec could "shape their own destiny." As a result, critics in Quebec tended to overlook precisely the historical and political implications of *Kamouraska*. By presenting eternal themes in the context of Quebec's "prehistory," the film implies indeed that little has changed despite the apparent transformations brought about by the Quiet Revolution. The idea that Quebec does not have a history is itself historicized by a narrative that centres on the effects of a lack of freedom. Quebec is trapped in mythic time because it has been deprived of historical agency.

Jutra's stress on the powerful underlying cultural effects of colonialism anticipates Denys Arcand's *Le Déclin de l'empire Américain* (*The Decline of the American Empire*, 1986). In this film, a group of intellectuals (most of them history professors or students) discuss sexuality, food, and the decline of Western civilization but virtually ignore the specific problems of Quebec's past or present. Whereas Arcand's film confronts us with a postmodern society in which Quebec no longer exists because it has been absorbed into the "American empire," *Kamouraska* depicts a "premodern" world in which the status of Quebec is equally impossible.

Despite the lack of symbolic historical information (dates and so on), *Kamouraska* differs from Arcand's film because of the imaginary (mythic) presence of the past (settings, costumes). It is through the tension between myth and history that Jutra develops a fable that speaks to the present. In this sense, the concern with historical authenticity signals a difference in approach from *Mon oncle Antoine* but not a difference in effect.

As my argument so far will have suggested, the cultural meanings of the film are closely tied to the relationship between the historical situation of Quebec and the desires and actions of Elisabeth as its central character. Before exploring the way the film represents this relationship, we need to look at the issues at stake in the controversy over the impact of its production on the Quebec film industry.

"Our First Historical Superproduction"

In breaking with the Canadian tradition of low-budget direct cinema films, the producers of *Kamouraska* had to confront the budgetary implications of reconstructing the past. The extensive publicity surrounding the making of what one journalist called "our first historical superproduction" emphasized that it would be "the most expensive picture ever made in Canada."[23] The involvement of Geneviève Bujold, who had established a reputation as "the Canadian cinema's only international star," gave the project commercial viability, but the large budget required the investment of a French coproducer.[24]

Jean Pierre Lefebvre complained that the production contributed to a "climate of inflation" that threatened the survival of Quebec cinema. He argued that expensive coproductions encouraged a denial of cultural roots because of the need to appeal to international audiences. According to Lefebvre, this approach led to a number of problems, including loss of control over the production (the casting of foreign actors, for example), exploitation of the folklore image of Quebec, and the imposition of a conventional film language that suppressed not only Quebec's direct cinema tradition but also the personal voice of the *auteur*.[25]

Lefebvre's argument is compelling in the cultural and economic context of filmmaking in Quebec, but the effects of the folklore image and the use of film language in *Kamouraska* are as complex as in *Mon oncle Antoine*. The production circumstances did lead to the casting of French actors as Elisabeth's two husbands, but the most obvious "foreign" actor played her lover. Since this character is an American sent to Canada as a child by his Loyalist family, the casting of an American actor, Richard Jordan, could be justified by the demands of realism rather than the conditions of the coproduction agreement. Some fascinating alternatives were considered, however, before Jordan was cast in the part.

If George Nelson had been played by Robert de Niro, whom Jutra interviewed with the part in mind, the effect of the character and of the gender dynamics in the film would have been very different.[26] Jutra also considered playing the role himself, a choice that would have radically altered the tensions around gender and language in the film.[27] Although some critics complained about the final choice because of Jordan's alleged lack of presence, it is difficult to separate the actor's persona from the character's lack of reality as a product of Elisabeth's imagination. Hébert commented that "Jordan is the very type of the foreigner who is suddenly parachuted into a drama that he does not control," an ambiguous judgment that could refer to the actor's unease with the production or to the character's relationship to the murder plot, or to both.[28]

As this discussion of the casting of foreign actors suggests, the effects of the complicated production process were apparent in the film itself and must have affected the way spectators responded to it, although these effects were more ambiguous than Lefebvre admitted. Lefebvre was concerned not so much with a single film as with the impact of such productions on the Quebec film industry, but his objections were later taken up by Vlada Petric, who cited Lefebvre's own personal cinema as a culturally responsible alternative to the trend "leading toward commercialism" of which *Kamouraska* was the prime example.[29] As Lefebvre himself pointed out, however, the film version of *Kamouraska* was not simply a commercial endeavour but an art film that appropriated the cultural and aesthetic values associated with the novel. Because Hébert had been living in Paris since the mid-1950s, her work was often seen as the product of French rather than Quebec literary traditions, and the adaptation of her novel thus falls between two stools, represented by Hollywood and European art cinema.

In this respect, *Kamouraska* shared the dual allegiance that was later to be successfully exploited by the British heritage films, but at the time it was more often seen as a failed Hollywood epic. Much to Jutra's annoyance, one journalist repeatedly compared it to *Gone with the Wind*.[30] With a budget reported to be around $750,000, *Kamouraska* was hardly a large-budget film by Hollywood standards, and it could not be expected to rival the special effects and spectacular grandeur of the most successful historical epic ever made. Jutra pointed out that the film would have cost four times as much if it had been made in Hollywood, where the period settings would have been constructed in a studio.[31]

The film's intimate and claustrophobic style, very different from the spectacular approach favoured by Hollywood, was to some extent dictated by the budget. "There are very few long shots," Brault explained, "because we didn't have enough money to reconstruct entire streets."[32] But, as Lefebvre might have pointed out, there were other options. In Lefebvre's own *Les maudites sauvages* (*Those Damned Savages*, 1971), for example, the narrative is set in seventeenth-century Quebec, but the continuity between past and present is underlined by locating much of the action in modern settings. The intrusion of powerlines into a long shot early in the film seems like an error but introduces an anachronistic aesthetic that forces the spectator to engage with the present meanings of historical events. By shooting *Kamouraska* on location while excluding all signs of the present, Jutra took what seemed to be a more conventional approach both to filmmaking and to history, one that led to attacks on the film for its betrayal of Quebec's cultural autonomy *and* for its lack of Hollywood production values.

The debate over *Kamouraska* raised some key issues about the relationship between art and commerce in the development of an emerging national cinema. As a commercial film that failed commercially, *Kamouraska* was, as Lefebvre argued, a warning signal to the Quebec film industry; but as Vallières effectively pointed out, it also fell victim to a lot of muddled thinking about the relationship between film and literature and about the political implications of cultural texts.

From Novel to Film

The film is an adaptation of a novel that itself deviates considerably from the social and psychological realism of the traditional novel. When dealing with such aberrant novels, most film (and television) adaptations tend to flatten out any peculiarities of the narration and to present the events from the linear third-person perspective of classical narrative cinema, using techniques derived from the realist novel. Literary critics seem to regard the adaptation of *Kamouraska* as an example of this kind of reworking. In his monograph on

Anne Hébert, Delbert W. Russell claims that the film "sacrifices much of the psychological complexity" of the novel in favour of its presumably less valuable "gothic elements."[33] Similarly, Robert Harvey asserts that the filmmakers decided to make a straightforward period piece so that the film would be "accessible to a large public, thus returning the enormous sums which had to be invested in it."[34]

The problem of adaptation thus comes up against the economic and cultural issues discussed by Lefebvre. Of course, to the extent that the motives behind the adaptation were commercial, it was a failure. But the reviewers, whose lukewarm or negative responses certainly contributed to the lack of public interest, made some very questionable assumptions about what is appropriate to novels and to fiction films and about the relationship between the two media.

One reviewer thought that Jutra had succeeded in making a film "very much in the tradition of the Victorian novel," a sort of "*Wuthering Heights* on the St Lawrence."[35] This description, which stresses the gothic elements and might equally be applied to the novel, glosses over the fact that *Wuthering Heights* is hardly a conventional Victorian novel. Most reviewers, however, stressed the resistance of the novel to cinematic re-presentation. Thus, although he described the film (rather inaccurately) as Quebec's first real example of "novelistic" cinema, Scully also argued that, because Hébert is a poet rather than a novelist and because her novel is "unipersonal," the screenplay based on it inevitably "lacks drama."[36]

The confident and casual way these prescriptive remarks assume clear-cut distinctions and relationships between and among film, poetry, novel, and drama does not exactly serve to clarify the issues at stake. Scully's response also illustrates how questions of adaptation became intertwined with generic expectations derived from Hollywood cinema. He argued that Hébert's novel was a poor choice as the source for a historical epic both because it lacked the backdrop of actual historical events required by the genre, like the American Civil War in *Gone with the Wind*, and because "it also lacked the elements of simple everyday reality" that could be found in the Victorian realist novels.[37]

As Harvey points out, the novel uses a style marked by the "predominance of narration over story" with the result that, "contrary to the logic of the traditional novel, the plot in *Kamouraska* is often betrayed by multiple anticipations and is shown from the beginning of the novel to be secondary, serving more as the context of the narration itself than as its principal content."[38] The novel thus creates an inner landscape of the kind that Proust felt cinema could not reproduce. As we have seen, the pressures and gaps caused by involuntary memory also led to the "predominance of narration over story" in *À tout prendre*, and after due allowance is made for the differences in budget and genre, the strategies adopted in *Kamouraska* are not so distant from those of the earlier film.

Like most of the critics, the adapters felt that their major challenge was to translate the abstract written text into concrete visual images. Hébert collaborated on the screenplay with Jutra and expressed approval of the film version, but she suggested that it did perhaps have "a certain nostalgia which is absent from the novel because it unfolds in a precise setting while the whole novel is an inner monologue, conveying a more naked and poignant passion."[39] Jutra agreed that the major problem posed by the novel was the subjective narration shaped by Elisabeth's passion and felt that "in the film, because everything that happens becomes more concrete, this passion is automatically diminished."[40]

Jutra, however, rejected Scully's claim that the novel lacked "the elements of simple everyday reality," insisting that "there is an abundance of details and gestures that, taken individually, are not spectacular but which, by accumulation, add up to a psychological whole of great richness."[41] The film's physical and visual re-creation of the world in which the story takes place may diminish the passion but it also reinforces the tension between reality and desire in Elisabeth's experience.

Far from straightening out the story into a conventional linear narrative, the tensions in the film, which were only intensified by the effect of the cuts in the released version, often led to charges of "incoherence" (to borrow Lefebvre's term). As Perreault pointed out, the film's depiction of "Elisabeth's inner drama" results in the neglect of such questions as "her trial, her second marriage, what happens to Nelson."[42] Robert Fulford complained that mixing up the "time elements" in the film provided audiences with "puzzles where they are entitled to simple stories," and he castigated Jutra for not being able to "make a film that answered its own questions."[43]

It would have been fairly easy to construct a story of the kind Fulford wanted from the historical materials that served as the inspiration for the novel, and thus for the film. Jutra described the basic story in terms that might serve for a classic film noir like Billy Wilder's *Double Indemnity* (1944): "The narrative is very simple. It is the story of a married woman who takes a lover and who asks this lover to kill her husband." In the film, as in the novel, the complexity lies in the way this story is narrated. It becomes, in Jutra's words, "a film-mosaic which leaps continually from one place to another."[44]

The events leading up to the murder are narrated in flashbacks as Elisabeth remembers them, while she cares for her second husband who is dying in their home on the rue du Parloir in Quebec City. The film's temporal structure has the effect of "a slow dissolve," as Jutra put it: "You are in the rue du Parloir, this dissolves gradually into the past where you remain for a certain time; and then gradually the rue du Parloir returns to the foreground."[45] This description may suggest a fairly conventional flashback structure (like that of *Double Indemnity*, for example), but the interplay between past and present, inside and outside, in the film version of *Kamouraska* creates a narration at least as complex as that in the novel.

The flashbacks in *Double Indemnity* also represent the memories of a narrator under considerable psychological pressure. Walter Neff describes how he became involved in a murder plot in an effort to reveal the truth before his own imminent death. In *Kamouraska*, Elisabeth does not consciously set out to narrate the events of her own past but instead tries to suppress the truth. Exhausted from nursing her husband, like the devoted wife that she appears to be, Elisabeth drifts in and out of sleep, and the narration takes on a dreamlike quality in which the forces of censorship attempt to deny the reality of the buried past.

Although the cuts required by the producers inevitably added to the sense of disorientation experienced by many critics, most of their complaints apply equally to the novel. Indeed Perreault expressed his concern about Jutra's failure to resolve the narrative enigmas at the same time as he argued that the film was too close a "copy" of the original literary version.[46] While it is true that the adaptation is unusually faithful, we have already seen that other critics accused the adaptation of betraying the spirit of the novel because of cinema's bias towards objective visual reality or because of the film industry's commercial imperatives.

Jutra made no secret of his own attraction to the gothic elements in the novel that alienated some of the critics. He noted that "on the back cover of the book it says it is the story of snow, love, and blood," but he also claimed that he worked against the melodramatic potential of the subject.[47] Contrary to conventional melodramatic practice, for example, he pointed out that "there is no music at the strong moments of the film."[48]

Kamouraska also undercuts some of the basic conventions of space and time in classical narrative cinema. As Jutra pointed out, Hébert's complex use of flashbacks in her novel is just one example of the influence of cinema on the modern novel, even though classical narrative cinema tends to privilege the linear narrative structures of the traditional novel.[49] The narration in the novel immerses the reader in Elisabeth's fragmented consciousness, while the film, following the grain of the medium according to Proust and many others, places more emphasis on the physical and visual environment. However, rather than reverting to the realism of the traditional novel and classical narrative cinema, the film version of *Kamouraska* sets up a struggle between the subjective perspective of the central character and the medium's supposedly objective reproduction of visual reality.

Instead of the smooth continuity between subjective and objective perspectives, between the look of the character and the look of the camera, basic to the language of classical narrative cinema, these two dimensions of the cinematic fiction never quite come together, and the resulting tension creates an uneasiness and instability in the deployment of the third look: that of the spectator.

According to André Bazin, "the objective nature of photography confers on it a quality of credibility absent from all other picture-making."[50] By shooting on location and using only available light, Jutra and Brault respected the objective bias of the medium, but this realist approach resulted, ironically, in images that were often praised for their painterly qualities. As in *Mon oncle Antoine*, what Hébert called the film's "nostalgic" tendency depends on a tension between the photographic presentness of the film images and the pastness of their referents.

The difficulty of reconstructing the past is itself vital to the narration in both the novel and the film. Images that seem to provide evidence of what really happened in the past may be the product of an imagination shaped by the pressures of present reality. By following the novel in confining the narration to Elisabeth's subjective vision, the film allows the tension between past and present to shape its visual style. Cinema has, of course, often used "the objective nature of photography" to create fantastic or dreamlike images. Indeed, Jean Baudry has argued that cinema produces "a fusion of the interior with the exterior," like that experienced in dreams.[51]

The norms of classical narrative cinema encourage this fusion, enabling spectators to identify with characters while also having the best possible view of the action. Although *Kamouraska* purports to represent Elisabeth's experience of the "return of the repressed" in a dreamlike state, its strategies create tension rather than fusion and involve the spectator in the struggle between the oppositions (interior/exterior, dream/real, past/present) inherent to the medium.

Two Beginnings

The novel opens with two paragraphs, narrated in the third-person, describing "Madame Rolland" watching over her husband's deathbed. Only in the third paragraph does the narration shift clearly into the first-person stream-of-consciousness mode that will dominate this subjective novel. Elisabeth begins by reflecting on her sense of being spied on in the streets of Quebec City and then quickly summarizes the events that led to her present notoriety. We learn that she has been married twice, that she was imprisoned for two months, that her lover abandoned her after "the tragedy at Kamouraska," and that she remarried to restore her "honour."[52]

Despite what Jean-Pierre Tadros called the novel's "splintered structure" and "extremely interiorized" narration, virtually all the necessary narrative information emerges from this opening in an only slightly elliptical way, establishing a framework that assists the reader in dealing with the fuller, but sometimes delirious, account of the events in the rest of the novel.[53] These first paragraphs also provide a lot of information on Elisabeth's immediate situation: notably, that she has been married to her second husband for eighteen years and that she has given birth to eleven children in twenty-two years, three of them during her first marriage, although the last of these is actually her lover's son.

Elisabeth thinks that she has been "nothing but a faithful belly," but her initial musings also foreshadow the association of sexuality with a desire for the freedom that her marriages have denied her. She invites the reader to "see for yourself" that she still has her good looks and expresses her desire to be able to exchange glances with "every man in the street."[54]

The novel thus makes clear that Elisabeth's quest for sexual freedom is doomed from the outset. Her confinement in the present colours the narration in its very form since the inner voice must remain *secret*. Elisabeth identifies her own view with that of the reader as she describes her body, perhaps looking in a mirror at a reflection that exists for the reader only in her words. The use of an apparently omniscient third-person narrative voice, which returns briefly at the beginning of the second section, further destabilizes the narration. Since Elisabeth's subjectivity dominates the rest of the novel, this "objectivity" suggests that she is viewing herself from the outside in her public role, defining herself through her second husband's name just as she had earlier done through the names of her father and her first husband.

The opening sequence of the film draws on the second section of the novel in which Elisabeth peers through the blinds of the bedroom window. Because it is the middle of the night, she can see nothing, but she hears a gutter banging in the wind and a wagon passing in the street.[55] In the opening shot of the film, the camera is outside the house. After the credits have appeared over trees swaying in the wind at night, the camera pans slowly to the left and upward. Rain begins to pour down, and the camera passes a broken gutter banging against the wall. Finally it comes to rest on a window at which the face of a woman appears. Before the shot ends, we hear shouts, and there is a cut to a high-angle shot of an expanse of snow across which a man drives wildly towards the camera in a sleigh.

This "impossible" reverse shot quickly sets up the film's primary oppositions, most notably between inside and outside and between present and past, and establishes that these will be developed in a style that disrupts normal continuity and sound/image relationships. Elisabeth is in a dark interior, in which she is imprisoned by the demands of respectability. As the point of view shot of the sleigh reveals, her spirit is outside in a snowy landscape that represents both freedom and danger and is associated with her lover and with the violent death of her first husband. The past exists only inside Elisabeth: the film proclaims its ability to show what she sees with her inner eye but also implies that her memories may be distorted by the pressures and desires of the present.

Of course, the meanings of this opening montage effect will vary according to whether or not the spectator has read the novel. Those familiar with the plot would recognize the man in the sleigh as Nelson and would understand the significance of Elisabeth's voice-over description of him as "my only, my terrible love." Others might be aware of the basic situation from the publicity surrounding the novel and the film. However, the shock effect of the film's second shot seems designed to short-circuit stock responses and to place all spectators, as far as possible, in the position of the naive spectator who is unaware of what is to come. In any case, the reverse shot establishes that the images from the past may be "contaminated" by Elisabeth's imagination, thus blurring the distinction between past and present.

The opening sequence of the film provides less precise information than the opening of the novel. It eliminates the summary of the story and many of the details of Elisabeth's immediate situation (for example, the number of her children). In some ways, the initial impression is less coherent than in the novel, despite the apparent security offered by the generic indebtedness to the historical epic and gothic melodrama. The relationship between incoherence and convention becomes a tension that is vital to the film's vision and to its form.

The intercutting between Elisabeth and Nelson ends when a second shot of Nelson, still shouting loudly, is interrupted by a close-up of Rolland shifting uncomfortably in his bed. It seems as if he is reacting to the shouts, but he then complains about the noise of the broken gutter. This prosaic explanation dispels the momentary suggestion that he is aware of what is going on in his wife's mind, but the hesitation draws attention to the film's (and the spectator's) voyeuristic operations. A little later, Rolland asks his wife to read aloud from a volume called *Poésies liturgiques* and directs her attention to a marked passage that declares that God can see into people's hearts and will eventually punish hidden sins. When she stops reading, a close-up of Rolland shows him looking at her with quiet satisfaction.

This exchange confirms that Elisabeth has something to hide, as the opening shots have already suggested, and implies that her husband is aware of her complicity in his predecessor's murder despite his outward function as guarantor of her innocence. Her reading is a public act of forced ventriloquism and contrasts with the private expression of her inner thoughts, which we can hear but her husband cannot. She now insists on her separateness from her husband and gains a momentary triumph when he fails to comprehend the short laugh that is the involuntary outward sign of her inner speech.

Before the sequence ends, three flashbacks begin the narration of the past events. The first two deal with the aftermath of the murder. As she rushes down a staircase to fetch the sugar necessary to administer Rolland's medicine, Elisabeth's rapid movement past the banisters sets off a memory of a sleigh crossing a covered bridge before her arrest at the border. After her careful attempt to count the drops of medicine arouses fears of being suspected of a second murder, she closes her eyes, and there is a cut to the dark interior of the prison in which she was confined for her part in the murder of her first husband. In the next shot, she leaves the prison, but her sense of moving "from one prison to another" is reinforced by the immense grey wall that fills the screen behind the black carriage that awaits her.

The final flashback in this sequence takes us back to the beginning of the story. It begins when the sight of a wagon outside the window disturbs Elisabeth. She lies with her head on her husband's shoulder and then reaches out to touch his hand. As she does so, her attention is attracted by the sleeve of his nightshirt whose frilly white material evokes the lace curtain from behind which Elisabeth appeared in the opening shot. It also acts as a transition to a flashback that begins with a close-up of the legs of a young woman whose white pantaloons peek out beneath her long gown. After the camera has moved up to reveal the young Elisabeth walking in the woods, there is a cut, apparently cued by her gaze, to a close-up of the bare feet of another young woman splashing through a stream. The camera reveals her to be poorly dressed and shows her lighting a pipe surrounded by a group of admiring boys.

This sudden shift back in time, made even more jarring by the contrast between the dark interior of the bedroom and the sunlit exterior from the past, emphasizes the difference between the respectable middle-aged woman that Elisabeth has become and the sixteen-year-old girl first discovering the temptations and constraints of the adult world. While Elisabeth's decorously clothed legs suggest that she is already caught up in the social pressures that will later lead to her masquerade of respectability, the bare legs of the other young woman imply a freedom that Elisabeth envies.

Although the film does not take over from the novel Elisabeth's invitation to look at her or her expression of a desire to share the male privilege of looking, it uses the fact that the spectator *can* look at her to link the act of spectatorship to her recollection of a failed attempt to break free from sexual and cultural constraints. The tensions that surround the act of looking first emerge when Elisabeth turns away from her husband's bed to look at herself in a mirror. While she speaks of keeping herself young for the sake of her lover, Rolland can also be seen in the mirror surveying his wife's image. In the flashback, Elisabeth looks at another woman, evidently from a lower class, who indulges in the "male" activity of smoking a pipe but who, in doing so, becomes the object of the gaze of a group of boys.

As the young woman lights her pipe, Rolland's voice intrudes into the flashback, asking for the name of "the girl who smoked a pipe." The question brings Elisabeth (and us) back to the present, again creating the disturbing impression that he has read her mind. When Rolland answers his own question, we discover that the pipe-smoker is Aurélie Caron. As the plot develops, we learn that this young woman became Elisabeth's servant and that the lovers drew her into the murder plot. While her social position allows her to behave in ways forbidden to Elisabeth, her freedom is limited, and she serves two years in prison while her mistress is released after only two weeks.

The flashbacks that punctuate the opening sequence function not only to introduce narrative enigmas but also to make clear that time and space in this film will move fluidly between the realistic and the imaginary. While the opening sets up the basic oppositions already noted (interior/exterior, dream/real, past/present), it also establishes that the boundaries separating each pair of oppositions will be permeable and unstable. The effect is to place the spectator in a position in relation to the film analogous to Elisabeth's in relation to her past, but this is not achieved simply through a process of identification. Although the plot is filtered through Elisabeth's consciousness, the film frequently disrupts the identification process to remind the spectator of the mechanisms of voyeurism and projection involved in her involuntary memories and also in the cinematic experience itself.

Spectatorship Inside and Outside the Film

Elisabeth's first attempt to escape from her social situation is through her marriage to Antoine Tassy. Since he is the squire of Kamouraska, this is a good marriage from a social point of view, but she is seduced by his animal vitality and disregard for social conventions. She quickly realizes her mistake when, on their wedding night, Tassy gets drunk and ignores her romantic expectations as well as her sexual desires. The camera looks down on the bed from the ceiling of the room in the inn as Tassy moves on top of her, and there is a cut to a close-up of Elisabeth crying out. There is just enough time to register that the cry actually occurs in her sleep in the present before there is a cut back to a shot of Tassy asleep beside her wakeful and pensive younger self.

The time shift masks the moment at which she loses her virginity, the expected climax of the sequence, thus negating the apparent voyeuristic motive for the "impossible" camera position. It is impossible both because it violates the norm of classical narrative cinema that the camera should not call attention to itself and because it is physically detached from Elisabeth's point of view, although it may suggest that she is viewing herself from the outside, as in the use of third-person narration in the opening of the novel.

Camera position also creates a strong awareness of voyeurism when Nelson and Elisabeth make their affair public by standing naked in front of a window. This scene is taken from the novel, but there the viewpoint remains inside with the couple. Since the gesture is directed towards (unseen) viewers outside, who have already been spreading rumours about the affair, it gains an added dimension when visualized in the film. Jutra reinforces its implications by cutting away from the lovers as they undress, thus denying us a close view of their bodies, and placing the camera outside in the night. It moves round the house and eventually comes to rest on a long shot of the naked couple at the window. Nelson declares that "tomorrow everybody will know" and tells Elisabeth to turn out the lamp. The shot fades to black accompanied by the sounds of their love making.

By exhibiting themselves to the gaze of the people presumed to be outside the window, Nelson and Elisabeth denounce the hypocrisy of a society in which their affair is a subject of gossip but is tolerated as long as it remains more or less hidden. The couple do what is expected of them, but by doing it visibly, they expose the prurient fascination that is the other side of public disapproval. In terms of the film's narrative, it is possible that there is nobody outside the window and that the couple's sense of being spied on derives from their own guilt feelings. However, the camera movement outside the house underlines that there is a voyeuristic gaze, mediated through the camera, and that it is ours.

While the narrative may invite us to identify with the couple in their defiance of restrictive social conventions, the visual style places us uncomfortably in the presumed position of the guardians of social order. Although we occupy this position only temporarily, such shots raise the possibility that the cinematic pleasure in looking is in itself complicit with the social gaze that condemns the couple. Cinema caters to a desire to "see inside," in the sense both of entering forbidden places and of gaining access to the consciousness of characters whose experiences we can enjoy vicariously, and *Kamouraska* offers both kinds of pleasure. Yet the film also explores the implications of looking at and into other people's lives without questioning the cultural context that shapes our own ways of seeing.

The tensions involved in the act of looking become most apparent in the film's representation of the murder, the traumatic event that Elisabeth does not wish to remember. As in *Mon oncle Antoine*, sexuality and death come together in an act of violence that Jutra himself called "the supreme coitus."[56] Perreault applied this sexual metaphor to the film's narrative structure when he argued that the general "dissatisfaction" with the film was the result of the marked contrast between the murder "where one witnesses an enormous release of energy and the rest of the film in which everything happens in a kind of suspended sentence."[57]

Elisabeth seeks release through her affair with Nelson, achieves it briefly as a result of the murder, but is then condemned to a suspended sentence in her second marriage. The vivid contrast between the bloody murder and the restraint of the rest of the film is another effect of the concreteness of film language. Hébert thought that the major difference between the two versions was that, in the novel, the murder "takes place as in an hallucination," whereas in the film, it becomes "bluntly realistic."[58] However, the distinction is not clear-cut: the novel has its gothic elements, and the film does not allow the spectator to forget that the murder, despite its graphic representation, is a traumatic event that takes on a hallucinatory force in Elisabeth's imagination.

The murder first appears in the film when, after the birth of her first child, Elisabeth's mother and aunts decide to rescue her from Tassy's brutality and take her away from Kamouraska. On the journey back to their home in Sorel, where she will soon meet Nelson for the first time, she looks out of the window of the carriage and "sees" the bloody figure of her husband lying in the snow. This vision accurately predicts the circumstances of Tassy's death as we see them later in the film. It is either an uncanny premonition or an involuntary memory in which the traumatic event tries to appear before its time. An abrupt cut takes us from a close-up of Elisabeth's face at the carriage window, screaming in silence at the sight of the murdered man, to the present as Elisabeth's daughter rushes to her mother who has cried out in her sleep. The sound of the scream (which we never hear) migrates across time, and we are again reminded of the subjective dimension of the narration.

Similarly, when the murder actually occurs, its objective status is very unstable because Elisabeth participates imaginatively in Nelson's long journey to Kamouraska even though, in reality, she stays behind in Sorel. When Nelson takes out his gun, Elisabeth cries out and sits up in bed in Sorel with her aunts in attendance; when he shoots Tassy, she cries out in the rue de Parloir. The event itself is thus doubly mediated through Elisabeth's powers of projection and memory.

The murder does, however, take on a great visual immediacy, when Nelson shoots at the body again after dumping it in the snow and then clubs the head with the butt of his gun. On his return journey, he becomes obsessed with washing the blood from the sleigh and from his clothes and invents a story about a pig being slaughtered. He describes to Elisabeth his horror at being alone "with that poor man bleeding away," but his remorse seems to contradict the excessive violence of the murder itself. This may be explained by his anger at the way Tassy has treated Elisabeth, but it also seems that he is simply an agent of her desire for "justice." On the one hand, the objective existence of the blood is attested to by the witnesses at the trial; on the other, the bloody killing seems like a ritual generated by Elisabeth's subjective fantasies.

Jutra emphasized the second possibility when he explained that the murder is a "blood bath" because this is how it is "imagined by Elisabeth." He also used the argument that the film is shaped by Elisabeth's imagination to justify the lack of information about what happens to Nelson after the murder, insisting that "even in Elisabeth's mind, Nelson is almost an abstraction: it is an ideal but impossible love."[59]

The unreality of this ideal love is captured in an early image in which Nelson is part of an idyllic family circle, watching the young Elisabeth contentedly sewing a sampler while one of her aunts plays romantic music on the piano. This apparent flashback shows an impossible past since Nelson was never part of the family in this way. It occurs just after Rolland has remarked that Elisabeth was lucky to have been able to save her honour by marrying him after her release from prison, and she has replied that she would have been free if it were not for him. Her inner voice then speaks of the murder as a "sacrifice," and there is a dissolve from her face into a soft-focus shot of her younger self seated next to Nelson. The mist that frames this shot testifies to its imaginary status, while the use of the aunt's music as an accompaniment to later meetings of the lovers suggests that their whole affair is as impossible as this utopian fantasy.

If this image represents the freedom that Elisabeth claims she could have achieved through the sacrifice of her husband, it also points to the ideological forces that prevent her from realizing her ideal or, to be more precise, that make it possible for her to envisage freedom only in an impossible form. Although she tells Rolland that she would have been able to "remake" her life, her ideal image represents a regression to the past and envisages Nelson integrated into the genteel middle-class family that has limited her options in the first place.

The violent murder of Tassy inevitably fails to turn this dream image into reality. After the murder, the lovers separate, not just because of the power of the law but also because their passion seems to depend on the impossibility of its fulfilment. During their one meeting after Nelson's return from Kamouraska, he tells her that they are "free" but then describes the horror of the bloody killing. As they embrace, the camera frames Elisabeth looking over his shoulder, apparently realizing that the murder has simply confirmed that their relationship is impossible. Although we know that Elisabeth did try to join her lover in the United States, the aftermath of the murder as depicted in the film's plot quickly establishes the process by which a concern for appearances wins out over desire.

The disappearance of Nelson from the film is not as absolute as Jutra and the critics suggested, since we do learn (even in the shorter version) that he has escaped to the United States and that a letter from him to Elisabeth was intercepted by the judge. In any case, the effect is far less radical than the disappearance of Claude at the end of *À tout prendre*. A parallel effect in *Kamouraska* would be the disappearance of Elisabeth, the site of subjective consciousness in the film. Even slight deviations from narrative norms are, of course, less likely to be tolerated in a (relatively) high-budget historical film than in a low-budget independent project. As with *Mon oncle Antoine*, critics again accused Jutra of selling out to Hollywood and of not having mastered the elementary principles of classic narrative cinema.

The contrast between the insubstantiality of Nelson as a character and the brutal murder of Tassy contributes to a tension between abstraction and embodiment like that found in *À tout prendre*. In *Kamouraska*, this tension shapes both the spectator's experience of the narrative and the images and Elisabeth's experience of her cultural environment.

Elisabeth and Quebec

The tensions between visual style and narrative also affect the relationship of the actors to the characters. As in the case of most adaptations, critics complained that the film's actors did not match up to the psychological complexity of the literary characters. One critic, for example, argued that Philippe Léotard made Tassy "too sympathetic" to capture "the ambivalence of the character in the novel."[60] Hébert felt that the character in the film does have the complexity of his counterpart in her novel, and the sympathetic dimension of Léotard's performance helps to motivate Elisabeth's initial attraction to Tassy's animal high spirits.[61] As she discovers his brutality and self-destructive tendencies, he also emerges as a victim of a culture in which, even as the squire of Kamouraska, he has no real power.

It was the performance of Geneviève Bujold as the film's "star" that raised most questions about the embodiment of the novel's characters. In the novel we see with Elisabeth's eyes, but in the film we also look at the body of the actor. Because we see Elisabeth only briefly and indistinctly in the first two flashbacks, we are introduced to her at points in her life that required Bujold to act first older and then younger than she was at the time. The "real" Geneviève Bujold emerges only when we finally see Elisabeth at the time of her affair with Nelson. Much was made in the publicity of the challenge of portraying Elisabeth at different ages, and the film's flashback structure makes it into a meditation on time and on the cinema's ability to represent it.

Bujold's performance is central to *Kamouraska* as a fable in which a woman's sufferings under a patriarchal society represent Quebec's colonial dependency. A few critics did notice this political allegory, but, as might be expected by now, the effect of the interaction between personal and cultural meanings is not as simple as it might appear. Vallières affirmed the contemporary relevance of the film by insisting that *Kamouraska* more "forcefully describes the situation of women in Quebec" than the explicitly feminist strategies of Mireille Dansereau's *La Vie revée* (*Dream Life*, 1972).[62] Jutra himself agreed that "there is a dominant feminist theme" in the film and claimed that Elisabeth represented "woman in a given context" that forces her to behave "in an excessive manner."[63]

This feminist reading forges links between the personal and the political and is also apparent in John Hofsess's description of Elisabeth as "the spirit, the soul of Quebec, radically innocent yet treacherous to all who love her."[64] Hofsess might be accused of simply imposing a stereotypical femininity on Quebec, but the film itself does not endorse such a sweeping equation. Elisabeth is a woman trapped in a patriarchal society, but she is also a member of a privileged class, and it is her (female) servant who is punished by the legal system for the murder plotted by her masters. Elisabeth is neither an innocent national heroine like Maria Chapdelaine, in Louis Hémon's 1916 novel and Gilles Carle's 1983 film adaptation, nor a *femme fatale* like Phyllis Dietrichson in *Double Indemnity*. She hovers uncomfortably between these two positions as she tries to fulfil herself "within suffocating limitations."[65]

Elisabeth's idealization of Nelson brings her close to Hémon's (and Carle's) heroine, who discovers the full meaning of her roots in Quebec only after the death in a snowstorm of her idealized lover, François Paradis. There is a stark contrast, however, between Maria's innocent love, passive suffering, and final epiphany and Elisabeth's illicit affair leading to murder. Yet Nelson's departing words, as reported by his assistant ("It is this damned woman who has ruined me"), are not fully convincing as an attempt to cast her as a *femme fatale*. Apart from downplaying his own role in the affair, they ignore the film's concern to establish the way the cultural context pushes Elisabeth to act as she does.

Nelson's words are quoted in English by his francophone assistant, and this moment is the culmination of a process that links the cultural context to the politics of language. English is the language of authority and is first introduced into the film through an invisible cut that transports Elisabeth from her present home, where her daughter is tidying her hair, to the courtroom. As the camera pans away to reveal the trial in progress, an off-screen male voice reads the charges against her in heavily accented and hesitant English.

The camera eventually comes to rest on the clerk of the court as he finishes reading the indictment, the disembodied voice of authority located in an ordinary, middle-aged man struggling with a foreign language, an act of ventriloquism like that of Elisabeth reading the accusatory text selected by her husband.[66]

Since the indictment claims that the crime has disturbed the Queen's "peace," Elisabeth is accused in the name of a patriarchal order, whose head is a woman, by a man whose subjection to a foreign power is apparent from his linguistic difficulties. In Lacanian terms, this "colonial" society is one in which the imaginary and the symbolic are completely divorced from each other. The result is madness for those who cannot accept the way things are, as exemplified in the self-destructive behaviour of Tassy and the excesses of Elisabeth who, as Hofsess puts it, has been "raised in a genteel household of women" but is "going mad with normal passion."[67]

The contradictions involved in living in a society whose symbolic order originates elsewhere are also apparent in the irony that the object of Elisabeth's desire is an English-speaking "foreigner." While Nelson left his homeland and was educated in Quebec because of the Loyalist sentiments of his family, his ties to the British colonial establishment are doubly contradicted by his American persona and by his childhood friendship with Tassy. He is bilingual and usually speaks to Elisabeth in French, becoming a non-threatening other, an alternative to the physical abuse she endures from Tassy. But his combination of virility and tenderness itself becomes a sign of the impossibility of their love in this social context. His language marks him as an outsider, but their passion leads to a transgression that subjects them to the power of the (English) law, condemning her to a passionless second marriage and him to exile in his own country.

By making Nelson the idealized object of Elisabeth's desire, the film emphasizes the lack of eligible males in the community. Elisabeth is brought up in an all-female society composed of her mother and her three unmarried aunts, and when she marries Tassy, she finds herself subjected to his domineering mother. Tassy initially seems to be an attractive rebel against social constraints, but his boyish charm masks a refusal or inability to take on the responsibilities of an adult male in a social order in which the authority of the lord of the manor is bound to be illusory. In contrast to Tassy's frustrated brutality, Nelson offers a romantic ideal that is abstract and impossible, while Rolland provides a social respectability in which desire gives way to duty.

Elisabeth bears children by each of these men, but, as in *À tout prendre* and *Mon oncle Antoine*, the emasculation of Quebec society leads to a difficulty in assuming the role of father. As in so many Quebec texts, Elisabeth's own father is absent, apparently dead, unmentioned but the source of her aristocratic maiden name. Her mother and aunts provide a traditional feminine environment, while Tassy's mother takes on the stern patriarchal role that her son refuses. At Kamouraska, she lectures her daughter-in-law on the need to accept, or at least to pretend to accept, the way things are. She dismisses the "nervous crisis" that the marriage has provoked in Elisabeth as mere "theatre."

A repressive presence, dressed in black and with a club foot, Madame Tassy runs the manor at Kamouraska and indulges her son's weaknesses. After the murder, she moves quickly to prevent a scandal, apparently arranging Elisabeth's release from prison and insisting that they be seen together, placing the need to demonstrate innocence in public over any private grief that she might feel for the death of her son. She claims that Elisabeth is "condemned to innocence," and it is the order restored by Madame Tassy, and confirmed by Elisabeth's marriage to Rolland, that prevails at the end of the film.

In the final sequence, Elisabeth is again at her husband's bedside. Having received the last rites from a priest, Rolland is confident that God has forgiven his sins. In a sense, the process of reconstructing the past seems to have brought Elisabeth to a state of calm like that which Rolland obtains from the ritual. Yet the results in her case are far more enigmatic. After a shot of Elisabeth approaching the bedroom, framed in the narrow opening of the door, there is a cut to a "subjective" shot in which the camera moves past the foot of the bed. A servant looks towards the camera and speaks to the priest of her mistress's grief. The final shot shows Elisabeth sitting on the other side of the bed. When she speaks of her fear, Rolland reassures her that he is there, and the camera moves in on her face, excluding Rolland from the shot, as she weeps silently.

This medium close-up of Elisabeth weeping is held for a long time before the final image eventually fades away. Although the previous shot allows us to share her optical point of view, we can now only infer Elisabeth's state of mind from her appearance. If Madame Tassy represents a social order that believes that inner experience must conform to external circumstances, the film has developed a vision in which the relationship between inside and outside is both less stable and more challenging. Elisabeth's idealized view of her affair with Nelson opposes the dominant order by attempting to make reality conform to inner needs, and her tears at the end are a lament for the impossibility of acting out her desires.

Although Elisabeth is physically attracted to Tassy and even shows some affection towards Rolland, her desires cannot be satisfied by either of these impotent males. As Jutra put it, she is able to affirm herself only "in an excessive manner by destroying all the males around her." He added that she joins with the women around her in "an enormous plot against a society that is masculine," but this formulation tends to conceal the difficulty of being masculine in a society in which effective power and authority exist elsewhere.[68]

The absence of fathers in *Kamouraska* even extends to the priesthood. In both *À tout prendre* and *Mon oncle Antoine*, the traditional figure of the priest as "father" and spiritual guide emerges briefly before being discredited, whereas in *Kamouraska*, although we do see Elisabeth receiving lessons in piety from her aunts, the Church seems to be totally irrelevant to Elisabeth's quest. A priest does appear in the final sequence, to administer the last rites to Rolland (in Latin, the language of spiritual authority), but this comes too late to overcome the sense of a society whose males lack the power and the authority associated with the father in the symbolic order.

Because of his age, Rolland functions as a kind of father figure for his wife, who prides herself on her youthful appearance, but the effect only underlines his inappropriate role as her second husband. The stability that he has provided depends on the construction of a "normal" patriarchal family in which sexual "duty" is only an aspect of the wife/mother's reproductive function. In any case, the film is framed by sequences set at the deathbed of this pseudo-father-figure, and Elisabeth's "excesses" are seen as a response to a situation in which male privilege is itself a masquerade (which, nevertheless, has real effects) since real power resides elsewhere and speaks in a foreign language.

The freedom that Elisabeth desires is ultimately impossible in any cultural context, but in the culture depicted in the film, the lack of political autonomy and economic resources places additional constraints on desire. These constraints are also cinematic in that film language can never fully capture either the past or the inner life of the characters, and Quebec cinema lacked the resources even to create the illusion of doing these things. Unlike Lefebvre, Jutra did not respond to this situation by constructing an alternative mode of production and a cinematic style clearly marked off from classical narrative. Instead, he created a text that attempts to work within the system, while using the genre of the historical epic to bring out the cultural contradictions built into its own creation. As with Jutra's earlier films, this strategy was vulnerable to misrepresentation, and *Kamouraska*'s complicated meditation on Quebec's colonial heritage fell victim to its publicity, its producers, and its critics.

Above: The married couple (Jutra, Monique Miller) in a domestic setting (Pierre Lamy)

Below: Bernard and Hélène during their musical number (Pierre Lamy)

A HAPPY FILM?

Pour le meilleur et pour le pire

In many ways, *Pour le meilleur et pour la pire* was the follow-up film Jutra had wanted to make after *À tout prendre*. His involvement as director, screenwriter, and actor matched his multiple roles in the making of the earlier film and contrasted with the shared authorship of the intervening films. The new film also represented a return to a more modest budget after the comparative epic grandeur of *Kamouraska*. Accordingly, Luc Perreault welcomed Jutra's latest effort as a "renewal with the spirit of his first real feature-film."[1]

In addition to the parallels between the two films, however, Perreault noted one major difference: whereas *À tout prendre* "virtually laid bare the private life of Claude Jutra," the new film dealt with "a problem that is completely foreign to his private life." This "problem" was marriage, and critics immediately and often compared Jutra's film with Ingmar Bergman's *Scenes from a Marriage* (1973), which enjoyed considerable success at the time both as a television miniseries and as a film. As Jutra himself pointed out, Bergman was something of an expert on the subject since he had been married several times. In contrast, Jutra was, in his own words, a "hardened bachelor," a thinly veiled allusion to his homosexuality, but he insisted that a detached perspective was an asset for his film.[2]

Most reviewers, however, thought the film suffered from the director's inexperience, and their lack of enthusiasm certainly contributed to the film's commercial failure. Since *Kamouraska* had also disappointed its producers, this second setback left Jutra once more without prospects at a time when the Quebec film industry was itself struggling to survive. In the case of *Kamouraska*, the passage of time and the belated appearance of the director's cut have led to some revival of interest in the film, but most accounts of Jutra's career and histories of Quebec cinema have virtually ignored *Pour le meilleur et pour le pire*. This is unfortunate because, as a Jutra film and as a

Quebec film, it is a symptomatic text that reveals much about the director's relations to his cultural context.

Jutra's Musical Comedy Project

The film's origins go back to the period after *À tout prendre* when Jutra planned to make a film called *Cinq filles*. At one point, the NFB and Radio-Canada expressed interest in coproducing this film, but Jutra also took the project to at least one Hollywood studio. His idea was to make what he called a "musical comedy," not "in the American sense of the term" but rather "a comedy with songs in a style closer to the Europeans."[3] One recent film that may have influenced his thinking was Jacques Demy's *Les Parapluies de Cherbourg* (*The Umbrellas of Cherbourg*, 1964) in which all the dialogue is sung, but he did not completely reject the Hollywood model. His new film would pay homage to the musicals of Vincente Minnelli but would translate them into "our cultural framework."[4]

In planning the film, Jutra clearly wanted to appeal to spectators who had experienced difficulties in identifying with the characters in *À tout prendre*. The hero of *Cinq filles* was to be a man with five daughters but who wants a son, and Jutra hoped that the spectator would fall in love with the five daughters and "even with the father" by the end of the film. *Pour le meilleur et pour le pire* inherits the attempt to place the Hollywood musical in the context of Quebec culture, but the musical content has shrunk to a single sequence in a film that is far from being the "happy film" that Jutra originally envisaged.[5]

Its plot deals with a day in the life of a married couple, Bernard and Hélène, opening with the rituals of getting up in the morning and ending as they retire for the night. But in the course of this single day, the seasons gradually change from spring to winter and their daughter grows from a baby to a teenager who leaves home with her boyfriend. In the meantime, the couple are haunted by a strange "mad woman," who initially seems to be a ghost, and Bernard sets up a confrontation between Hélène and a man he thinks is her lover. Shifting frequently between grotesque comedy and emotional crisis, the film builds to a violent climax in which Bernard and Hélène threaten each other with a gun.

As this summary suggests, rather than breaking with the aesthetics of failure that complicated spectatorship in *À tout prendre*, Jutra increased the distancing devices in *Pour le meilleur et pour le pire*. As a result, many of the complaints made about the earlier film resurfaced in discussions of the new one. Léo Bonneville summarized much of the critical response when he claimed that the "clichés, tricks, nonsense interminably wear down the spectator."[6] Critics again accused Jutra of borrowing from "almost everywhere" and stuffing his film with "the most worn-out symbols."[7] Frederick Edell described it as "a smart-aleck wise-ass movie," revealing a "nasty misanthropy" in a filmmaker whose earlier work had established him as "the Quebecois heir of Renoir and Truffaut, a warmly generous humanist, tolerant and gentle, soft and loving."[8]

Another reviewer, however, felt that the new film did reveal the influence of Renoir (by way of Truffaut), pointing out that "Renoir can be tart as well as warm" and that Jutra's film "deliberately deals in the commonplace in order to point out an eternal verity or two."[9] Whether the verities treated in *Pour le meilleur et pour le pire* are "eternal" or not, Francine Laurendeau, in one of the most favourable reviews in the Quebec media, argued that the film was a "mature work" by a true "*auteur*" that explored marriage as an "institution" in the same way that Bergman called into question "the existence of God" in *Winter Light* (1962) and *The Silence* (1963).[10]

Despite these attempts to turn the comparison with the European "art cinema" to the advantage of the film, the uneasiness evident in most reviews points to the way it disrupts established norms of spectatorship and genre. Its reputation has hardly recovered, although one recent "dictionary" of Quebec cinema does claim that, while critics did not recognize the film's qualities at the time of its release, "the ironic dimension and the audacity of the narrative structure" now "stand out to advantage."[11]

Show Business

As the allusions to Bergman and the Hollywood musical already suggest, *Pour le meilleur et pour le pire* is an unstable mixture of elements that refuses to settle into a clearly defined cinematic identity.[12] The mixing of genres creates a jarring clash of tonalities between different aspects of the film, an unsettling effect anticipated by its title. At first glance, the idea of "for better or worse" is simply an allusion to the marriage vows that bind the couple together, but it also evokes the tension between the film's playful address to the spectator, evoking the artifice and utopian vision of the musical comedy, and a bleak vision of male-female relationships worthy of the plays of August Strindberg, the troubled Swedish playwright who deeply influenced Bergman.

The utopian desire that things could be "better" and the dystopian sense that they could not be "worse" set up the polarities that govern the film's style and structure. What these two apparently mismatched traditions share, however, is a strong sense of the importance of theatricality in everyday life. This is very evident in stage and screen musicals, in which theatricality enables the construction of an alternative, "better," reality, a vision of community based on the translation of inner experience into the spectacle of the dance, the exhilaration of the music, and the romance of the lyrics.[13]

On the other hand, the naturalist tradition apparently seeks to eliminate any sense of theatricality in the effort to create an illusion of reality. But the very effort to eliminate the theatrical results in a return of the repressed, as the characters put on masks, so to speak, and manipulate language so that outward signs do not clearly express their inner selves. These characters construct alternative, but worse, realities and find themselves trapped in situations where the existence of a true reality behind appearances is called into question. Thus, the climax of Edward Albee's *Who's Afraid of Virginia Woolf?* (1965), a play squarely within the Strindbergian tradition, turns on the revelation that the child to whom the couple have referred many times during the play is a figment of their imaginations.[14]

Both traditions stress the power of the theatre to construct artificial worlds, and Jutra plays them off against each other in his highly theatrical film. He referred to yet another theatrical tradition when he appealed to the example of Brecht to justify the collision of generic elements in the film.[15] This appeal fell on deaf ears, and the unsettling generic and tonal clashes simply annoyed most reviewers, who also dismissed the film's theatricality as an affront to cinematic realism.[16] But the relationship between cinema and theatre is far from mutually exclusive, and it is precisely this interest in exploring the theatricality of life through the medium of film that Jutra shared with such different filmmakers as Renoir and Bergman.

While there is only one musical number in *Pour le meilleur et pour le pire*, the sequence holds the key to what Jutra called the film's prevailing "stylization."[17] It thus provides a useful starting point for an analysis of the unusual strategies to which this term refers. When the couple try to escape from the pressures of their present relationship by remembering their early days together, Hélène reminds Bernard that he took her to see a film called *Rio Rita* on their honeymoon. The title, actually used for two undistinguished Hollywood musicals made in 1929 and 1942, evokes the familiar generic motif of escape to the tropical South, and the couple remind each other of their favourite old films and Hollywood stars. Under the influence of this shared nostalgia, Bernard declares (in English) that "those were very good times, after all," and Hélène replies in the same spirit: "Ah yes, weren't they." These words lead into a musical number in which the lyrics switch into French and from romantic nostalgia to vicious insults. The couple sing about their mutual feelings of boredom and even their disgust with the other's sexual organs.

In the Hollywood musical, romance substitutes for sexuality, and the graceful rhythms of the dance act as a sublimation of the sexual act that cannot be represented. The choreography makes the spectator aware of the bodies of the performers but, at the same time, creates the illusion of transcending the limits of the physical body. In *Pour le meilleur et pour le pire*, the musical number allows the couple to express feelings that normally remain unspoken, but their less-than-graceful dancing exposes the sexual meanings that the genre normally confines to a discreet subtext. The collision between the romantic and the grotesque also betrays the effects of time on the bodies of a couple who are no longer in good enough condition to imitate the stars that they admired in their younger days.

This sequence thus depends on a tension between romance and reality very much like the contrast between idyllic fantasy and brutal murder in *Kamouraska*. In both cases, the implication is that the stress on romance in popular culture generates idealized expectations that can only be disappointed by an imperfect reality. According to their joint reminiscences about the past that precede the musical number, Bernard once thought of Hélène as Cinderella, and she imagined him to be Prince Charming. These fantasies have inevitably failed to survive the passage of time, and they have now reached the point where, as Hélène tells Bernard, they know each other so well that they have nothing left to say to each other.

Bernard works for an advertising agency, and his current project is a toothpaste commercial that also conflates the appeals of romance and sexuality.

Jutra may be alluding to Allan King's *A Married Couple* (1969), a documentary on a couple caught up in a similar claustrophobic relationship, in which the husband also works as an advertising copy writer. In both films, the cynicism of the advertising industry suggests that sexuality has now become commodified to an even greater degree than in the classic Hollywood musical.

Bernard's proposed commercial features a glamorous woman whose smile, as his boss tells the clients, "represents consent." According to the accompanying jingle, the smile says "oui" because the woman uses Diamond-T, thus rhyming sexual promise with the brand name of the toothpaste. Hélène suggests a revised version that undercuts masculine complacency, while preserving the rhyme, by substituting "maybe" (in English) for "oui."

Hélène's use of the slogan as a weapon in her power struggle with Bernard suggests the infiltration of advertising imagery into people's everyday behaviour and even into their inner lives. In the opening sequence, she uses Diamond-T – emphasized by a close-up that evokes television commercials – to brush her teeth in the morning before returning to bed with the apparent aim of seducing the still-sleeping Bernard. Bernard later imagines the completed commercial with Hélène running in slow motion through an idyllic natural landscape towards the man he suspects of being her lover.

Bernard's fantasy occurs while he listens to classical music through headphones. His isolated immersion in music from the "high" culture of the past contrasts with the couple's shared and interactive, but certainly not idealized, response to the Hollywood musical. Bernard uses the music of the past to escape from the complications of the present, but he is only able to do so through the mediation of modern technology, and the music comes to function as background to a private fantasy presented through the clichés of commercial advertising. The complex interconnections between romance, sexuality, and commerce in the Hollywood musical are thus also at work in contemporary Quebec culture. The power of modern technology and advertising has "colonized" the unconscious or fantasy lives of the couple.

The influence of Hollywood and the requirements of the business world both lead to the frequent use of English and to the intrusion of English words and phrases into the French dialogue. What the film seems to offer, then, is an extremely bleak vision in which the domestic frustrations of married life are mapped on to the manipulative power of the mass media and then on to the decline of Quebec culture. Yet while the depiction of marriage disturbed many reviewers, there was little recognition of the film's broader cultural dimensions.

The critics also tended to deplore the film's "stylization" without addressing the way it distances us from the negative implications of the narrative and allows a utopian dimension to emerge. Although the couple's romantic expectations lead to disillusionment, their stormy relationship also reveals the need for fantasy and desire if the actual situation is to change. They choose to remain together at the end of the film, realizing that they prefer their flawed relationship to the prospect of individual isolation. This ending is quite consistent with one of the central motifs of Bergman's films, but by breaking with realist conventions, Jutra's film encourages the spectator to seek out the utopian potential within the negative account of the present situation.

Style and Spectatorship

In a review published in *Cinéma Québec*, alongside Francine Laurendeau's positive assessment, Richard Gay argued that the film was a failure because the distancing devices prevent the spectator from "communicating with the emotions of the characters."[18] From Jutra's perspective, of course, this was precisely what he intended, but he insisted that the stylization effects did allow for a "second-degree identification."[19] As in Brechtian theatre, there is a constant tension between identification with the characters and distancing devices that invite us to think about how the characters came to be in the situations depicted.

In *Pour le meilleur et pour la pire*, the disruptive strategies remind us that it is impossible to ever really know or claim to represent another person's experience (for reasons that I have discussed with regard to *À tout prendre*). The detached perspective also reveals the shaping of the characters' situations by their social and cultural context and asks us to view the characters not as unique individuals but as exemplary figures who serve the needs of the fable.

Because of his objections to these strategies, Gay blamed the actors for not matching the "intensity" of the performances in *Scenes from a Marriage*. He argued that, while both films "rely almost exclusively on two actors," the two central performances in *Pour le meilleur et pour le pire* pale in comparison with those of Liv Ullmann and Erland Josephson in Bergman's film. He found Monique Miller as Hélène to be "too theatrical, too insistent," and blamed Jutra for casting himself as Bernard, thereby proving yet again that he was a "filmmaker not an actor."[20]

There is, however, a major difference between Bergman's psychological exploration of a complex interaction between two individuals evolving over many years (even the abbreviated theatrical-release version is almost three hours long) and Jutra's compressed fable in which individual psychology is about as important as it is in a Hollywood musical or a Brechtian play. Nevertheless, in striking contrast to Gay, Laurendeau praised the "real characters" and "the intelligence, the subtlety of the actors" in Jutra's film.[21]

All responses to acting and performance must be at least partially subjective, but, in this case, they are complicated by the effects of the overall stylization. There are two main distancing devices at work throughout the film: the inclusion of black-and-white sequences in a film shot mainly in colour, and the shifting time schemes. For spectators at that time, these devices might evoke memories of the play with colour and time in Claude Lelouch's *Un Homme et une femme* (*A Man and a Woman*, 1966), whose idealized vision of the couple is in marked contrast to Jutra's depiction of a marriage on the verge of breakdown. Another recent film that used the alternation of black-and-white and colour sequences as part of an overall strategy of stylization was Lindsay Anderson's *If...* (1968), in which realism, fantasy, and satire blend (and clash) in a way much closer to the tone of Jutra's film.

As with *If...*, there were budgetary reasons for the use of black and white, but Jutra incorporated this economic constraint into his aesthetic purposes.[22] In *Wow*, he had used colour for the dream sequences and black and white for the interviews; in *Pour le meilleur et pour le pire*, sequences set inside the high-rise apartment building in which Bernard and Hélène live are in colour, while the outside world appears in black and white. Since the couple do not leave their apartment after returning home in the late afternoon, the second half of the film is entirely in colour. Colour thus evokes the intensity generated by the confined living quarters while black-and-white images represent the mundane urban environment, a contrast similar to that in Michel Brault's *Les Ordres*, in which colour represents the pressures on the victims of the War

Measures Act when they are in prison. In *Pour le meilleur et pour le pire*, this pattern completely cuts across the distinction between reality and fantasy.

Like all such effects, the shifts into black and white invite the spectator to speculate on the reasons for the change and thus increase awareness of the cinematic apparatus. After the opening sequences (in colour), which introduce us to the life of the family through the rituals of getting up in the morning, Bernard leaves for work. The first black-and-white shot shows him getting into his car in the underground parking lot, with the effect that the absence of colour initially seems to be the result of the poor lighting. As Bernard tries to start the car, he seems surprised by something he sees through the windscreen, and a reverse shot reveals a woman staring back at him. He shines the headlights on her, but when he looks again she has disappeared. This is the "mad woman," whose function in the film will be discussed later, but her unexplained disappearance raises the possibility that she is imaginary, a ghost or Bernard's hallucination, and immediately discourages the spectator from assuming that black and white will simply represent mundane reality.

Although this first shift into black and white alerts the spectator to the reflexive dimension of the film, the perceptual disruption is minor compared to the effect of the play with time that starts to become apparent in the following sequence. The film conforms to the usual two-hour running time, but its plot develops three distinct time frames that are simply laid on top of each other: a day, a year, the years it takes for a baby to grow into an independent young woman. A visual clue to the film's multiple time schemes is provided by an M.C. Escher print on a wall in the couple's apartment, first seen when Hélène goes to the bathroom in the opening sequence. It is a reproduction of the woodcut called *Day and Night* (1938), one of the artist's perceptual puns, showing what could be either a flock of black birds flying in one direction or a flock of white birds flying in the opposite direction. What Escher does with spatial perception in his witty images, Jutra does with the perception of time in his film.

Just as the ambiguities of space only gradually become perceptible in an Escher print, so a key part of the spectator's experience of this film is the gradual awareness of the different layers of time. Whereas the opening shots in *Kamouraska* immediately plunge us into the fragmented time schemes of Elisabeth's consciousness, the opening of *Pour le meilleur et pour le pire* establishes the time and space of the action in ways that seems quite normal. Before the credits, we see shots of the sky at sunrise, and the camera pans across and up high-rise buildings in the early-morning light. This establishing shot ends with a cut that takes us from outside to inside the apartment, where the camera pans over the bodies of the couple, as they sleep in their double bed, until it reaches their faces.

Once the camera has entered the personal space of the couple, the state of their relationship emerges in a sequence that introduces hints of the film's double vision. The process of getting up in the morning is represented both as a routine activity that has been performed many times and as a singular and unpredictable event. Hélène's manipulation of the schedule that defines the working day is the first example of temporal confusion. After quietly getting out of bed, she goes to the bathroom to brush her teeth and tidy her hair, returns to bed, and sets off the alarm. She has to shake Bernard to wake him, but her efforts seem to bear fruit when he asks her how she manages to be so "pretty" in the morning. He is sorry that he does not have time to stay in bed with her, but she points out that she has created time by advancing the alarm.

However, this prelude to love making comes to nothing because a baby starts crying. The couple immediately get into an argument, and she complains of his bad breath. This rapid emotional shift points to a diagnosis of the marriage as a "love-hate" relationship. While Hélène later declares that she loves Bernard so much that she hates him, the sudden argument in the opening sequence also works against such pat definitions by making clear that the film will not take the "normal" time to provide cues to assure us that we know why the characters act the way they do. The abrupt shifts in tone led André Leroux to complain that the spectator is "projected from one tension to another without having been prepared for what surges up abruptly on the screen."[23] Similarly, the spectator has to adjust and then readjust as the different time schemes come into play.

The perception of time begins to take on broader cultural implications during the couple's conversation at the breakfast table. Bernard predicts that the company will reject his proposal for the toothpaste commercial because of the costs of shooting in Spain to avoid the Canadian winter. When Hélène points out that it is still only spring, Bernard details the time-consuming bureaucratic process by which the commercial must be approved in Quebec City, Toronto, Ottawa, and New York. The effect is to place the couple's situation within the context of constraints, both temporal and spatial, with which Jutra was very familiar as a Canadian filmmaker.

Although Hélène loyally comments that administrators dislike Bernard because he is an "artist," there is an irony in Jutra's decision to cast himself in the role of an artist who is not a filmmaker but a writer of advertising jingles. The treatment of the commercial is a symptom of social and industrial processes that impose a linear schedule, apparently rational but in fact dictated by an absurd logic, on natural time and on human creativity. Time becomes a factor again when Hélène informs Bernard that he is two minutes late leaving for work and then tells him that she will not answer the telephone if he calls at noon.

After the destabilizing effect of Bernard's encounter with the "mad woman" in the parking lot, the film begins to make apparent the ways it will disrupt normal continuity. He is already suspicious about what Hélène will be doing at noon and, when he takes a taxi because his car will not start, he hears a message over the radio calling a taxi to their apartment. Meanwhile, the cab driver's casual remark that "spring's gone too fast" seems to contradict Hélène's reference to spring in the previous sequence. In the next sequence, however, Hélène visits Loulou, her friend who lives on the floor above, and tells her that she has just taken her daughter in a taxi for her first day at nursery school.

This explanation, of course, depends on the assumption that several years have passed since the breakfast sequence, when the daughter was still a baby, rather than the few weeks suggested by the cab driver's remark on the weather. But Hélène goes on to tell Loulou of her threat not to answer the phone if Bernard calls at noon, implying that this is still the same day on which they had their earlier argument. There remains the possibility that an argument about a noon phone call is a common occurrence in the life of the couple, but the next sequence, in which Bernard loses his job because his jealousy has caused him to miss an important meeting with representatives of Diamond-T, re-establishes the sense of the action occurring during a single day.

As the film progresses, the disruptions caused by the different time schemes become less severe as they become more predictable. The linear plot centres on Bernard's jealousy, which provokes him to follow a stranger into a bar and invite him to the apartment in the evening so that he can confront Hélène with the man he takes to be her lover. During the afternoon, the now-unemployed Bernard walks home from school with his young daughter, who becomes a teenager by the end of the evening and leaves home with her boyfriend, after expressing her contempt for her parents' way of life. When their guest arrives promptly at half past five, they chat uncomfortably about the weather, and we learn that it is now summer. Later that evening, as they prepare for bed, Bernard looks through the window and sees that it is winter.

The film draws further attention to its play with time when Hélène, searching for something to say when she first meets their guest, comments that "spring went so fast," and when, in the final sequence, Bernard's watch goes haywire with its hands speeding around the dial. In a similar way, the visitor reminds us of the shifts from colour to black-and-white, well after the last black and white sequence, when he rather oddly refers to the couple's television set as "black and white on the exterior, colour on the interior."

For many critics, these reflexive devices simply keep the spectator from becoming involved with the characters. But the main point of these "distractions" (as Gay called them) is that they demand the kind of "distracted" viewing called for by Walter Benjamin (a great admirer of Brecht) in which the spectator is not absorbed into the fiction but analyzes its meanings in their social and cultural contexts.[24] This critical perspective does not prevent identification and may lead to more powerful emotional effects because the personal circumstances of *this* couple illuminate the dynamics of social relations in which the spectator is implicated. Unfortunately, very few actual spectators seem to have responded to the film in this way.

Gender and Family Life

The problem of identification, however, is not only a question of form. If Jutra is apparently dealing here with a situation of which he had no personal experience, he still places the male at the centre of the action. Even though he is absent from a few early sequences involving Hélène and Loulou, our involvement with the film is filtered through Bernard's consciousness and his jealousy drives the narrative. Jutra emphasizes his centrality by playing the role himself, but, far from being in control, Bernard continues Jutra's line of males who lack any of the traditional patriarchal authority.

As we have seen, the crisis of masculinity in Jutra's films is symptomatic of a culture deprived of its own symbolic order. While the rigmarole surrounding the process of approving Bernard's commercial playfully alludes to the film's dislocated time schemes, it also makes clear that ultimate power in the publicity business lies outside Quebec – in Toronto, Ottawa, and New York. His jealousy towards the man he suspects of being his wife's lover further exposes Bernard's insecurity, but it also introduces a rather different male response to the same situation. Bernard vaguely remembers that Hélène has spoken of an ex-boyfriend called Jerry, but he quickly adjusts when the man he has followed tells him that his name is Johnny. These English-sounding names suggest a desire to tap into the power associated with the language of the colonizer, and Johnny does boast of his sexual prowess with other men's wives. Yet he is a salesman for "National Lumber," selling Quebec's natural resources to the highest bidder, and during his evening with Bernard and Hélène, it becomes clear that he is married and that he uses sexual innuendo to mask an insecurity as great as Bernard's.

The masculine pretensions of both men are repeatedly undercut by the use of the term "con." Translated as "schmuck" in the English subtitles, the French word also carries overtones of femininity through its vulgar usage to refer to the female sexual organ. It is first used by Hélène when she gets stoned with Loulou and ridicules Bernard because smoking makes him sick. In the bar, Johnny uses the term to describe the husband of the woman with whom he is currently involved, an insult that Bernard takes to himself. Hélène later applies it to Johnny to his face and then, after pointing out Bernard's mistake over the names, recalls that Jerry was also a "con." She says that she broke off with him because he asked permission to make love to her, and Bernard only reinforces her contempt for masculine inadequacy when he asks permission to shoot her during their final struggle.

As the only significant male characters in the film, Bernard and Johnny seem to justify Hélène's contempt for men. In the gender politics of the Strindbergian tradition on which the film draws, the emasculation of the males is the result of the castrating power of the woman as *femme fatale*. In Jutra's films, however, gender politics intersect with cultural politics in often contradictory ways. In this case, the battle of the sexes is mapped on to the effects of a social order in which modernization, represented by the apartment building and Place Bonaventure where Bernard works, disrupts traditional modes of personal and gender identity. While Bernard blames Hélène for his frustrations and anxieties, the film makes clear that her erratic behaviour is the product of her own frustration as wife and mother, trapped in the apartment and in a culture in which traditional family values no longer function to give these roles meaning.

There is one other male figure in the film who (like Jerry) remains unseen but who embodies the ideal of masculine potency that Bernard lacks. This absent character, significantly named Léo, figures prominently in the final confrontation between the couple. When Hélène accuses Bernard of "screwing around" on his business trips even though nothing happens in their own bed, she threatens to go on the streets and telephones Léo to ask him to find her a customer. When Loulou comes down to investigate the noise they are making, Bernard rather pathetically asks if she will let him come to her apartment, but she quietly refuses because Léo is already there. Finally, Hélène reveals that Léo supplied her with the gun. He thus represents a masculine power that is both absent and criminal, and thus doubly unavailable as a solution to the crisis of gender codes that threatens the couple's relationship.

As a married couple, representing a central social institution, Bernard and Hélène lack the marginal status of most of Jutra's characters. Nor do her cultural and sexual frustrations quite lead Hélène to the "madness" attributed to Elisabeth in *Kamouraska*, although the whole film injects an element of destabilizing madness into the life of the couple and the spectator's experience of it. In this film, madness is itself marginalized in the figure of "la folle," the mad woman who, according to Jutra, "symbolizes everything that disturbs the couple."[25]

After her first brief apparition in the parking lot, the mad woman next appears when Bernard hangs up after trying to phone Hélène from a crowded shopping concourse. Once again, she disappears mysteriously, reinforcing the sense that she is a figment of his imagination. However, she is next seen by Hélène as a ghostly reflection in the window of the balcony of the empty apartment next door. While she may be a projection of the couple's anxieties, she comes to seem much more real when she approaches Hélène in the elevator and gives her a letter for Bernard, casually remarking that he has an "interesting penis." Later, Bernard admits that he once had a casual affair with the woman before he knew Hélène, making her the counterpart of Jerry of whom he has been so jealous.

The uncertain status of "la folle," as both projection and victim, complicates responses to her extremely disturbing final appearance. Shortly after Johnny has left, the doorbell rings and Hélène finds the mad woman outside. Presumably as a result of the pressures that have been building up during the evening, Hélène repeatedly slaps the woman until she collapses in the corridor. A neighbour emerges from the elevator but does not intervene, and Bernard finishes off the assault by kicking the helpless woman. The brutality is excessive, despite the threat that she represents to the couple and her symbolic status as the embodiment of their repressed fears. Occurring just before the musical number, this sequence reinforces the instability built into the spectator's response by the film's refusal to settle for realist or fantasy explanations for its events.

If the mad woman, whether actual or imaginary, is an extreme image of the oppression of women in a society that depends on the institution of marriage, there are two other women in the film who suggest possible alternative approaches. One of these is Loulou, whom Jutra regarded as "the healthy character ... a truly liberated woman."[26] She is first introduced through a close-up of the cello she is playing, and she later describes the musical instrument as a source of sexual satisfaction that she has been unable to obtain from men. However, although she tells Hélène that happiness depends on constant change, her liberated status does not seem to be fully satisfying. She admits that the cello does not really make her happy but simply prevents boredom. The happiness achieved by the two women when they share a joint is, as with the drug culture in *Wow*, both temporary and based on a denial of their actual situations.

What Loulou does offer, like Barbara in *À tout prendre* (both characters are played by Monique Mercure), is a refusal to take men seriously. As in the earlier film, laughter deflates male pretensions. Under the influence of the pot they have smoked, both women laugh at a male stranger who steps out of the elevator. Later, the camera pans up Bernard's body in pyjamas and Loulou giggles, saying that he reminds her of Bach's third cello suite. As when

187

Barbara and Johanne laugh at Claude in *À tout prendre*, the main point is the disturbance caused by the laughter rather than deciding whether it represents a liberated point of view.

The other female character who offers a possible alternative to the dominant gender codes is, of course, the couple's daughter, Martine. Like the young people in *Wow*, she belongs to a new "liberated" generation, but Jutra remains ambivalent about what this alternative entails. When Martine is a schoolgirl, she solemnly tells her parents that the children have voted against doing math, implying an approach to education that Jutra advocated in *Comment savoir* but that here hardly has progressive results. As a young adolescent, she defies gender norms by practising baseball in her room, but the room is decorated with posters of Clint Eastwood and Paul Newman, attesting to the continued influence of Hollywood on sexual fantasy.

The long-haired youth with whom Martine leaves home at the end represents a very different kind of masculinity associated with the counterculture and with the loud rock music they have been playing in her room. Although the young couple break with the constrictive cultural codes that have shaped the parents' marriage, the rock music suggests that this break will also involve a loss of contact with the great achievements of Western culture, such as the music of Bach, which Bernard and Loulou both love.

According to Laurendeau, the child does not represent a "sure value" for the future, but she does develop "outside the influence of the family."[27] In other words, people's lives are not totally determined by their familial (or cultural) environments. Martine survives to make her own mistakes, just as the marriage of her parents will continue on the basis of their mutual contempt and need for each other. The film's detached perspective makes possible its own version of Brecht's goal of "complex seeing" that exposes both the extent and the limits of cultural conditioning.[28] There are no simple answers, it implies, to the problems of the couple, of mass society, or of Quebec. Yet its negative vision also recognizes the needs on which the present arrangements depend even as they prevent their complete fulfilment.

The Logic of the Everyday and the Absurd

Many of the critics who rejected *Pour le meilleur et pour le pire* compared it to familiar media representations of the life of the couple. Thus, Gay commented that the film looks like "a poorly televised play," while Leroux objected that the plot consists of marriage crises assembled by a computer programmed from "our worst *téléromans*."[29] These judgments seem to be in tune with the assessment of mass culture in the film itself, but they ignore the utopian undertow to its negative vision.

The film is "an acerbic and surrealist comedy" that constantly calls into question the stereotypes and assumptions to which it alludes.[30] Jutra himself stressed the importance of "humour," which, he argued, "best expresses all human situations, including anguish." Of course, humour does not usually express anguish, and it is the film's defiance of conventional expectations that allows it to develop what Jutra called a "logic of the everyday and the absurd."[31]

The same tension between constraint and disturbance is evident in responses to the film's characters and its depiction of marriage. Leroux found the lack of psychological motivation symptomatic of a refusal to accept that the problem is not marriage in itself but the failure of the partners to recognize "their personal limitations."[32] Edell similarly felt that film denied the couple any alternatives so that their failure came to seem "predestined."[33] This emphasis on limitation and constraint is a response to the narrative structure that the film works so hard to undercut through its stylization and generic instability. Once these are taken into account, *Pour le meilleur et pour le pire* emerges as "one of the most successful fictions on the subject" of marriage and "the life of the couple."[34]

Despite the verdict of many of its reviewers, the film does not represent the marriage simply in terms of failure. At times of crisis, the couple act together against the common enemy. The beating of "la folle" is just the most extreme example of this. Two other instances illustrate the film's comic dimension and the couple's complicity. After Bernard has been fired, he meets Hélène in the shopping concourse and claims that he told his boss to "eat shit." We know that he has not stood up for himself at all, but when she sees the boss with some clients, she attacks him for destroying a family and ignoring genius. She tells him to "eat shit" before walking off arm in arm with Bernard. Near the end of the film, after Bernard has apparently shot Hélène with a bullet that turns out to be a blank, they put up a united front to disturbed neighbours and police, claiming that the shots were fired by burglars.

The film is not so much about a failed marriage as about the effects of time on any human relationship. That the relationship in this case is a heterosexual marriage, thus representing the central social institution for managing sexuality, is certainly significant, but the vision is not unlike that of *Who's Afraid of Virginia Woolf?*, which has been interpreted as a disguised representation of a gay relationship.[35] As they exchange confidences in the bar, Bernard tells Johnny that he loves Hélène but that it is difficult to always be together. At one point, she suggests that she is "too old" for him and that women age faster than men. He replies that the solution is to grow old together, to be the same age.

The playful manipulation of time within the two-hour experience of the film also gives the lie to the "happy ever after" fantasies of the romance tradition. As the film suggests, age is to some extent a subjective condition, since mature people are capable of behaving like children. However, the couple have to come to terms with the passage of time that has changed their very sense of themselves. When Hélène accuses Bernard of keeping a photograph of another woman, she is embarrassed to learn that this is an image of her younger self in a bathing costume.

After the perverse euphoria of their musical number, Hélène suggests that they should have a night out, but when they find that they cannot get into their old clothes, they decide to go to bed instead. At this point, Hélène smiles at Bernard and agrees that the last word of the jingle should be "oui" rather than "maybe." This quiet moment precedes the couple's final showdown in which she declares that the fog has cleared away so that she can "see hell" – which is at least better than seeing nothing. The film depicts a process whereby the couple lose their last illusions about each other but then stay together.

This ending refuses to allow the spectator the assurance of knowing whether the life of the couple will improve as a result of their experiences. Yet time is also a factor in the film in relation to the social changes that have called the institution of marriage into question. Hélène suggests that she and Bernard are the "last of a dying species: the married couple," but despite the "hell" within which the couple are struggling, the film does not end by simply welcoming the extinction of an outmoded institution.

After they have driven each other to the brink of murder, the couple begin to make love on the floor amid the debris that they have created around themselves. A close-up of Bernard's hand on Hélène's body, in which his wristwatch is prominently visible, stresses the sense of mortality that lurks behind the motif of time and the act of physical love. When Martine and her boyfriend interrupt the love making and look down on their elders in disapproval, the effect is as ambivalent as everything in this film. That Martine will continue to develop outside the family suggests hope for the future – but it is a hope tinged with a sense of loss.

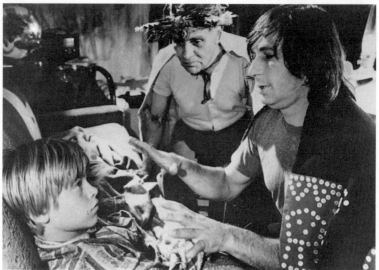

Above: Jenny (Anne Anglin) observes Ada (Janet Amos) from her hospital bed in *Ada* (Canadian Broadcasting Corporation)

Below: Peter (Ian Tracey with the old man (George Clutesi) and his mute companion (Jacques Hubert) in *Dreamspeaker* (Canadian Broadcasting Corporation)

INSTITUTIONAL MADNESS
Ada and *Dreamspeaker*

After the commercial failure of *Kamouraska* and *Pour le meilleur et pour le pire*, Jutra's future as a filmmaker looked very bleak indeed. Ironically, the Canadian film industry had just entered a boom period as a result of the Capital Cost Allowance Act (CSA) of 1974. This act "created a tax shelter for investors, enabling them to deduct one hundred per cent of their investment in features certified as Canadian from their taxable income and thus defer taxes until profits were earned."[1] Although many films were made under this scheme, the complicated regulations meant that the main beneficiaries were lawyers and that few projects were controlled by filmmakers. In any case, the increase in production rarely benefitted the filmmakers associated with the direct cinema movement whose work did not accord with the emphasis on production values in commercial Hollywood cinema.

In order to take advantage of the Capital Cost Allowance Act, it was necessary to attract potential investors who usually had little knowledge of, or interest in, the Canadian film industry. Since there was a general assumption that these films had to succeed in the US market, producers placed great emphasis on the need for "international" appeal and usually cast minor stars from Hollywood or from network television in the leading roles. As we shall see, Jutra's next theatrical film, *Surfacing*, fell victim to the economic and cultural pressures that dominated film production under these conditions. The film did not appear until 1981, however, and in 1975 – only four years after making *Mon oncle Antoine* – Jutra found himself virtually unemployable in the Canadian film industry.

Because the NFB was also going through one of its many difficult periods, television seemed to offer the only likely source of funding for film projects that did not have the ingredients to satisfy the CCA producers and investors. But French-language television had a strong commitment to the production of *téléromans* (the indigenous form of the soap opera) and variety shows, both of which were extremely popular with Quebec audiences. Thus, despite his reluctance to leave Quebec, Jutra accepted an offer to work in English for CBC television, which had just embarked on the production of a series of innovative television dramas.

As a result of this decision, Jutra worked outside Quebec on English-language television and film productions for almost a decade, in conditions that ranged from excellent to poor and with results that included some of his best work as well as some of his least convincing. Jutra was not the first Quebec filmmaker to pursue this option: in 1976 Gilles Carle contributed *A Thousand Moons* and Francis Mankiewicz *What We Have Here Is a People Problem* to a new CBC series called "Camera '76." It was for this series, now renamed "For the Record," that Jutra directed *Ada* and *Dreamspeaker* (both made in 1976 and first broadcast in 1977).

Jutra and "Dramatized Documentary"

One of the most successful series ever produced by the CBC, "For the Record" offered a small number of dramas on topical issues during every season from 1977 until 1985. The series originated in an initiative by John Hirsch, who became head of television drama in 1974. Hirsch believed that "art has a social responsibility," and he set out to produce dramas that would be as relevant to "mainstream Canadian experience" as the CBC's well-regarded current affairs programming.[2] He recruited Ralph Thomas as executive producer of the new series, and Thomas in turn recruited directors drawn mainly from the pool of Canadian filmmakers with experience in direct cinema.

At the end of the first season under its new title, Marc Gervais praised the series for drawing on "the richest tradition in Canadian filmmaking" and for treating topical social and political issues with a powerful, but often contro-versial, blend of fictional and documentary strategies.[3] Eight years later, as the series was coming to an end, Gail Henley stressed its difference from the products of American network television: whereas "an American TV drama would create an artificial dramatic reality and invariably resolve the issue emotionally to the detriment of the issue itself, but at the same time reinforc-ing the mainstream ideology," the "For the Record" dramas were less con-cerned with "whether viewers agree or disagree" than with enabling them "to relate to the situation, to understand the dynamics of the situation, and to make decisions based on expanded knowledge."[4]

"For the Record" became a flagship for the CBC, and its efforts to inform and challenge viewers gained the support of those who saw public television as an island of cultural nationalism in a sea of American media. Although there are evident parallels between the direct cinema tradition and the televisual challenges of "For the Record," the television series achieved greater public and critical recognition partly because it also appealed to the norms of television journalism and partly because Canadian content regulations for television ensured that the programs were shown in prime time.

After the first season, however, Gervais expressed concern that the series would win neither popular nor cultural success because it did not offer the usual pleasures of television viewing. On the one hand, he argued, viewers used to US network programming would find no "superstars" and "no outlet for living out their sex-and-violence fantasies," while, on the other, more discriminating viewers "surely will find no Fellini or Bergman among these Canadian TV offerings."[5] This judgment reveals the contempt for mass culture found in much writing on Canadian popular culture, as well as the equally common assumption that Canadian filmmakers cannot match the achievements of their European counterparts. In other words, "For the Record" had to define itself against a cultural background very similar to the one with which Jutra was familiar as a filmmaker.

The main difference was that the television series could exploit its anthology format to respond quickly to topical issues, building on the apparent "liveness" of the medium and ensuring that its offerings would attract public interest and even controversy. Although critics often refer to these television films as "docudramas," the CBC resisted the term, with its strong implication that the events and characters depicted are non-fictional. This resistance is understandable in view of the action for libel taken against one of the episodes from the 1977 season. Peter Pearson's *The Tar Sands* was a thinly disguised account of a recent scandal over dealings between the oil industry and politicians in Alberta. The fear of legal repercussions delayed the broadcast for several months, and the libel action ensured that it was never shown again.[6]

There were other films that dealt with specific topical issues, including Don Haldane's *Someday Soon*, also from the 1977 season, about the struggle of Manitoba farmers against the Garrison Dam project in the United States. Yet the format of the series also allowed for episodes on specific social issues but not tied to actual cases, and Jutra's contributions clearly belong to this group.

Jutra had refused Thomas's first invitation to become involved in the series, made during a visit to Montreal in 1974. According to Thomas, Jutra insisted that "only in Quebec could he find a cultural environment in which he could 'create'," and he also made clear that he had little interest in making what Thomas called "dramatized documentaries" or "dramas with a social theme." Jutra told him that he was working on a film that would take place "entirely in one house, if not one room." Although the setting in *Pour le meilleur et pour le pire* was slightly less constricted than this description suggests, it must have confirmed Thomas's belief that Jutra's "tastes were leading him towards intimate drama, confined to as small a space as possible." A year later he was thus able to persuade Jutra to come to Toronto to make *Ada*, whose action would be "circumscribed within the walls of a single building, a psychiatric institution."[7]

From Page to Screen

Both *Ada* and its successor, *Dreamspeaker*, were adaptations of literary works written by women, and Jutra found himself in a situation that resembled his collaboration with Anne Hébert on *Kamouraska*. *Ada* was based on Margaret Gibson's short story of the same name first published in 1974 and then collected in *The Butterfly Ward* (1976). The origins of *Dreamspeaker* are a little more complicated: the screenplay was by Cam Hubert, a pseudonym used at the time by Anne Cameron, who published a short novel based on the same material in 1978. Jutra got sole credit for the screenplay of *Ada* but received no credit for that of *Dreamspeaker*. The two films nevertheless have images and motifs in common that link them to each other and to other films by Jutra.

In both cases, Jutra was clearly attracted to the original material, but the adaptations reveal subtle yet significant differences from the published works. These differences suggest that, despite the apparent compatibility between the director and his material, the projects also involved elements that were quite alien to the treatment of similar situations in Jutra's previous films. Martin Knelman thought that *Ada* suffered from "an excessively poetic masochism," while *Dreamspeaker* exhibited a "sentimental phoniness" foreign to Jutra's sensibility. He applied these judgments equally to the original works and to the television adaptations and claimed that Jutra limited himself to reproducing the authors' visions because of his discomfort at working in English and for the CBC.[8]

Other critics were more sympathetic and stressed the continuity between the two television films and Jutra's previous work. According to Louis Goyette, "*Ada* and *Dreamspeaker* share wholly in Jutra's personal themes."[9] Gervais also saw them as "personal" films that reveal "the Jutra poetry" in their depiction of doomed "outsiders" and their overall mood of "adolescent, anarchistic romanticism." In fact, Gervais even argued that Jutra's new working conditions had a beneficial effect because they restrained him from indulging in the "artistic showiness" that had proved so controversial in his earlier films.[10] The generally respectful reception of Jutra's first two works for the CBC suggests that Gervais's view was widely shared.

Poetic Masochism: Ada

The first transmission of *Ada* took place a few months before the well-publicized theatrical première of *Outrageous!* (Richard Benner, 1977), based on another story from *The Butterfly Ward*. Although its director was American, *Outrageous!* is perhaps the quintessential English-Canadian film, a bittersweet fable about a schizophrenic woman and a female impersonator struggling for acceptance in Toronto but eventually finding happiness in New York, a "happy" ending not found in the original story. While Gibson's fiction grew out of a personal struggle with mental illness, which is central to her own biographical legend, these two adaptations suggest that her stories also speak to more general Canadian cultural concerns about identity and marginality.

The short stories in *The Butterfly Ward* all deal with women whose madness is both a symptom of and a protest against an absurd and cruel social order. For Gibson madness is both a label by which society protects itself from disturbing realities and a sign of the return of what has been repressed. It becomes a potential source of alternative values that are defined as "feminine," but it remains unclear whether this label depends on a sense of essential gender differences or on cultural definitions of male and female behaviour. This ambiguity gives the stories much of their power.

Ada, both the story and Jutra's adaptation of it, deals with two women whose experiences in a mental hospital expose the fragile basis of social norms. The title draws attention to Ada, whose "madness" was once apparent mainly in her intense love of poetry, but who has been transformed by a botched lobotomy into a pitiful figure begging for chocolate and struggling to remember nursery rhymes. There is an equally strong focus on the situation of another patient, Jenny, whose struggle with her own mental problems is complicated by her anger at the treatment of Ada and the other patients.

In Gibson's story, Jenny is the first-person narrator. Although there is no voice-over narration in the adaptation, her perspective remains central. She observes Ada and the other patients and cues flashbacks that allow us to see Ada before the operation. Jenny thus becomes a surrogate for the spectator, an indignant but impotent observer of conditions in the hospital, vulnerable to mental pressures that are only made worse by the way they are treated.

In both versions, the confinement of the action to the hospital creates a sense of entrapment. The adoption of this strategy in the television version gives it the intimacy that Thomas thought Jutra wanted, but it also results in a theatrical rather than cinematic structure, an effect enhanced by a cast "made up almost exclusively of actresses from the theatre."[11] *Ada* thus looks more like a television play than does *Dreamspeaker*, which was shot mainly on location in British Columbia. The sense of confinement in *Ada* is reinforced by the limits imposed by the usual fifty-minute format of the "For the Record" series, whereas *Dreamspeaker* was allowed to expand to seventy-five minutes, bringing it close to the normal length of a feature film.

In an interview with Louise Barrière in 1977, Jutra commented on his equal love for cinema and theatre, suggesting that "these two forms of expression are very closely related" while "television is situated half-way between the two."[12] This placement of television between theatre and film is highly relevant to *Ada*, despite its literary source. Jutra sets up a tension between the cinematic observation of reality, expected of the "For the Record" series, and the "theatrical" connotations of its confined setting and cast.

The casting of stage actors serves Jutra's purpose because of the emphasis on role-playing in the everyday life of the mental institution. Most of the patients act out their madness either by refusing to restrain their emotions (in which case theatricality, as "overacting," is identified with being unreasonable) or by obsessively taking on a specific role (like the character referred to only as "the Virgin"). In this context, the (male) doctors become the audience, but their scientific detachment is itself a role, assumed in the face of what one of the (female) nurses refers to as their "fear" of the women. The patients invent dreams for the doctors to analyze but are bitterly resentful of the presence of a woman whom they accuse of only pretending to be mad to gain attention. Since normality also depends on playing roles assigned by society, the ultimate fear would seem to be that there is no certain way to distinguish between the sane and the mad.

Knelman dismissed *Ada* as "R.D. Laing filtered through the feminine mystique," and the depiction of insanity in both the story and the film certainly owes a major debt to Laing's "anti-psychiatry."[13] In his practice and books, which deeply influenced the youth culture of the 1960s, Laing argued for a new approach to madness that would treat it as a defensive reaction to living in a mad society. He insisted, for example, that "there is no such condition as 'schizophrenia,' but the label is a social fact and the social fact a *political event*" through which a person is "inaugurated not only into a role, but into a career of patient."[14]

The influence of Laing is made explicit in both versions of *Ada* when a doctor invokes his name to settle an argument during a group therapy session. However, the doctor's appeal to Laing as a way of asserting his authority involves a denial of the full implications of a theory that insists that doctors have much to learn from their patients, and he is immediately attacked by a patient who insists that she knows Laing "backwards and forwards."[15] The group therapy session supposedly involves a free exchange of ideas, but it breaks down because the doctors will only listen when the patients adhere to the script in which they are supposed to be the objects of analysis. This script also has implications for gender roles since the doctors are all male and the patients female, while the female nurses try to mediate between them.

The doctor who cites Laing is the one whose operation resulted in the "accident" that transformed Ada from a hyperactive young woman, enthusiastically quoting poetry, into a childlike adult who ranges the ward begging for money to buy chocolates. In the adaptation, the flashbacks suggest that Ada was originally diagnosed as mad because of an unruly imagination encouraged by her passion for literature. The treatment she undergoes merely takes to an extreme (it was a "mistake") the way in which normality is defined in terms of a reduction of sensation and a refusal to think about the disturbing ideas and feelings aroused by the work of poets and artists. In one of the flashbacks, Ada declares that what is regarded as "genius" in people outside is treated as "madness" inside.

In the short story, Jenny describes Ada's case with the avowed aim of exposing the inadequacy of the institution. Although Jenny's narration disappears in the adaptation, her perspective functions rather like that of Benoît in *Mon oncle Antoine.* In other words, we are invited to share her point of view, but we are not confined, as we are in the story, to her consciousness. Jenny mediates between us and the world of the "insane," from which she is distinguished by her clear-sighted awareness of her situation but to which she belongs because of the intermittent fits brought on by the visitations of a "black bird." We do not see this bird, but we do hear its wings beating, a sound that apparently emanates from inside Jenny's head. The bird's status, somewhere between inner and outer reality, corresponds to our position in relation to Jenny and thus suggests the vulnerability of all to irrational fears.

This tension between identification and detachment also has implications for the question whether the women are suffering from a medical condition and can thus be treated by brain surgery, shock treatment, or drugs, or whether (as Laing would argue) they are victims of a patriarchal social order to which the doctors are trying to make them conform. The nurses are caught between these two possibilities as they carry out their professional duties in close contact with the patients. They are either assisting medical science or supporting an oppressive system, but it is difficult to distinguish between the two positions. At one point, a cut identifies a nurse with the "black bird" that Jenny fears, but later she chats with a sympathetic nurse who tries to maintain a balanced attitude to the patients and the doctors.

While there are male patients, who become excited by the presence of the women as they file past on their way to the dining-room, they remain peripheral in the film, as in the original story. Hence the question of the relationship between madness and gender is left open to some degree; but it is the male doctors who hold positions of power in the institution. Although the outside world appears only in the opening shot of cars in a parking lot, dimly seen through a pale blue window, the tensions and relations in the hospital reflect the hierarchies and structures of so-called normal society.

The only intruders from the outside world are Jenny's mother and brother, whose brief visit offers an image of society outside the institution as banal and unappealing. Their evident discomfort and inability to communicate with Jenny expose an underlying fear that leads to an insistence on a clear-cut definition of insanity in order to maintain the boundaries of normality. The mother's primness and prurience derive from her upbringing in a past cultural order that frowned on the open expression of feelings and desires, but her son's crude allusions to his sexual exploits suggest less the potential of a more liberated society than a "dirty" attitude to sexuality quite consistent with the moral codes he apparently rejects. The new morality does not represent progress over the past but simply a different configuration of the same desire to master nature, and the need to separate inside from outside remains constant.

By implication, it is poetry that offers the possibility of overcoming this separation. The passages quoted by Ada deal with sexuality and death, linking them in a way that is familiar from Jutra's earlier films. While her immersion in the world of poetry may be a compensation for Ada's inability to come to terms with the outside world, the film makes clear that the problem is cultural rather than simply personal. The instability of the women diagnosed as mad is, at some level, a rejection of the terms on which social stability depends.

Both art and madness are marginalized, so that Jenny's mother and brother can only see her paintings as a symptom of her insanity. *Ada* thus refuses to resolve the question whether madness involves role playing as a response to cultural pressures or whether it is a medical condition. Each of these explanation becomes dominant at various points, and the conclusion seems to be that they are not mutually exclusive. Each case may be different, and the women themselves may not be aware of the forces influencing their behaviour. This lack of awareness is not a sign of insanity, however, since the film also implies that normal behaviour is equally a product of social roles, cultural pressures, and deep-rooted obsessions.

The ending works to heighten rather than resolve the tensions surrounding the representation of madness. In the middle of the night, Jenny finds Ada strangling another patient who has earlier taunted her for her childish behaviour. After this act of violence, Ada repeats the lines of poetry that she quoted in the opening sequence and asks Jenny not to "tell on me." This sudden recovery of her memory and her literary sensibilities leaves it unclear whether her mental powers have just returned or whether she, too, has been playing a role. If the former is the case, the capacity to appreciate poetry cannot be separated from the act of violence that occasions the "miracle"; if the latter, Ada has defeated the medical establishment by exaggerating the state of childlike obedience to which it tried to reduce her. In any case, the effect of Ada's "recovery" must be set against the final image in which Jenny lies down on her bed and hears the wings flapping again.

The Golden Age: Dreamspeaker

When the French version of *Dreamspeaker* was shown on television in Quebec, Louise Cousineau described it as a film about "the universe of childhood" and "the incapacity of the system to tolerate marginality."[16] Her description presents the television film as a continuation of Jutra's earlier work, and in general critics have treated it as a worthy successor to *Mon oncle Antoine.* Marginality appears in this film, however, not only in the isolation of the disturbed child but also in the native spirituality that he discovers when he runs away to the forests of Vancouver Island and meets an old Indian shaman (or "dreamspeaker"). This aspect of the film clearly derives from Anne Cameron, who has since become well known as the author of a series of books that retell Indian legends in terms that appeal to the so-called New Age sensibility.

As I have already noted, Knelman felt that Jutra simply tried to convey Cameron's vision and that *Dreamspeaker,* as a result, is merely "sentimental" and nostalgic. A few critics have shared his view, and it is certainly plausible in the light of Tony Reif's description of Cameron's *Dreamspeaker* script as "a fable about the golden age, the lost time before the world became an object and people merely manipulators and manipulated."[17] On this account, the film simply recycles the myth of the noble savage and advocates a retreat from the complexities of modern urban society.

While the film certainly does depend on a basic opposition between modern science and traditional spirituality, its emotional power belies the claim that Jutra had no personal commitment to the project. As Cousineau noted, the themes of childhood and marginality are familiar from his earlier work, and there are several important differences between the film and the short novel published after its first broadcast. Whether Cameron subsequently revised her screenplay or whether Jutra freely departed from it, the differences between the strategies and meanings of the two works are even more substantial than those between *Ada* and the short story on which it was based.

The utopian image derived from the past is a common feature of Jutra's films, most visibly in the dreams in *Wow* but also in the treatment of history in *Mon oncle Antoine* and *Kamouraska* and in the role of memory in *À tout prendre, Pour le meilleur et pour le pire,* and *Ada.* Such images expose the dystopian qualities of the present, but they are always accompanied by an awareness that the past was not really a golden age, that the roots of present problems lie in the past, and that the confusion of the imaginary and the real can block attempts to construct a better future. In the case of *Dreamspeaker*, present and past, real and imaginary, are yoked violently together in an unusual ending on which interpretations of the film seem to hinge. In order to assess the effects of this ending, we need to examine how the film sets up its tensions and to note the implications of its departures from Cameron's version.

Jutra plunges us into the story without the benefit of an establishing shot: the first image is a close-up tracking shot following the feet of a young boy. At the end of the shot, the camera pans up as the boy opens a door, but it still does not reveal his face. The next shot shows him in a classroom where he pulls books and papers from the desks and sets them on fire, while the framing still prevents us from seeing his face. A shot of flames shooting up in an unidentified space leads into a series of four shots that alternate between a burning building and close-ups of the boy's face as he quietly watches. The last close-up ends with a cut to a long shot of heavy traffic moving slowly on a highway.

The novel begins with what amounts to an establishing shot of the highway, with the traffic described as "a long segmented snake" or "serpent." This metaphor anticipates the "snake-thing" that frightens Peter and that the old man identifies as Sisiutl, a "double-headed sea-serpent."[18] Through its opening sentences, the novel thus establishes a narrative perspective that is attuned to the spiritual meanings beneath physical appearances. The traffic becomes a mechanical embodiment of a spirit that usually takes the form of a monstrous animal. Peter's attacks are the result of his fear of the monster, which haunts him because he has not adjusted to the unnatural life of modern society. In this way, the novel validates in advance the old man's attempt to convince Peter that his visions are real and not the product of his imagination.

In the film's second sequence, the traffic moves along a curved stretch of highway and, seen from a high angle, offers a precise visual equivalent to Cameron's verbal description. Yet there is nothing to compel the spectator to think of a snake. Metaphor in film is highly dependent on context, and the only context here is the abrupt shift from the darkness and confinement of the opening sequence to an exterior long shot in daylight. The image of traffic does suggest a link between the boy's behaviour and modern urban life, and some spectators might remember its snakelike appearance when the old man describes the snake to Peter; but there is no need to read the visual similarity as a sign of underlying spiritual significance. Nor is there any reason, before Peter meets the old man to attribute his seizures, which closely resemble Jenny's attacks in *Ada*, to the supernatural power of a sea-serpent.

The two openings also differ in the way that they introduce us to Peter. In the novel he is first described sitting in a car between a man and a woman identified only as "the people." After a brief shift into first-person narration as he contemplates escaping from the car, the third-person narrator reports what Peter is thinking: "He knew his face betrayed nothing." Immediately, however, we are given the woman's view of the boy as "the child all white middle-class parents hope will be theirs." Although we are soon told that little is known about Peter, the narration reveals that his mother was a drug addict who came from a fundamentalist family and was abandoned by Peter's father, and that Peter had been in nine foster homes by the time he was six.[19]

As in the adaptation of *Kamouraska*, the film suppresses most of this background information, but, whereas the earlier film filters images from the past through Elisabeth's imagination, in *Dreamspeaker* we are allowed only brief access to Peter's consciousness at moments of great psychological pressure. The framing that conceals the boy's face in the opening shots draws attention to our lack of information, and the film also denies us any account of his past that might explain his behaviour. In the novel, the fire is not even mentioned until the old man tells Peter that he heard about it on the radio, but the film uses it as a striking opening image that associates the boy's troubles with elemental forces and suggests that they can never be fully explained.[20] Whereas the novel begins with social and psychological information that is then displaced by an awareness of spiritual forces, the film maintains a high degree of ambiguity, refusing to settle for either the rational or spiritual explanations.

The long shot of the highway shows a car driving on to an exit ramp, and the next shot shows Peter sitting between a man and a woman in what we assume is the same car. His relationship to these two adults is not immediately apparent, and we might assume that they are his parents. The man is driving, but when they arrive at what appears to be a detention centre, the woman takes charge, and her brisk handling of the situation reveals that she is a social worker. In the novel, the narration adopts Peter's perspective when it refers to his companions as "the people," but it quickly reveals that the woman is a social worker called Anna, assigned to Peter's case just after leaving university.[21] It is through her memories that we learn about his past.

The film does not give the woman a name and reveals nothing about her past or her thoughts. Instead it invites us to make inferences about the situation based on the behaviour of the three characters. Peter is presumably there as a result of the act of arson, but this is never mentioned and he remains sullen and silent while he is being admitted. The man sits rigidly in the background in the waiting-room, his silence and withdrawn manner making him appear like an older replica of the boy. Is he just a male attendant, required by the system and ill at ease in his surroundings, or does he have a relationship with Peter (father? foster father?), and, if so, is he trying to hold back anger or grief?

When he gets up to leave, he finds that he has chewing gum stuck to his pants, much to the woman's amusement. This incident refers back to an earlier moment in the car when she unwrapped some chewing gum and silently passed it to Peter. His acceptance signals the only successful contact with him before he meets the old man during his escape, while the man's discomfort only underlines his lack of control over the situation. The contrast between the woman's warmth and efficiency and the silence and apathy of the two sullen males introduces questions of gender into the social and psychological problems posed by Peter's case. The receptionist at the institute is also female, but the only other women to appear in the film are Peter's "dream mother" (so identified in the final credits) and Queen Elizabeth II. These two women appear only briefly, but they represent the pressures of sexuality and power that provoke Peter's apparently irrational behaviour.

His dream of the "mother" occurs shortly after he has been admitted to the institution, whose exact status is never explained but which seems to be a cross between school, hospital, and prison. When Peter stands in front of a window in the dormitory, his hand moves over the bars on the window and the focus changes to show a fence topped with barbed wire outside. He does not respond when a man introduces himself as his counsellor, and he silently submits to a medical examination, a procedure he has clearly been through many times before. Two sequences then bring out a "schizophrenic" division in his personality between an obsessive desire for order and outbursts of violence: in the dining hall, an older boy taunts him for his care in laying out his cutlery, and Peter pushes his soup bowl into the boy's face and violently attacks him; when the other boys rapidly change in a locker room, he carefully folds his clothes before compulsively swimming up and down the pool.

The dream occurs after the counsellor has pulled him from the pool, and there is a cut to Peter lying on his bed. It begins with a fat woman, humming and smiling suggestively at him, reminiscent of similar figures, combining maternal and sexual attractions, in several films by Federico Fellini. She hikes up her skirt and laughs as she sits on a counter, whereupon a man grabs her and pushes her down, exposing her naked thighs. Their embrace dissolves into flames, like those seen in the opening sequence, from which emerges a close-up of Peter's horrified face. The sequence ends as he falls back on his bed in tears, and there is a cut to a shot of a wet sheet.

His counsellor insists that this is a normal occurrence that "happens to a lot of the guys." Yet, like Benoît's distorted view of his uncle eating in *Mon oncle Antoine*, the grotesque dream mother links Peter's fears to the excesses of the unruly body. This dream does not speak, in the sense that it does not really explain why Peter set the fire, but it does create an image cluster in which flames become inseparable from bodily functions. Presumably the dream derives from his memories of one of the many foster homes in which, according to the novel, he has spent his childhood; but the film does not define his relationship to the couple or suggest the extent to which the dream may be a distortion of reality. He later tells the old man that he lived with "some people" who taught him good table manners by threatening to take his food away. While the institution is more liberal and progressive in its approach to discipline, Peter is clearly a product of a society based on a rigid division between a daylight world of order and discipline and a nightmare world of repressed fears and anxieties.

If the dream mother is an imaginary figure (since we see her only through Peter's dream) who embodies the desires that threaten the stability of the social order, Queen Elizabeth is a symbolic figure who authorizes the exercise of power within that order. In this respect she functions in *Dreamspeaker* much as Queen Victoria does in *Kamouraska*, and, as in the earlier film, she is the head of state in whose name the legal system operates. After the police forcibly remove Peter from his cabin, the old man breaks down in tears, and there is an abrupt cut to a portrait of the queen. As the camera pulls back, a male voice speaks of the need for "mercy and compassion" in a "civilized society" and admits that this society has been "unable to find an answer to Peter's problems." In a single take the camera pans past the judge, whose voice we are hearing, across the courtroom and into a close-up of Peter who lets out a long scream when he realizes that he will be sent back to the institution.

In *Kamouraska* Queen Victoria has a clear ideological function: the charge against Elisabeth is read out in English, stressing that the court's authority comes from outside Quebec, while the patriarchal legal system derives its authority from a woman. Although the language issue does not come into play in *Dreamspeaker*, Jutra draws attention to the ideological significance of the Queen by using the portrait instead of a conventional establishing shot. She is an absent authority figure whose gender masks the patriarchal values that the law upholds. The judge tries to redress the admitted inadequacy of the system by granting the old man and his companion parental visiting rights, but he cannot envisage a solution that would allow Peter to grow up outside the system. By using a single take, Jutra binds together the queen's face, the judge's words, and Peter's scream into a condensed expression of the logic on which the culture depends.

The judge exercises power through language, using words to deny any personal stake in his verdict (he speaks for the queen in the name of "civilization") and to create the impression that he is simply confirming the "solution" that Peter has found for himself. In the courtroom, as we see it, everyone else is silent, and Peter's scream becomes an anguished protest against the symbolic order that authorizes the judge's speech. Peter has earlier tried to escape from this order by refusing to speak, frustrating the adults at the institution but also denying the spectator verbal explanations for the character's thoughts and behaviour.

As in Ingmar Bergman's *Persona* (1966), observers both inside and outside the film cannot be certain whether the silent character refuses or is unable to speak. In Peter's case, there is also the problem of the causes and meaning of the recurring "fits" (as the doctor calls them) in which he seems to be trying to strangle himself. The first of these occurs after some boys have accused Peter of breaking a window and he has maintained his usual silence when asked if he did it. Although the counsellor does not take silence as an admission of guilt and instead punishes the other boys, Peter suffers an attack when he is left alone, and his hands on his throat seem to be a self-inflicted punishment for his inability to communicate. The doctor can find no medical explanation, but the counsellor insists that it would be impossible to fake such an attack. Peter overhears them discussing his case, and, while they are absorbed in conversation, he silently leaves the room and escapes.

When he first meets the old Indian, Peter tries to get away but runs straight into the arms of a younger man. They reassure him and take him back to their cabin. Peter finally acknowledges that he can speak after the old man explains that his companion cannot because he has "something missing in his throat." Although muteness is in this case a medical condition, the old man suggests that it is also a logical response to a world in which "people won't listen anyway." The old man himself speaks a lot, but he tells Peter that this is because he has to speak for two, and he is proud of his ability to argue aloud "for both sides at the same time." His speech, like that of the judge, is sanctioned by tradition, but it is open to other voices and does not depend on legal authority.

When the mute makes signs to indicate that Peter is "half-crazy," the old man responds that they are all a bit crazy. He refuses to take himself seriously, but he also insists on the sacred meanings of the dance that he had to learn in order to become a dreamspeaker. His attitude to language and education undoes the effects of a system that has convinced Peter that he cannot learn because he has a "learning disability." According to the old man, learning was easier in the "old days" because it did not involve listening to the words of a teacher but allowed children to do the things that interested them, an account of traditional ways in native communities that makes them sound like the progressive methods documented in *Comment savoir*.

The old man urges Peter to try his hand at carving and makes him a belt that illustrates the structure of the universe in which symbolic creatures represent the four elements. His spiritual wisdom helps Peter by giving him confidence in himself and by providing a sense of order grounded in nature rather than in discipline and repression. Yet Peter does not passively accept his teachings. When the old man demonstrates his dancing, the boy quickly loses interest and starts to wash the dishes. After the old man has explained the meanings of the symbols on the belt, Peter shows that he has learnt the names, but then he suddenly attacks the traditional beliefs as "just words" and repeatedly yells "bullshit" before running away from the cabin.

Peter does return, and the old man silently touches his hand just before the police arrive. The violence of the system confirms Peter's distrust of language, which he expresses through the inarticulate scream with which he interrupts the judge's liberal platitudes and then through his repeated response to a psychologist that all the blots he is shown look like "shit." The reduction of language to a scream and obscenity is his response to a culture that uses words to define and control the natural world rather than to refer to it, but the final effect is quite different in Cameron's and Jutra's versions.

In the novel, when Peter asks the old man's name, he replies that he has "a whole raft of names" but does not say what they are. The other man, who may or may not be an Indian, has been adopted by the old man who explains that some people call him "Loony" but that his "spirit name" is "He Who Would Sing." Before Peter's court appearance, he insists that he wants to go home with "my grandpa and my uncle," but nobody pays attention. During the legal hearing, they are referred to as Mr Seward and Mr Thomas, which Peter realizes are their "real" names.[22] These names, given by a culture to which the men do not belong, underline the way the culture uses language to label things and people regardless of their own traditions and identities.

The presentation of these characters in the film obviously depends on the physical appearance of the actors. In the novel, the old man is described as being "so incredibly old you couldn't even begin to guess when he'd been young," suggesting that we see him through Peter's eyes but also that he may be older than possible for a normal human being. The actor in the film may be old, but there is no attempt to suggest that he is exceptionally old. Similarly, the film has no equivalent to the old man's attempt in the novel to remember how many children have "come to him in his lifetime."[23] There is no discussion of his name, and the only reference to the mute's name is the old man's comment that "some people call him Loony." The compression of the legal proceedings at the end means that there is no chance for Peter to identify the men as his family or for them to be addressed by their so-called real names.

Apart from Peter and two workers at the institution, none of the characters in Jutra's *Dreamspeaker* is named. The film thus adopts a perspective close to Peter's, outside the adult world in which names are so important. But names are significant for the old man's teachings. When Peter has another attack, the old man asks for the name of what he sees. To name it is to give it an existence outside the mind. He insists that children are especially vulnerable to "spirits" and that, because adults cannot see them, they blame the children.

The problem is not the spirits themselves but the fear that they inspire. Fear, according to the old man, attracts ghosts and "ugly things," a claim that seems to explain Peter's "dream mother" and his bed wetting. Since "educated city people" do not believe in spirits, they live in a culture of guilt and fear.

These city people have also lost contact with nature. The two men introduce Peter to their way of life, which consists of loafing around, visiting beautiful areas in their surroundings, and making sculptures out of wood. Their life is not entirely natural, however: the old man ridicules Peter's attempt to eat raw oysters, and they spend their evenings playing cards and listening to the radio. While the escape from the city relieves the pressures on Peter, the experience of nature does not address his fears of sexuality. Sex is virtually absent from the lives of the two men, although the mute does mime a dirty joke when the old man pauses in his dancing and says that he used to be able to "go at it all night." When the old man gets sick, the other two care for him, and the old man rejects Peter's claim that "men can't be mothers." The group seems self-sufficient, and a utopian image of the boy and the mute swimming together in a lake, with the old man laughing on the bank, displaces the bad dream of the "mother" and her erotic laughter.

This return to nature does carry connotations of the "golden age," and it is destroyed by the intervention of the legal system serving the modern urban society. When he returns to the institution, Peter expresses his frustration by transgressing the limits that society imposes on natural functions. He deliberately urinates on his bed, pours his food onto the table, and smears excrement on the washroom walls. His defiance of the rules leads to a general uprising, suggesting that the tensions shown in the film are not limited to one particular case.

The riot leads into the film's controversial final sequence in which the three main characters all die. The old man dies in bed after telling the mute that they did not know how lonely they were until Peter came. There is a cut from the old man lying on his bed to a shot of Peter lying in roughly the same position. He seems to hear the old man saying that there is nothing to fear from death, which "doesn't mean it's finished, only means it's complete." After a shot of the mute preparing the old man's funeral in a tree, fulfilling his request for a traditional burial, the counsellor finds that Peter has hung himself. The mute then places a shotgun in his mouth and pulls the trigger.

As the shot rings out, there is a cut to the place where he and Peter played in the stream. We are allowed to register their absence, but another cut reveals the old man laughing on the bank, and then the final shot shows his two companions in the water, while his voice is heard reiterating that "death makes us complete."

Like Knelman, Mary Jane Miller found this ending "sentimental."[24] Yet it is certainly more disturbing than the ending of the novel, in which the deaths occur in much the same way but the final image is of the old man and the boy listening to He Who Would Sing "singing for the matriarch and her women, singing for the ears of creation, for the men who would one day be Dreamspeakers and the men who had been Dreamspeakers, singing for the women who had been Dreamspeakers and the women who would be Dreamspeakers, singing to the ear of creation, singing with the voice he had always known was his."[25] Instead of this final moment of transcendence, Jutra's ending sets up an extreme contrast between the dark and morbid outcome of the narrative and the utopian "golden age" image of what has been destroyed.

The deaths go beyond what is normally expected of a television film, but they are the logical outcome of the social processes that it has depicted. Ironically, it is the boy's presence that disrupts the peaceful but marginal existence of the two men, while the old man's teachings inspire Peter to end a life that is palpably not "complete." The return to the idyllic moment by the stream seems almost like wish fulfilment on the part of a spectator unable to bear the brutality of the real ending, but its status hovers uncertainly between flashback, after-death experience (as in the novel), and utopian image of a possible but unreal alternative way of life.

While native spirituality functions in *Dreamspeaker*, much like poetry and madness in *Ada*, as an expression of what has been lost in the development of modern industrial and technological society, the ending of the film does not simply affirm, as does the novel, the superiority of native values and traditions. The conflict is not between two specific cultures but, as Peter Morris puts it, between "the alienating world of reason and order and a world where love is the norm in human relationships."[26] The violent clash between the real and the utopian endings leaves us to confront not only the implications of the gulf between the two but also the complexity of the issues that must be addressed if the gap is to be narrowed.

Above: Kate (Kathleen Beller) emerges from the lake in *Surfacing* (Beryl Fox)

Below: Helen (Patty Duke Austin) and Angie (Sara Botsford) in *By Design* (Beryl Fox)

MISSING FATHERS
Surfacing and *By Design*

After making a successful transition from film to television, and from French-to English-language production, Jutra was rather less fortunate with his subsequent projects for the CBC. *Seer Was Here* (1978), another contribution to the "For the Record" series, was a dark comedy about life in a men's prison whose main characters are once again alienated from mainstream society, but this time the focus is on a group of adult males. Although it was apparently the most popular of Jutra's three contributions to the series, it received some intense critical abuse in the press even before it was broadcast and has since languished in the CBC archives.[1]

The Wordsmith (1979) was better received by the critics, but this comic story, about a writer who lodges with a Jewish family in Montreal during the 1950s, owes less to Jutra than to Mordecai Richler, who wrote the screenplay based on his own short stories. Jutra does seem to have effaced himself here behind his literary source, although the writer's story is told from the point of view of the adolescent son. The narrator reflects on his earlier fascination with the writer who embodied the promise of a world beyond the constraints of family and community life, but the main focus is on Richler's satiric depiction of the Jewish community.

Jutra did later make one other English-language television film, *My Father, My Rival* (1985), which was completed shortly before his death and shown on the Global Television Network. As the title suggests, Jutra's involvement in this fairly routine project probably came about because of its depiction of an adolescent whose widowed father becomes his rival for the attentions of his teacher. By the time he made this television film, Jutra's return to French-language film production in Quebec had resulted in a less than triumphant homecoming. During his period of exile, however, Jutra directed two English-language films that added little to his reputation but reveal much about the processes of Canadian film production at the time.

Just before the release of *Surfacing*, Ray Conlogue speculated that Jutra had agreed to direct the adaptation of Margaret Atwood's novel "in the absence of other film work, and perhaps out of a hankering to get out of theatre and TV and back to where his heart lay."[2] As these comments suggest, it was not Jutra's own project. He became involved at the last minute when the original director, Eric Till, left the production. Jutra's contribution to the pre-production process was thus very limited, and the fascinating prospect of a collaboration between Jutra and Atwood resulted in a film that betrayed the visions of both filmmaker and novelist.

This outcome was especially unfortunate because there are strong affinities between the narrative voice in Atwood's novel and the unstable I/eye in Jutra's films, as even a brief plot summary reveals. An unnamed woman returns to her childhood home in the northern wilderness of Quebec or Ontario in search of her father, who has been reported missing, and goes through a period of "madness" before she emerges with a stronger sense of her own personal identity. Through her experience in the wilderness, the woman comes to recognize that she lives in a mad society.

The therapeutic experience in the wilderness evokes the ideas of R.D. Laing with which Jutra would have been familiar from his recent work on *Ada*, but the combination of madness and the filtering of events through a woman's consciousness in Atwood's novel also suggests a close kinship with Anne Hébert's *Kamouraska*. As novels by women who are also poets, they lack the linear, cause-and-effect structure of the traditional novel and substitute the intensely subjective vision of a female narrator. According to John Hofsess, Geneviève Bujold kept a copy of *Surfacing* in her room during the filming of *Kamouraska*.[3]

Jutra's experience in adapting *Kamouraska* to the screen, his ability to see through the eyes of a woman as demonstrated in *Kamouraska* and *Ada*, and his interests in dream and inner speech ought to have made him an ideal choice to direct *Surfacing*. But the film makes little attempt to find cinematic equivalents for the admittedly difficult subjective and poetic dimensions of the novel.

As in the case of *Kamouraska*, *Surfacing* was a critical and commercial failure, but the two films were made and released under very different conditions. Jutra worked closely with Hébert to produce a screenplay that captured the intensity of the novel's subjective narration. The failure of *Kamouraska* could be attributed to the cuts demanded by the producers and to the adverse publicity generated by its production circumstances. On the other hand, Atwood did not contribute to the adaptation of *Surfacing*, and Jutra was able to make only last-minute changes to the screenplay (by Bernard Gordon), which was in place before he joined the production. The result was a film that distorted and diluted Atwood's vision and probably would not have succeeded even if it had received adequate distribution.

Surfacing fell victim to the pressures of a film industry whose reluctance to take risks prohibited an imaginative approach to adapting the novel. Unfortunately, the producers failed to recognize that the novel explores issues of subjectivity and perception in a style that is highly cinematic, although not in the manner of classical narrative cinema. It should be noted, however, that the only other film adaptation of an Atwood novel to date, an international version of *The Handmaid's Tale* (1990), directed by Volker Schlöndorff from a screenplay by Harold Pinter, did little better on a much-larger budget.

Apart from the weak screenplay, the most obvious sign of trouble in *Surfacing* was the casting. In keeping with the practice of the Canadian film industry during the Capital Cost Allowance period, the two main roles went to American actors. Joseph Bottoms, a young Hollywood actor, appeared as Joe, the heroine's boyfriend. He is adequate in this role, but the fact that he received top billing does not inspire confidence in a film based on a novel whose central character is a woman. Kathleen Beller, a young and virtually unknown American actress, was cast as the protagonist, but her wholesome and athletic persona was quite remote from Atwood's deeply disturbed and rather older character.

Canadians did appear in the other major roles, with ironic effects that I will discuss later, but Bottoms and Beller were clearly chosen for misguided commercial reasons despite the inevitable distortion of the novel's exploration of personal, cultural, and national identity. These choices reveal the degree to which the English-Canadian film industry had been "colonized" by Hollywood, or at least by Canadian producers' confused sense of what made Hollywood films popular. Ironically, Atwood had turned down a better offer from a US producer to provide an opportunity for a Canadian woman, Beryl Fox, well known for her work as a documentary filmmaker but now producing her first feature film with a considerable investment of her own money.[4]

Although Fox wanted to direct the film herself, she was unable to find backers willing to invest in a film directed by a woman with no feature-film experience.[5] Apparently, there was no thought of hiring a more experienced female director like Mireille Dansereau, whose *La Vie revée* appeared in the same year as Atwood's novel and dealt with similar issues of female subjectivity and the colonization of inner life. Unfortunately, these issues had largely disappeared from the screenplay that Jutra inherited.

As Conlogue noted, the screenplay was a product of the idea that "the whole story ... had to be liberated from the viewpoint of the central female character" in order to become cinematic. Although Jutra expressed agreement with this assumption, he may have been trying to be tactful, since he added that he had managed "to see an entire story through the eyes of one character" in *Kamouraska*.[6] Fox hoped that *Surfacing* would "justly represent Atwood's vision" despite the changes that had been made "due to the commercial considerations of filmmaking," but the changes did not, in fact, enhance the film's commercial prospects.[7] What they did was to diminish the range and power of the novel's vision: as Martin Knelman put it, they "transformed Atwood's unfilmable quest allegory into a simple-minded feminist equivalent of a woodsy *Boy's Own* adventure story."[8]

My discussion of the film's relationship to the novel explores the implications of the assumption that the novel was unfilmable and had to be made more cinematic. Whereas Jutra's other films unsettle such categories, *Surfacing* tries to abide by them; but its failure exposes key issues involving both adaptation and Canadian cultural identity.

Making the Unfilmable Cinematic

Since 1972, when Margaret Atwood's second novel was published to much acclaim, critics have tended to attribute its success either to its universal mythic themes, associated with the influence of Northrop Frye, or to its more specific Canadian and feminist concerns. It is the interaction of these two dimensions that gives the novel its power, creating an experience that resembles the treatment of myth, gender, and identity in two Canadian films that appeared in the same year. Paul Almond's *Journey* also features an unnamed heroine who moves from city to wilderness, from present to past, and through whose consciousness the narration is filtered. Gilles Carle's *La Mort d'un bûcheron* (*The Death of a Lumberjack*) deals with a woman whose search for her missing father leads to a confrontation with her own personal and cultural identity.

The women in the novel and in the films are all victims of what Frye has called Canada's "obliterated environment," moving uncomfortably between nondescript urban environments and a sparsely inhabited wilderness.[9] Frye's influence on the novel comes through quite unmistakably when the narrator declares that her father "split us between two anonymities, the city and the bush."[10] Although the novel presents this division as a specifically Canadian experience, it associates the anonymity of the city with people whom the narrator designates as "Americans." They seek to control nature, and when they appear in the bush, they take the form of tourists and hunters.

The narrator uses a cinematic metaphor to convey her fear of these people: "They spread themselves like a virus, they get into the brain and take over the cells and the cells change from inside and the ones that have the disease can't tell the difference. Like the late show sci-fi movies, creatures from outer space, body snatchers injecting themselves into you dispossessing your brain, their eyes blank eggshells behind the dark glasses. If you look like them and talk like them and think like them then you are them, I was saying, you speak their language, a language is everything you do."[11]

This outburst is provoked by the discovery of a dead heron, which has been wantonly killed by hunters who, as she has just discovered, are really Canadians. She insists that they are "still Americans," but it is she who is really the alien because she cannot become an American and cannot find a basis for identity in her own environment and traditions.

The reader shares her sense of dislocation because, as gradually becomes apparent, she is an unreliable narrator. As we learn that we cannot always trust what she writes, we also come up against the problem of language. Words divide reality into segments to enable us to communicate, but, in the language of the "Americans," they become a way of dominating reality. In resisting this use of language, the narrator loses control both of her syntax and of her memories. As we plunge into her confused perceptions and slowly move to the surface, we realize that these problems are the result of a mistaken conception of the self and its relationship to the environment.

In an introduction to a reading of her poetry in 1973, Atwood made a distinction "between self and ego," arguing that "to define self as ego is to posit absolute separation between a conscious subject and its object," and that "such a view leads to the projection of a static hierarchic system of dichotomies upon all non-ego." Instead, Atwood preferred "to define the self phenomenologically ... – as a place in which things happen, where experiences intersect."[12] Such a view of the self helps to explain the difference between novels like *Surfacing* and *Kamouraska* and conventional linear novels. These are not texts where one thing leads to another but where experiences intersect.

Atwood's phenomenological view of the self suggests that a fully cinematic version of *Surfacing* might look something like Jack Chambers's *Hart of London* (1970), which uses a kaleidoscopic array of overexposed and superimposed images to suggest a consciousness responding to newsreel images showing the hunting and killing of a deer trapped in the streets of London, Ontario. The destruction of the hart in the city parallels the killing of the heron in the bush in *Surfacing*, and both works contain images that associate looking through binoculars with the killing of animals. Because Chambers was a visual artist whose experimental films occupied a marginal position in the Canadian film industry, there was no chance that the adaptation of a best-selling novel would follow the example of a work that departed so far from the familiar norms of classical narrative cinema.

The credits sequence immediately reveals that *Surfacing* will work within these norms at the expense of the novel's more subjective approach. Whereas the novel opens with the narrator and her three companions on the road north, the first image in the film shows cliffs rising behind a lake and a woman diving from a small boat. The film's title and the first credits appear over shots of her swimming under water. A dissolve then takes us from a plant rippling under the water to a high-angle long shot of a city. The camera gradually picks out a young woman on a bicycle and looks vertically down on her as she pulls up at a traffic light. On the soundtrack, the sweet voice of Ann Mortifee sings about a woman who "should have been gypsy born," and, after a cut to a close-up of the brooding face of the bicycle rider, the song assures us that "she'll find her way."

The shots of the swimmer in the lake amount to a flash forward, and the dissolve sets up the contrast between country and city. But in both environments the woman is the object of the camera's gaze, and the narrative will clearly not be filtered through her consciousness. Instead of the first-person narration of the novel, we have the song whose third-person description of a woman is inevitably associated with the woman on the screen. The lyrics foreshadow the outcome of the narrative and the reduction of the complex process of self-discovery depicted in the novel to the glib feminist moral offered by Beryl Fox: "a woman is not free to love until she's free."[13]

The first sequence after the credits quickly establishes that this woman is not free. It opens with a close-up of a reel-to-reel tape deck that is switched on by a man's hand and plays electronic jazz music, quite unlike the pseudo-folksong we have just heard. We then see two men listening to what is evidently their music, while a woman lies down smoking and another dances, much to the annoyance of one of the men who insists that it is not dance music. A technological masculine ambiance contrasts with the female "naturalness" associated with the folksong and the bicycle rider in the credits sequence. When this woman arrives at the apartment, her presence breaks up the gathering, and we discover that one of the men, Joe, is her partner. She shows them a telegram with news of her father's disappearance, and it is Joe who decides that they should go north to look for him.

In the novel, one of the effects of the first-person narration is that we never learn the narrator's name. Her period alone in the bush begins when she refuses to answer to her name and ends when Joe returns and calls her name, but that name is never revealed.[14] Although it is obviously more difficult to withhold the name of the central character in a film, there are examples even within the classical narrative tradition. Both *Rebecca* (Alfred Hitchcock, 1940) and *Letter from an Unknown Woman* (Max Ophuls, 1948) are narrated by women whose names we never learn, and both draw on the "gothic" romance tradition that also lurks behind Atwood's novel. The effect of leaving the woman apparently nameless differs in each case, but it does suggest an uneasy relationship with the symbolic or patriarchal order within which naming is a way of controlling nature. In any case, this disturbance does not come into play in the film version of *Surfacing*, since the woman is addressed as Kate as soon as she enters the apartment.

Whether its characters have names or not, a novel can represent them only through the medium of words, even when a distrust of language is part of the meaning of the work. Films represent their characters more immediately through the bodies of the actors. In Atwood's *Surfacing*, the narrator slashes her clothes and lives naked in the woods during the time of her madness. The exposure of her body becomes an outer sign of an attempt to free her consciousness from the patriarchal culture that has shaped her life. This process leads to the discovery of her father's body in the lake, and the novel ends when she clothes herself and expresses her recognition that "for us it's necessary, the intercession of words."[15]

In the film, the meanings associated with the body change drastically as they become part of the spectator's own voyeuristic relations to the screen. Shortly after they arrive at the cabin, Joe and Kate take a walk in the surrounding forest. He starts to unbutton her blouse and sets up what Florence Jacobowitz called "an interesting tension between the uncovering of a female body for the pleasure of the audience – the kind of thing the cinema has long habituated us with – and Kate's impulse to cover up."[16] The tension dissipates as Kate reveals that she is still disturbed by the pressure he placed on her to have an abortion, but it soon reappears in a bedroom sequence that ends with the expected glimpses of naked bodies.

Kate's later decision to remain alone in order to continue the search for her father is much more conscious and rational than in the novel and occurs only after Joe has been injured in a climbing accident. When she dives into the lake to search for the petroglyphs that her father had discovered, she wears a modest black bathing-suit, and she only strips naked at the end, when she bathes in the lake in a form of ritual cleansing, revealing what Jacobowitz called her "very sexual Playboy-centrefold body."[17] She has exorcised the spirit of her father, and the film ends as she is reunited with Joe, apparently freed from the anxieties that disturbed their earlier relationship.

The shot of Kate bathing does suggest an attempt to create unease around "the uncovering of a female body." Taken from the shore, with the body framed by trees, it seems to adopt the point of view of an unknown lurking presence. Since Kate has earlier found her father's body in an underwater cave, he cannot be the source of this look, but the camera was in a similar position on shore when the boat carrying the visitors first arrived at the dock in front of the father's cabin. The possibility that he is watching them disturbs Kate when she and Joe prepare to make love in the bedroom, and there are a few suggestions that her intense relationship with her father may have been incestuous. However, the film does not really develop the disturbing implication that its viewpoint may be that of the absent patriarchal figure.

The disturbances in the field of sexuality are instead displaced on to the other couple, Anna and David, who travel to the wilderness with Kate and Joe. They are described as "sex fiends," and their relationship alternates between physical obsession and verbal abuse (not unlike the couple in *Pour le meilleur et pour le pire*). Jacobowitz described Anna as "the extreme of the victimized woman," while David is cynical and domineering.[18] Like Jenny's brother in *Ada*, David exhibits a "dirty," schoolboy attitude to sexuality, associated with modern urban life and with the aggressive behaviour of the hunters who come north just to kill animals.

All of these elements come together in a sequence in which David tries to rape Kate, after insinuating that Joe and Anna are making love elsewhere in the forest (a possibility that the film does not explore). He loses interest when Kate reluctantly starts to undress herself, but the drunken hunters interrupt their confrontation. After killing a moose, one of the hunters turns his gun on David, who urinates in his pants from fear but then manages to grab the gun and hold it to the hunter's head, ordering him to urinate. This ugly scene exposes the equation of sexuality with power, also found in David's relationship with Anna, but hunting is itself an assertion of power over nature.

The natural body in its relations to death and sexuality is also central to the film's treatment of the dead heron. In the novel, David and Joe film the heron, which the hunters have killed and hung from a tree, while the two women wait.[19] In the film, David forces Anna to strip for his camera and dance around the heron while Kate and Joe wait.[20] While Anna dances, Kate and Joe sit beside the lake and, when Kate expresses her disgust at what is happening behind them, Joe tells her that she does not have to look. She refuses to "pretend it isn't happening" and takes action by opening David's film cans and unrolling the spools into the lake. The spectators, however, unless they close their eyes, have not only to watch the dance but also to see much of it through David's camera. The film thus seems to become complicit with his humiliation of Anna, while Kate's protests enable it to disavow this complicity.

Earlier in the film, when the couples first meet the hunters at a gas station, David tells them that he shoots animals with his camera which, to their discomfort, he then turns on them. Although he is mocking the hunters for their desire to kill, he again uses his camera as a weapon when it becomes an extension of his verbal abuse of Anna. This equation of camera and gun is a trace of the novel's much more extensive critique of the camera as a technological and masculine way of relating to the world. At the opposite extreme to the Hollywood genre films from which the narrator takes the metaphor of the "body snatchers," David and Joe are making an experimental film called *Random Samples*, in which they try to "capture" all the unusual sights that they encounter. The deadly camera may also have caused the death of the narrator's father, a scientist attempting to photograph petroglyphs that have been submerged because engineers have raised the level of the lake.

The death of the father thus represents the contradictions inherent in modern science and technology. After the art produced by native peoples who lived close to nature has been destroyed in the name of progress, scientists then try to record and preserve it. The "random" sampling of reality in David's film project is as much a protest against scientific classifications as against the generic codes of Hollywood cinema, but his film still depends on the separation of the observer from what is being observed. In the novel, this attitude to filmmaking contrasts with the psychological and physical processes by which the narrator becomes aware of the interdependence of inner and outer experience.

From the perspective of the novel's narrator, the camera is an object of intense suspicion. The film version of *Surfacing* evidently wants to clear itself of any such suspicion. A title at the end informs us that the heron was not killed for the film but had been found dead in a barn two years earlier and kept frozen until it was needed. We are also informed that the moose was shot with a tranquillizing dart. When Kate destroys David's film by exposing it to natural light, she not only discredits technology's claim to power over nature but also helps to dissociate *Surfacing* from this claim.

Yet the film's conventional narrative structure also leads to a more external view of nature than the novel advocates. In particular, there is a long "shooting(!) the rapids" sequence in which first Kate and David, and then Anna and Joe, are carried through dangerous rocks in their canoes. As expected, Kate proves her competence, while Anna screams hysterically, and after the second canoe capsizes and breaks up, it is Kate who enters the water to perform a heroic rescue. As in most wilderness adventure films, nature is a challenge, a force beyond human control that becomes a test of endurance. Equally conventionally, but more successfully, nature provides spectacle, often compensating for the weakness of the acting and the screenplay. The images of trees silhouetted against a lake often recall the Canadian landscape paintings of Tom Thomson and the Group of Seven.

These images of nature – perhaps inevitably, given the subject matter – become an allusion to one of Canada's best known artistic achievements. If the allusion is recognized, it would seem to replace the novel's allusions to native arts and traditions. The petroglyphs remain as one of the clues to the father's disappearance, and we do see a drawing of one of them when the couples first enter the cabin, but their significance is not really explored. They function as a narrative convenience, although in a rather unconvincing way. Joe's departure is motivated by the injuries he suffers in a fall from a cliff face after he finds petroglyphs, but this accident occurs just before Kate realizes that the water level has been raised so that the petroglyphs are now under water.

The film also eliminates the French Canadians who live in the region and almost all explicit references to the characters' nationality, although David does call Anna a "Canadian tart." Most notably, it omits all reference to the "Americans" who, in the mind of the novel's narrator, represent the negative tendencies in modern culture. Although she comes to admit that the term refers not to a country but to a state of mind, her own state of mind allows the novel to bring together contemporary debates on Canadian nationalism and sexual politics. Some critics found the novel strident and didactic, but the filtering of these issues through the consciousness of an unreliable narrator gives it a poetic ambiguity in which identity becomes "an unstable, multiple or shifting construct," very much as it does in Jutra's earlier films.[21]

Unfortunately, the adaptation of *Surfacing* simplifies the novel's feminist politics by eliminating any suggestion of unstable identities and it erases all issues of national identity in its efforts to look like an "American" film. As we have seen, the most visible sign of the latter process was the casting of Americans in the leading roles. An apparently unintended irony emerges from the casting of Canadian actors, Margaret Dragu and R.H. Thompson, as Anna and David. Their troubled and tormented relationship is the outcome of the urban and American culture whose values the encounter with the wilderness calls into question. Kate is clearly out of place in the urban environment to begin with, and she and Joe have to build a new kind of relationship that will respect her freedom. The effect is that the American actors portray characters who are often disapproving witnesses of the ugly and insensitive behaviour of characters played by Canadian actors.

If, as the producers clearly assumed, spectators recognized the American stars, they would also be aware that the "normal" couple is American. Perhaps the effect is an unintended confirmation of the fears of Atwood's heroine that Americans are indeed taking over Canadian culture.

When Beryl Fox approached Jutra with the offer to direct *Surfacing*, he initially refused because he was already working on *By Design*, a Vancouver-based comedy about two lesbian fashion designers. Since potential investors doubted the commercial prospects of this project, Jutra changed his mind about *Surfacing* when Fox agreed to produce *By Design* as well.[22] Although a script existed before Jutra became involved with the project, he was able to rewrite it thoroughly in collaboration with playwright Joe Wiesenfeld.

Jutra also contributed to the casting decisions. Although there was still a felt need to cast an American star in one of the major roles, the negotiations and compromises that often take place around the casting of a Canadian film had a much happier outcome than in the case of *Surfacing*. The original plan was to hire an American actor to play the male lead, a fashion photographer named Terry; but this role went to Saul Rubinek, a Canadian who had appeared in *Seer Was Here* and *The Wordsmith* and whose screen persona was close to Jutra's own in some of his earlier films.

This decision eventually led to the inspired pairing of the diminutive Patty Duke Astin and the tall Sara Botsford as the film's "odd couple," Helen and Angie. The former, well known for her performance as Helen Keller – the deaf and blind child in Arthur Penn's *The Miracle Worker* (1962) – and as the star of her own television series, became the American connection, while the latter was a new face, a young Canadian who would go on to make a career in Hollywood before starring as a sexy news producer in the Canadian television series, "E.N.G."

An on-the-set report on the shooting of the film, published in *Cinema Canada*, made clear that Jutra was much more comfortable with this intimate comedy than with the conventional drama and outdoor action of *Surfacing*.[23] But commercially the film fared little better than its predecessor. Its poor reception at the Cannes film festival delayed its release, and when it finally reached Canadian cinemas, the reviews were mainly contemptuous. After promoting the film in an issue that contained the production report as well as an interview in which Fox and Jutra spoke enthusiastically about their new project, *Cinema Canada* published a review written by someone who had apparently not read the earlier issue and who offered a glib dismissal of the film, whose "vacuous nature" supposedly reflected Jutra's "emotional and artistic alienation in English Canada."[24]

This comment echoed Martin Knelman's earlier response to Jutra's CBC television films, but Knelman wrote one of the few appreciative reviews of *By Design*. Acclaiming the film as "easily the outstanding Canadian movie of 1982," Knelman declared that it was the first of Jutra's English-language works in which his "distinctive sensibility breaks through" and that it signalled "the re-emergence of Claude Jutra as Canada's finest writer-director."[25] Knelman's enthusiasm was shared by Pauline Kael, who called the film "a buoyant, quirky sex comedy" and praised Jutra's "light, understated approach" to the material.[26]

Ostensibly, the "quirky sex" ought to have been a selling point but as Knelman suggested, some reviewers seem to have been uncomfortable with "the whole notion of lesbianism as a subject for comedy." In the 1982 *International Film Guide*, the film was dismissed as "worthless" and "offensive" by Gerald Pratley who, according to Knelman, regarded "the Canadian film industry as a private finishing school for girls with himself as its shrill headmistress."[27] Pratley's discomfort may have had something to do with the photographic collage of naked female breasts that Terry displays on his bedroom wall and calls "Tits Transcendent," or with the sequence in which Helen has sex with Terry in his apartment while talking on the phone to Angie who is simultaneously engaged in an energetic sexual encounter in a motel.

More in tune with what she calls Jutra's exploration of "the whole modern supermarket of sex," Kael found this sequence "near to being irresistibly funny." She was also impressed with the moving depiction of the physically mismatched couple, insisting that "nothing that happens in the movie ever makes us doubt that these two love and need each other."[28] It is difficult to imagine a response more remote from that of the *Cinema Canada* reviewer, who wrote that "only a single, brief close-up of the two lead actors conveys their sense of love for each other."[29]

These critical differences may have a lot to do with the film's subject matter, but there was clearly a problem in coming to terms with its comic tone. While many of the situations could easily have been treated as broad farce, *By Design* is a muted comedy in which laughter is often contaminated with a sense of embarrassment or sadness. Patrick Schupp felt that the film failed to live up to Jutra's legend because its approach was "too reasonable" and therefore lacking in comic "madness."[30] He compared it unfavourably to the classic Hollywood comedies of Howard Hawks and Billy Wilder, but Kael made a more complex attempt to define the film's tone through reference to other directors. After noting that Jutra's "sensibility suggests a mingling of Tati and Truffaut," she also used Hollywood cinema as a touchstone by describing the film as "a Lubitsch sex comedy stripped of the glamour but not of the fun."[31]

A model closer to home might have been *Outrageous!* (based, as we have seen, on the same source as *Ada*), which was a similarly unstable comedy built around an unconventional relationship. But the depiction of the lesbian couple in *By Design* also draws on the treatment of sexuality in Jutra's own earlier comedy, *Pour le meilleur et pour le pire*. The troubled relationship of the heterosexual couple in that film is a consequence of the institution of marriage that defines sexual normality in a patriarchal, capitalist, and colonized society. In contrast, the lesbian relationship in *By Design* allows a glimpse of an alternative social order in which normality involves the acceptance of difference.

In the earlier film, Jutra drew on his own intimate experience of Quebec society but valued his detached perspective as an unmarried (read gay) man. In *By Design*, he had far less experience of the society depicted but must have felt closer to the problems of the lesbian couple. The utopian dimension becomes more visible, and the film avoids the overt stylization and "madness" that characterized Jutra's earlier work. Instead, as Kael argues, "*By Design* is so matter-of-fact in the way it tells its story that it may invite ridicule," and "Jutra is so unassuming he makes the film seem smaller than it is."[32] It offers a comic world in which laughter is no longer a way of marginalizing those who do not conform but a celebration of the diversity of human desires and behaviour.

The credits sequence sets up the kind of spectatorship that the film will invite. In some ways, it looks like the opening of a television situation comedy, situating the two main characters in their urban environment. Instead of the rapid montage of the typical sit-com credits sequence, however, Jutra starts with a long take in which the camera follows Helen and Angie from their home beside a harbour until they enter a building that appears to be a warehouse. The camera movement briefly excludes them from the frame, and there is a slight zoom in on the skyline of a modern city seen across the harbour. As in most sit-coms (and *Surfacing*), a song accompanies the credits sequence: in this case, it begins as a sultry torch song (sung by Kathleen Adair), but just as Helen stumbles going down a step on the wharf, the tempo changes to an upbeat Latin celebration of "Your Best Day."

226

The credits sequence thus appears familiar, but its use of a long take prepares us for a film that will invite the spectator to think about the implications of its images and effects. By detaching itself from the human figures, the camera asserts its independence and suggests that the two women live a somewhat marginal existence in a modern city. The shot of high-rise buildings at the beginning of *Pour le meilleur et pour le pire* carries similar connotations, but in that film, the couple are part of this modern world. In *By Design*, the couple live beside the water, whose redemptive qualities had been more heavily emphasized in *Dreamspeaker* and *Surfacing* but which here provides a circumscribed trace of the natural world within the metropolis. The most notable impression created by this opening shot is the physical disparity of the two women whose intimate relationship is evident even from a distance at which their voices can only be vaguely heard.

The film that follows this opening long take will be, in the strongest sense, a situation comedy but one without a laugh track to define what is funny and without clearly defined norms that dictate a correct response to its humour. Its low-key approach is especially unexpected given the potential for glamour and spectacle in a film dealing with the fashion industry. Kael commented on the "almost harsh" lighting that allows us to "read the grain of the faces" and to accept the characters "as they are."[33] As for the fashions, even Knelman noted that his "one serious complaint" about the film was that "the clothes are ghastly."[34]

When a businessman offers to market their designs, Helen and Angie lose the opportunity he offers because they refuse to work in "synthetics." The film simply shows them defending a position they believe in, and it hardly matters whether the position has any validity in the context of an international industry that thrives on illusion or whether their designs are "ghastly." While the businessman is only concerned with whether the clothes will sell, the film calls into question not only the commercial imperative but also the norms that enable Knelman to put forward his judgment as more than a matter of personal taste. As with Bernard's job in advertising in *Pour le meilleur et pour le pire*, the situation of Helen and Angie in the fashion industry is an uneasy reminder of Jutra's situation in the film industry, and he must have found the ending, in which their clothes achieve success in Los Angeles, especially ironic.

However, the narrative is less concerned with clothes and the industry that surrounds them than with the bodies in the clothes. Terry takes advantage of his job as a fashion photographer to watch the models in their dressing-room and to persuade women to undress for the sake of his collage. His behaviour is a reminder of the voyeurism involved in all cinematic spectatorship, but the film also seeks to rescue female nudity from the constraints of the male gaze, most notably in a beach sequence in which Helen tells Angie that she looks like a Botticelli Venus when she emerges naked from the sea.

In the same sequence, a naked young girl approaches the couple as they sunbathe, and the mother angrily accuses them of having removed her bathing suit. Despite the embarrassing end to this encounter, it reminds Helen of her desire to have a child, which is beginning to emerge as the main driving force of the plot. Her desire is not presented as a sign of an innate female need for motherhood or as a contradiction that undermines her lesbian desires. Angie does not share her desire, but she is willing to become a parent to satisfy her partner.

The only obstacle would seem to be a purely physical one, but their attempts to do without a father reveal the inadequacy of both the law and science. Their application to adopt a child is taken up as a test-case by a "progressive" female social worker but vetoed by her male boss, who reminds them that lesbian parenthood is against the law. They then quickly reject the idea of artificial insemination when they see an unkempt drunk emerging from the cubicle where he has donated sperm for beer money.

The lack of legal or scientific solutions sets in motion a search for a father that is a virtual parody of the one in *Surfacing*. Helen and Angie appropriate the power of the gaze, much to the discomfort of men who are not used to being looked at, reversing the gender dynamics of the fashion industry (which had also been a factor in *À tout prendre*). After a visit to a night club, where Angie dances with a male acquaintance and Helen runs away in disgust, the two women go to a lesbian bar where they dance contentedly with each other.

The search depends on the assumption that the male will provide the necessary physical assistance but will not assume the responsibilities of fatherhood. As in Jutra's earlier films, the culture is one in which there is a crisis in masculinity. The only "normal" father we see is the businessman, who is married to a submissive Japanese wife whose traditional kimono places her outside the codes of modern fashion. He is a relatively amiable representative of an oppressive social order from which men can escape if they are gay, like the designers who compete with Helen and Angie, or child-like, like Terry.

Terry's collage of breasts implies a mother fixation, which apparently accounts for his secret love for Helen, an older woman who makes no pretence to glamour. Like a child, he fails to notice Helen's sexual preference until he is disabused by Suzie, a model who has earlier complained about his acts of sexual harassment in the dressing-room. When Angie persuades Helen to take advantage of Terry's feelings by using him to father her child, the sexual act takes place while Helen talks to Angie on the phone and Terry leafs through pornographic magazines to maintain his erection in the face of her indifference. This unlikely union results in a male child that, however, is born dead, another example perhaps of the weakness of the male principle. But the film's utopian dimension prevails because Helen's desire for a child is fulfilled when Angie gives birth to a girl, conceived in a vigorous sexual encounter with an inexperienced youth that takes place while she speaks on the phone to Helen.

The film ends with the two women suckling their shared baby, but another phone call links them to Terry, who has moved to Los Angeles to promote their designs. Suzie has gone with him, and the film's final image reveals that she is pregnant. Although this shot seems like a conventional heterosexual "happy ending," it does not cancel out the more unorthodox personal and professional success of the lesbian couple. Terry's involvement with their scheme has given him a new maturity that makes it possible for him to look forward to becoming a father, the first (and only) such case in Jutra's work.

Terry becomes integrated into the adult world only by leaving Canada, just as the couple in *Outrageous!* find happiness in New York after the woman's child has been born dead in Canada. Jutra, however, at least suggests that there is hope for a utopian renewal north of the border. This relatively hopeful outcome is more convincing than the conventional happy ending of *Surfacing*, but there are clearly enormous obstacles in the way of significant cultural change. Even this shred of hope would again disappear beneath the surface when Jutra returned to Quebec and to the past for his next film.

Above: Agnes (Charlotte Laurier) with Sister Gertrude (Paule Baillargeon) (Pierre Lamy)

Below: The children and the artist (Gilles Renaud) in front of the mural (Pierre Lamy)

DREAMS OF ELSEWHERE
La Dame en couleurs

After Jutra's death, Brian Johnson described *La Dame en couleurs* as a "belated yet masterly return to his own culture," but his opinion was not widely shared.[1] When the film was released in 1985, many reviewers in Quebec dismissed it as curiously old-fashioned and ideologically regressive, and Jutra once again found himself living in the shadow of his own legend. The critical response is to some extent understandable because the film is set in a vaguely defined past and its main characters are children living in a mental hospital operated by nuns. *La Dame en couleurs* is almost self-consciously constructed to include virtually all the ingredients of Jutra's biographical legend, but there was now a widespread impression that this legend had lost any of the cultural relevance it may have originally possessed.

In one of the few appreciative reviews of the film, Michael Dorland argued that its strength lies in the power of "its searing despair, its stark bleakness, the harshness of its denunciation of the world."[2] For many critics, however, especially in Quebec, the film's bleak outlook was the product of a sensibility ill attuned to modern social developments, and there was even speculation that this allegedly morbid vision could be accounted for by Jutra's health problems.

In his history of Quebec cinema, first published shortly after Jutra's death, Yves Lever summed up much of the critical response to the film when he argued that, despite "an excellent initial idea" and "some inspired intuitions," it failed because of "a badly structured, incoherent screenplay, with dreadful continuity, poorly defined characters and an ending that could have opened out to a hope but opts for pessimism."[3] Commercial failure, in the face of hostile or lukewarm reviews linking the film's "pessimism" to its neglect of the rules of "continuity," was an all too familiar experience for Jutra. As we shall see, the film is in some ways a (courageous) response to the difficulties he was facing, but this does not mean that it was not also an important reflection of and on its cultural context.

In particular, the film's pessimism is far from simply a product of Jutra's personal outlook. As Ian Lockerbie has argued, "optimism in Quebec cinema is rarely unqualified and often threatened by a great pessimism," and this was especially true of many films made after the rejection of the separatist option in the 1980 referendum.[4] *La Dame en couleurs* was released just a few months after Jean Beaudin's *Mario* (1984), in which a deaf-mute boy escapes into an imaginary world but eventually commits suicide. While Beaudin's powerful but disturbing film may owe something to Jutra's previous explorations of similar territory, these and other films of the early 1980s clearly reflect more than just the personal preoccupations of their filmmakers.

Of course, to claim that a film is culturally relevant does not mean that one cannot deplore its version of the situation; but it must also be recognized that Jutra's biographical legend was itself very much a product of the culture within which it was constructed. That culture, whether defined as Canadian or Québécois, has always included a strong negative component, but the refusal of happy endings is not necessarily a sign of wilful pessimism.

A Dream and a Legend

According to Louise Rinfret, who collaborated with Jutra on the screenplay, the story originated in her dream about "orphans living in a psychiatric hospital."[5] As one critic put it, the film "progresses like a nightmare," and although the initial dream was not Jutra's, the nightmare packs together so many images and preoccupations from his earlier films that *La Dame en couleurs* becomes an intense retrospective of the filmmaker's entire body of work.[6]

It begins with the arrival of a truck full of children at a large old building. We quickly learn that the building is a mental hospital and that the children have been sent there because there is no room for them in the orphanages. This explanation leaves many questions unanswered, especially about the time and place of the action, and I shall return to these later. For the moment, it is sufficient to note that the film quickly introduces its three major groups of characters – the children, the nuns, and the patients – confronting us with three major elements in the Jutra legend.

The community of nuns reminds us of earlier Jutra films that represent the experience of marginality and confinement through a female consciousness.[7] However, nuns also figure prominently in the iconography of Quebec's past, and their presence helps to define the action as taking place before the Quiet Revolution. As in Babette's dream in *Wow*, the nuns in *La Dame en couleurs* offer refuge during what appears to be a wartime situation. They have withdrawn from an apparently disordered outside world, but they hold positions of power within the building, despite the crowded conditions they have to work in. They apparently accept their situation, with the exception of Sister Gertrude, who does not clearly express her discontent until she decides to leave at the end.

At first, the large building before which the truck pulls up seems to be a convent, but it soon becomes clear that the nuns are running a mental hospital. In depicting the treatment of madness in this historical film, Jutra was again drawing on his experience of the "miserable conditions" faced by patients in mental hospitals "during the Duplessis period."[8] As in many of the earlier films, madness is not so much a clinical condition as a refusal to conform to the demands of a culture hostile to the powers of the imagination. The key figure is the "mad" artist whose mural, secretly painted in the tunnels beneath the convent, fascinates the children and gives the film its title.

The character most fully involved in all aspects of the film's complex plot is Agnès, a fifteen-year-old orphan who has already been at the hospital for some time. She has an intense relationship with Sister Gertrude, who gives her private lessons; and she, along with the other children, discovers the network of tunnels where the artist paints his colourful mural. At the end, Agnès stays behind when most of the children escape, drawing back at the last moment, apparently afraid of life outside an institution whose constraints have given her a sense of security. A brief epilogue shows that she is still there at the age of forty.

Although the main focus is on Agnès and the other children, it is the interaction of the three groups that gives the film its meaning. Near the beginning, a deep-focus long shot quickly captures the basic characteristics of each group: as the nuns briskly go about their business, patients listlessly move along the corridors, while children organize a game of hide-and-seek. In their efforts to maintain control, the nuns are always rushed, with little or no time to pursue their spiritual vocations. The patients are unable to control themselves and alternate between inertia and sudden bursts of activity. Although the children perform menial tasks in the wards, it is through their games that they explore the possibilities of taking control of their own lives.

A Child is Dead

Why are there so many orphans? The opening image of the children on a truck, and the clothes they are wearing, suggest that they are World War II evacuees. In her review, Carole Corbeil stated bluntly that "the time is the '40s" and claimed that the film reconstructs an actual wartime situation in which "there was a surplus of orphans in Montreal" with the result that "some orphans ended up in insane asylums."[9] Yet the clothes may simply be old, like the truck at the beginning of *Mon oncle Antoine*; hence they do not clearly indicate when the action takes place. According to Dorland, the setting is "ostensibly the 1940s; but it could be anytime." He added that the children are "refugees from the emotional wars beyond."[10] Janick Beaulieu referred to "a kind of suspended time."[11] As we shall see, the ending implies a date some time in the late 1950s, and the children are always referred to as orphans, not evacuees or refugees.

Thus, as in *Mon oncle Antoine*, the action takes place in an ill-defined "some time ago." Although there can be little doubt that it takes place in Quebec, the film avoids stating this explicitly. When Agnès tries to comfort a small boy among the new arrivals, he asks her, "Where is here?" She shrugs and replies, "Just here." This apparent allusion to Northrop Frye's basic Canadian question may be coincidental, but it does introduce the problem of constructing a sense of identity in an "obliterated environment." When Agnès later speaks of her memories of the outside world, she has to admit that she is not sure whether she is describing real or imaginary places.

The effect is that the outside world (which we never see) becomes both a historical place, Quebec before the Quiet Revolution, and an alternative reality ravaged by some unspecified disaster. This science-fiction premise could also explain the presence in the hospital of uniformed and armed guards whose job is apparently to prevent the inmates from escaping. As in *Dreamspeaker*, the functions of hospital and prison seem to merge in one building, although here it is also a convent. Its secular medical and disciplinary functions coexist with the spiritual influence and cultural power of the Catholic church in Quebec's past.

But why is this hospital/prison so full of orphans? The answer would seem to be that the orphans are refugees from Quebec's literary and cinematic traditions. Children figure prominently in these traditions, and it is perhaps through his concern with the difficult passage from childhood to adulthood that Jutra's biographical legend has its roots most deeply implanted in Quebec culture. Not all children are orphans, of course, but there seem to be an unusually large number in the works of Quebec's novelists and filmmakers, and even those who have families would often prefer to be orphans.[12]

In a wide range of novels by writers like Marie-Claire Blais, Réjean Ducharme, and André Langevin, the child's perspective exposes the imaginary and symbolic poverty of the adult world.[13] In her study of *The Child Hero in the Canadian Novel*, Theresia Quigley describes the treatment of childhood in Quebec novels of the 1950s in terms that would apply equally well to Jutra's films. She argues that the object is "not to portray a realistic world of childhood but to use the child character as a symbol of a social condition" so that the "vulnerability of the child" signifies "the oppression of an entire people by centuries of outdated social values and restraints."[14]

While these literary precedents are an important part of the cultural context within which Jutra worked, most critics discussed the children in *La Dame en couleurs* in relation to earlier cinematic manifestations of this motif. Indeed, Dorland suggested that "the child is perhaps the most important single signifier in Quebec film" and argued that Jutra's film belonged to a tradition that began with *La Petite Aurore l'enfant martyre*, a film in which a child is beaten to death by her stepmother.[15] He was not the only critic to place Jutra's film within what Lever called "the pessimistic tradition inaugurated by *La Petite Aurore*," but while many critics viewed this affiliation as further evidence of Jutra's regressive tendencies, Dorland argued that the film transcends the limits of the tradition to which it alludes and on which it draws.[16]

Orphans appear so frequently in the films made in Quebec during the brief production boom after World War II that Christiane Tremblay-Daviault called it "an orphan cinema" in her important study of the "mental and social structures of Quebec cinema" at that time.[17] As Beaulieu pointed out, orphans are, by definition, "cut off from their roots," and in Jutra's film this condition also applies to the nuns and to the patients, although they are to some extent able to defend themselves against it through faith, in one case, and madness, in the other.[18]

The Catholic faith is, of course, a central component of Quebec's cultural roots, but here its values clearly belong to the past, even if its institutions retain a great deal of power. In the overcrowded hospital, the nuns desperately try to keep order and have little time to respond to the spiritual needs of the patients and children in their care. Their businesslike manner, however, is also a defence against an emotional response to the suffering around them, just as Sister Gertrude tries to keep her distance from Agnès's emotional demands. During one of their private lessons, she dictates a text that claims that "God protects His children against evil," but religion seems to have become simply a matter of forms and uniforms.

While religious traditions may be hollow and inadequate to the children's needs, the possibilities of art, although more promising, prove to be equally ineffective. The imaginary world created by the artist-madman offers an alternative source of spiritual values, as suggested by the film's title. Although the "lady of colours" refers most obviously to the artist's underground mural, the title could equally apply to the portrait of the Virgin Mary in the chapel. The mural replaces the religious icon, and the artist presents himself as a Christlike figure, alienated equally from the world and from the religious establishment. At one point, he asks that "little children come unto me" and offers to help "all those who are struck with sorrow or lost."

The children, however, reject both the old Christianity and the new Christ. They parody the official rituals in their underground ceremonies (with complex effects that I shall discuss later), and they finally turn on the artist (perhaps killing him) after he has discovered that adults and children "cannot understand each other."

A Man of Many Colours

The figure of the artist-madman is clearly in some ways a stand-in for the artist-director, and Jutra apparently thought of playing the role himself.[19] Even though he decided to remain behind the camera, the relations between painter and filmmaker were quite obvious, and Beaulieu even called the film an "impressionist drama," thereby echoing the comment of one of the nuns that the artist's paintings offer an "impression" of reality.[20] The artist is troubled by the losses of memory from which he suffers during the increasingly frequent black-outs that afflict him, suggesting that Jutra was expressing his own sense of anguish through a character with whom he closely identified.

Although the artist's real name is Leclair, implying that he ought to see clearly, his nickname is Barbouilleux, aptly translated in the English-dubbed version as Big Smudge. His paintings are expressions of his inner vision, but their artistic quality remains very much open to doubt. When the Mother Superior finds the mural in the tunnels, she is unable to see any difference between the artist's work and the "children's scribbles" on the walls beside it, and many critics were equally unimpressed with the painting that is clearly central to the film's meanings.

Dorland even suggested that the artist is so keen to paint in the tunnels because the light of day reveals "the poverty of his painting," but he added that "it is not clear whether the fact that his paintings are simply awful is deliberate or not."[21] As with the "ghastly" clothes in *By Design*, the film does not dispute this judgment but does call into question the confident standards that make it possible. The alleged gap between the artist's intentions and his paintings allows them to stand for the aesthetics of failure through which Jutra's films raise disturbing questions about their cultural context. Although Dorland felt that Jutra was successful in his final film because he distanced himself from the failed artist, the complexity and power of the film depends on the unstable boundaries between identification and critical distance.

The nuns are disturbed by the distortion of reality in the paintings. Although one of them refers to the artist as an impressionist, his avoidance of the light and the paintings that we see suggest that he belongs more to the expressionist or surrealist traditions. He responds to the charge that his landscapes are "twisted" by pointing out that "we all see things with different eyes," implying that he has been confined to the hospital because he refuses to see things in the accepted way. However, his paintings suggest that he sees through the eyes of other artists. His room is decorated with self-portraits that make him look like Vincent Van Gogh and that are painted in the style of that archetypal "mad" artist.

When two nuns search his room after his disappearance, they discover not only the pseudo-Van Gogh self-portraits but two paintings that look suspiciously like the work of Salvador Dali and Francis Bacon. The artist seems to be an unconscious plagiarist who reproduces the style and vision of other artists whose work has impressed him. Despite his evidently sincere efforts to express his anguish, he is only able to reproduce the visions of others.

In the outside world, however, he was an apparently respected artist, and the nuns allow him to stay in a private room so that he can prepare for an exhibition from which they hope to profit. The nuns who search his room decide that the paintings have no value, though they appear to be unaware of the original works Leclair has virtually reproduced. The paintings are certainly not great works of art, but the nuns dismiss them because they do not conform to aesthetic standards dictated by the art market.

Leclair himself seems unconcerned with market values. He speaks of confronting the darkness within and tells one of the children that his goal is to paint the "black sun," to "show the invisible." His efforts to give form to the unseen contrast with the photo-novels – which use photographic realism to lend credibility to romantic depictions of human relationships – from which the children derive their knowledge of the outside world. For the children, these photographs become what films were for Jutra in his childhood and, like commercial cinema, they activate the imagination even as they turn images into commodities. This conjunction of romance and commerce recalls the relationship between Hollywood musicals and Bernard's advertising job in *Pour le meilleur et pour le pire*.

The crucial image that brings the painter and the filmmaker together is, of course, the mural that Leclair sees as the culmination of his work. It owes more to art nouveau or pop art than to the surrealist and expressionist models of his above-ground work, and it would be difficult to argue that it is a great painting. A few years later, in *I've Heard the Mermaids Singing* (1987), Patricia Rozema suggested the ineffable quality of a supposedly sublime painting by representing it only as a mysterious glow shining from an apparently empty canvas. Jutra chose to show the painting and thus open it up to value judgments, leaving us to wonder whether the problem lies in the painting or in the film or in the aesthetic standards used to judge them. The question of value is deflected on to the question of meaning.

This second question is more interesting but even more difficult to answer. Corbeil described the figure in the painting as "a fantastical, beautiful woman who is surrounded by colours and shafts of light" and suggested that "to the children she becomes the symbol of the mother they have lost, and of all of the sensual delights that presumably lie in the paradise they have made of the outside world."[22] From a more political perspective, Beaulieu felt that "the Lady in question represents Liberty" in the allegorical tradition of Delacroix's revolutionary painting of *Liberty Guiding the People*.[23]

Although the orphans initially contribute to the mural as a communal project that promises to revive the artist's inspiration by uniting it with the uncontaminated vision of children, they quickly lose their enthusiasm for the painting. The first one to turn against the project is Agnès, who denounces Leclair's attempts to explain what the Lady means to him as "a pack of lies," apparently expressing her own fears of sexuality and the outside world. Her intense reaction foreshadows her refusal to escape with the others at the end of the film, but it also seems to reveal a fear that she will not measure up to the glamour through which the painting sexualizes the idea of freedom.

The painting may not live up to the artist's intentions, but it does evoke a dream-state whose meaning depends on the viewer's engagement. As an image that seeks to give external form to inner feelings, it gains its complexity not from its own aesthetic qualities but from its uneasy disturbance of the boundary between inside and outside. Leclair insists that the painting depicts a real woman "from the outside," but he admits that he is only able to paint her because she appears to him in his dreams and that she does not look the same every time.

Inside/Out

The image of the Lady thus refers to a reality that supposedly exists outside the hospital grounds but that the inmates can experience only through the inner life of the imagination. As the presence of the orphans makes clear, what goes on inside the hospital is deeply marked by what happens outside, and in this sense the relations between inside and outside are political. Although the film provides little information on the political situation, the period setting suggests a process of displacement similar to that described by Jutra when the October Crisis aroused memories of his own childhood fears during World War II.[24] Political and psychological responses thus come together through the power of memory and imagination. Just as the people inside the hospital draw on their memories or imagination of the outside world, the focus on madness allows the film to explore the relations between outer reality and inner experience, relations that Jutra had repeatedly explored in his earlier films.

These relations have, of course, always been crucial to the discourses of religion and art that underlie the narrative structure of *La Dame en couleurs*. As we have already seen, the religious discourse can no longer provide the basis for a stable sense of identity. Sister Gertrude unsettles Agnès when she tells her that it is the Devil who makes people "sick in the head" but then adds that the potential for good and evil exists inside everyone. Agnès is puzzled by the idea that the Devil is both an outside force and an inner experience, but she is especially disturbed by the implication that the "mad" may not be a clearly defined group, as she had believed. A little later, another nun disinfects the artist's scalp and remarks that his "head is full of strange but interesting things." The hygienic concern with the outside of his head suggests an underlying attitude to what goes on inside it. Both religion and art mediate between what is inside the head and the outside world, offering terms in which this relationship can be experienced, expressed, and regulated.

For the individual, this process of mediation has a great deal to do with the way the body is experienced as both inside and outside, as part of the self and yet as separate from the mind or "self." From the perspective of the nuns, who have taken a vow of chastity and conceal their bodies in their habits, the physical body is a source of temptation and evil that can be combatted only through self-denial. Agnès sets out to challenge this perspective in her relationship with Sister Gertrude, but her sexual experimentation reveals her own uncertainty about bodily experience and its relation to her sense of self.

When Gertrude cuts short their discussion of the Devil, Agnès asks what is wrong with their being together if they love each other. Just as the theological lesson unsettles Agnès, her physical presence disturbs the nun, and their relationship becomes a subject for gossip among the other nuns. Since she remains silent, we can infer Gertrude's feelings for Agnès only from her appearance and behaviour. She becomes very agitated when Agnès goes missing, and, after she hears that all the children have escaped, she removes her habit and leaves the hospital.

During another lesson, Agnès reads passages from the Song of Solomon in which the passionate imagery fuses the experience of spiritual and physical love. In so doing, she demonstrates that the Bible does not always endorse the Church's efforts to keep physical and spiritual desires separate. Despite these playful attempts at seduction, however, her own uncertainty becomes apparent in her relationship with Denis, another orphan of about her age. When they are alone in the tunnels, she restrains his physical advances by telling him that she does not want to "make children" but, after she guides his hand to her breast, declares that she is sure that God is "all mixed up."

The hospital setting intensifies the tension between spiritual and physical reality that torments Agnès. In his depiction of hospital life, Jutra places great emphasis on bodily functions. In one sequence, children collect and clean the patients' chamber pots; in another, two children make up the bed of a patient who has had a sudden bowel movement, apparently out of fear of another patient who runs screaming through the ward. Although Sister Gertrude blames madness on the work of the Devil, the existence of the mental hospital is an outcome of the scientific effort to distinguish between the mad and the normal and to treat madness as an illness.

As in many of Jutra's earlier films, the erotic life of the physical body cannot be separated from an awareness of its mortality. When a young orphan named Sebastien dies in the infirmary, the other children steal the body and take it down to the tunnels. The two nuns who discover the theft arrange a fake funeral at night in order to maintain appearances, thus creating an ironic metaphor for the denial of the body on which their order is based. Meanwhile, down below, the children conduct improvised but much more meaningful ceremonies in which they try to confront their own fears and anxieties.

The children have their own ways of pursuing freedom, but the film leaves open the question whether they are really able to break free from their ideological environment. Their activities in the tunnels may undermine the foundations of the official institution above, but their improvised rituals show the influence of the culture they have been brought up in. During the ceremony in which they promise to keep the secret of the tunnels, they adapt the imagery of the Catholic mass to their own purposes. Dorland argued that they create "a world that parodies the one outside as black magic parodies the practices of established religion," but this solemn mockery suggests a need for ritual that ties them to the old ways.[25] Like the artist's paintings, their attempts at self-expression are shaped by the cultural forms from which they are trying to escape.

These underground ceremonies function as a way to exorcise their fears, just as Agnès and another orphan pretend to undergo shock treatment in an attempt to drive away their fears of being contaminated by the madness around them. Because of the reality of these fears, they tend to fall back on the medical and religious practices of their everyday environment, but their rituals have a real meaning that is absent from the traditions and conventions on which they draw. There are two simultaneous funeral ceremonies for Sebastien: one in the tunnels, where the children stand in front of the body and offer it their most precious belongings or memories, and the other on the surface, where the nuns bury an empty coffin at night to avoid embarrassing questions about the missing body.

Rituals provide a reassuring sense of order, but for the nuns this order is merely a façade. The children need a sense of order and meaning as a defence against their fears and uncertainties, but they remain aware that the prevailing order is an illusion that contributes to their entrapment. While they desire freedom, it requires courage to opt for an unknown reality in which the rituals may no longer work. From the perspective of those brought up in an oppressive cultural order, freedom may seem like the loss of meaning (or madness). When some of the orphans do escape at the end, they run off in different directions, and we are left wondering whether they will be able to cope with whatever is going on in the outside world.

These questions also involve our response to the context in which the escape takes place. It is the outcome of a series of events that begins when the artist stumbles on Sebastien's body and then wanders in shock into the hospital storeroom, which connects with the tunnels. The children surprise him there and force pills into his mouth so that he will stop seeing strange things – like dead bodies in the tunnels. Somehow he finds himself in the infirmary, where the Mother Superior questions him and discovers the existence of the underground passages beneath the institution.

The children escape in the subsequent confusion, but they gain their freedom because of an act of cruelty towards a man who is as trapped as they were. Agnès, however, refuses to leave the security of the tunnels. When she returns to the hospital and discovers that Gertrude has left, she sits in a rocking-chair with Mario, the young orphan she befriended at the beginning. There is a slow dissolve that spans a period of about twenty-five years to show that she is still in the institution with Mario. He is now apparently her "fiancé," and they play a game of hide-and-seek that ends with them tickling each other as they roll on the floor. As two nurses separate them, the film ends with a freeze-frame.

The final credits indicate that Agnès is forty in this epilogue, suggesting (if we assume that the epilogue is set in the "present") that the main action took place in the late 1950s. This dating should probably not be taken too seriously, but the transition from nuns in habits to nurses in uniforms alludes to the changes in Quebec after the Quiet Revolution (often seen as originating in the election of a Liberal government in 1960). It is the continued entrapment of Agnès, along with the possible murder of the artist, that led to the charges of pessimism against the film. Despite the secularization of the hospital, the ending seems to imply that the changes have been purely external and that little has changed in the inner lives of the people of Quebec.

Beaulieu described *La Dame en couleurs* as "an allegory that invites us to a pertinent reflection on our more or less suicidal behaviour."[26] Insofar as it functions as an allegory, the film belongs to a group of Quebec films of the 1980s in which the intimate depiction of psychological experience displaces social and political themes, while "a surplus of meaning," as Ian Lockerbie puts it, "points to a second-level narrative." According to Lockerbie, this allegorical tendency is an expression of "that dream of a more inspiring elsewhere that nourishes the entire Quebec imaginary," and that we have already seen as an important motif in many of Jutra's films.[27]

The Lady certainly derives from an imaginary elsewhere, but the meaning of the dream depends on the desires that it activates in the spectator. As in *Mon oncle Antoine* and *Kamouraska*, Jutra's previous films set in the past, the fable or allegory remains essentially unstable. At the end of the film, Agnès settles for the stability provided by the institution, even as her rocking-chair suggests a desire for movement that she represses at the cost of becoming a fixture in the hospital.

Although the camera remains fixed on Agnès as she opts for a sterile security, the ending remains ambiguous. Her refusal to leave could represent the fear of freedom to which Jutra, as a separatist, would presumably have attributed the "no" vote in the 1980 referendum. However, it could also represent the fear of the outside world that prevailed in Quebec before the Quiet Revolution and led to a rejection of technological progress. These readings are not necessarily contradictory and correspond to positions that Jutra frequently maintained in interviews, but they also need to be held in tension with an awareness that there is something seriously wrong "out there."

The ending is disturbing primarily because Jutra rigorously refuses to show us the outside world and thus leaves us to imagine what happens to the escaped children and the former nun. Similarly, the film refuses to settle for explanations that stress the outside (politics, allegory) without taking into account the inside (imagination). Each unsettles the other, creating a final effect in keeping with what Lockerbie calls "the *precariousness* of the Quebec condition."[28]

As we have seen, precariousness, or instability, was always a key element in Jutra's legend, which is perhaps not as out of touch with "the Quebec condition" as some critics have claimed. *La Dame en couleurs* did not result in Jutra's successful and triumphant return to Quebec; hence it did not overcome the public indifference built into his aesthetics of failure. Dorland, however, asserted that, in the context of "our orphaned cinema," Jutra had shown himself to be "a man who is not afraid to reaffirm his deserved claim to paternity."[29] Typically, the "our" in this sentence remains uncomfortably poised between Canada and Quebec, but it does suggest that Jutra's final feature film transcended the refusal of "paternity" that had figured so prominently in *À tout prendre*.

CONCLUSION

Jutra's place in Canadian film history seems secure, but as my account of his films and their reception has suggested, it is difficult to define exactly what that place is. It is a little easier to situate his work if we limit ourselves to Quebec cinema, where he seems to occupy a middle-ground position somewhere between two of his most prolific contemporaries, Gilles Carle and Jean Pierre Lefebvre. All three were indebted to the French New Wave. Whereas Carle sought to adapt the new approaches to the demands of commercial film production, rather like Claude Chabrol in France, Lefebvre made low-budget films in which he was able to develop a more radical perspective on film language and Quebec culture, rather like Jean-Luc Godard in France. As early as 1962, one critic called Jutra "the François Truffaut of our non-existent New Wave," and the films of these two directors do seem to attempt to steer a middle course by adopting the strategies of what became known as "art cinema."[1]

Such comparisons are useful as far as they go, but they certainly do not do justice to the range and complexity of the work of all these filmmakers. As we have seen, Jutra met and worked with Truffaut, who made a cameo appearance in *À tout prendre*. Both were accused of retreating from the innovative style of their early work, and both avoided direct involvement with the political discourses that had such an important place in many of Godard's enormously influential films. There are other similarities, but if the comparison is pushed too far, Jutra can only emerge as a pale imitation of the French master. The "instability" and the "aesthetics of failure" that I have traced through my discussion of Jutra's films are certainly influenced by the French New Wave, but their effect is quite different from Truffaut's seductive explorations of desire and obsession.

One of the major factors in this difference is the existence of a long-established and relatively secure film culture in France within and against which Truffaut and his colleagues could develop their own thinking about cinema. As Jutra's career makes abundantly clear, this was certainly not the case in Canada, with the result that Jutra's films do not fit comfortably into existing models or traditions, and most critics could not respond to them on their own terms. Of course, other Canadian filmmakers found themselves in the same situation, and their very different responses often reveal strategies and tensions similar to those that I identify in Jutra's films.

This is why a "national cinema" approach, with all its attendant difficulties (especially in the Canadian context), still provides the most useful context for examining Jutra's aesthetics of failure. Michael Dorland recently argued that Canadian film critics have tended to measure the heterogeneous body of films produced in Canada against "the ideal of a Canadian national cinema" as defined by the critics themselves. This "prescriptive and moralistic" approach finds value in the "Canadianness" of those films that come closest to the ideal and rejects films that do not reflect the alleged national characteristics on which the ideal is based.[2]

In my study of Jutra's films and the critical discourses about them, I have tried to remain descriptive, although I clearly value the films highly and disagree with what most critics wrote about them when they were first released. My main concern has been to discover how the films work and why the critics responded to them as they did. The answers to these questions have a lot to do with the workings of the national culture, but they do not depend on an assumption that this culture should have been different from what it was. At least, I have tried to avoid making such an assumption despite my evident regret that Jutra's films were not well served by their critics or by a distribution system that had little interest in giving audiences an opportunity to see them.

We do need to learn from the past, and historical studies such as Dorland's provide an invaluable source of information about the evolution of film production and film policy. Learning from the past also requires looking carefully at the films that were made in the given circumstances and at what they have to tell us about the present situation. If there is a prescriptive side to my account of Jutra's career, it lies in the conviction that his films, and those of many other Canadian filmmakers, should not only be preserved but made accessible to contemporary spectators.

Dorland quotes Seth Feldman and Joyce Nelson who, in the introduction to their *Canadian Film Reader*, wrote of the challenge to "make a national cinema out of what we have seen," and he suggests that such an approach allows film critics to conceive of themselves as "nation builders." It should be noted that Feldman and Nelson do go on to suggest that Canadian cinema exhibits only "a frustrated unity" and that Canada itself is "an endless mass of contradictions," but it is true that discussions of national cinema usually involve a search for continuity in the discontinuous variety of actual film production.[3] The critical attempt to describe a national cinema is always really a process of construction and one that cannot be divorced from the ways people conceive of the nation itself.

Of course, the most evident sign of frustrated unity in Canadian cinema, as it affects our response to Jutra, is the "one cinema or two" debate to which I alluded in my introduction. Jutra himself believed that Canada's two official languages have produced two cultures that do not belong under one roof, and this view has been widely supported by critics from both sides of the cultural divide.[4] It depends on the dual claims that Quebec culture is distinct from that of the rest of Canada and that it cannot fully develop its potential because of Quebec's "colonial" status. By this view, Canada is the colonizing power but one that lacks a distinct culture of its own because English Canadians have apparently been absorbed into the cultural sphere of the United States.

In *À tout prendre*, Jutra used the relationship between Claude and Johanne to develop a vision of Quebec as a colonized culture. Although he certainly believed in this vision, however, it depends, in the film, on issues of racial and gender difference that both support and complicate the basic metaphor. In the culture at large, the Québécois identity may grow out of a sense of shared aspirations and grievances, but it tends to obscure differences among the population. Whereas Jutra allowed these complications to enrich his films at the expense of political clarity, Pierre Vallières used the "white niggers" metaphor for more radical political purposes, but his argument depended on a fusion of national and class interests to the point where it was unclear whether the title of his book referred to "the Quebec collectivity" or to "the working class."[5] For Vallières, the goals of the independence movement were completely bound up with the movement towards a socialist revolution.

More recently, the Parti Québécois has argued that independence will benefit all classes but has attributed its referendum failures to the growing "ethnic" communities in Quebec.

In comparing English-Canadian and Québécois films, Robert Fothergill once suggested that "it would be easier for a Torontonian, for example, to maintain a conception of himself as colonized ... if he were not so readily indictable as a colonizer of others – Indians, Eskimos, women and the Québécois."[6] Of course, all but the last item on this list would also apply to a white male Québécois filmmaker, and the list could easily be expanded. The colonial metaphor is likely to be unstable in most contemporary societies in which many different oppressed groups demand equal treatment and challenge traditional hierarchies. However, the ironic use of the figure of the queen in both *Kamouraska* and *Dreamspeaker* makes clear that this metaphor maintained its force for Jutra even when he worked outside Quebec.

There has been no shortage of arguments that Canada as a whole is "a colonized country divided by regional and linguistic barriers."[7] From the English-Canadian perspective, colonization is often synonymous with Americanization, as it is for Margaret Atwood's heroine in *Surfacing*. Although the Canadian colonial experience can be traced back to the nation's origins as a literal colony of France and Britain, the recent emphasis has been on the influence of US popular culture. Canada has long felt especially susceptible to this influence because of its geographical situation, but since technological developments have virtually eliminated distance as a factor in global communications, other national cultures now find themselves confronting the same problems. These developments have given a new urgency, for example, to debates about whether national cinemas should seek to produce distinctive films with roots in their own cultures or whether they should imitate Hollywood.

As Thomas Elsaesser has remarked, "Hollywood can hardly be conceived, in the context of a 'national' cinema, as totally Other, since so much of any nation's film culture is implicitly 'Hollywood.'"[8] This is not just a matter of imitating Hollywood; it also involves issues of the ingrained habits of spectatorship nurtured by the international dominance of popular Hollywood cinema. Stuart Hall has even suggested that postmodernism is "about how the world dreams itself to be 'American.'"[9] At the same time, however, the proliferation of images and information (amplifying political and economic changes) means that the meaning of "being American" is also changing, both in reality and in dream. The aesthetic and economic contexts in which Canadian films are produced and consumed can no longer be defined simply in terms of Hollywood domination.

According to Hall, the global impact of these postmodern developments has disrupted traditional notions of identity so that we all now share the migrant's experience of marginality. Despite the unsettling effect of this experience, Hall insists that "it is an immensely important gain when one recognizes that all identity is constructed across difference and begins to live with the politics of difference."[10] Canada has adopted an official policy of "multiculturalism" that recognizes and seeks to control these changes, with decidedly mixed results. However, some of the most important Canadian films are now being made by filmmakers from the ethnic communities. In a recent article, Peter Harcourt pays particular attention to *Rude* (Clement Virgo, 1995) and *Lulu* (Srinivas Krishna, 1996) and notes that, while "other-culture filmmakers have been less in evidence" in Quebec, *Eldorado* (Charles Binamé, 1995) "depicts the inherited alienation of *pure laine* culture that's beginning to unravel, that's beginning to trouble the easy confidence of what it means, in the 1990s in Montreal, to be Québécois – whatever one's language of birth."[11]

What this means in terms of the "one cinema or two" debate is that, whatever the eventual outcome of the seemingly endless political processes, the Québécois and Canadian identities each depend on the existence of the other, and that this other is never wholly other. Moreover, the postmodern condition is one that calls into question the opposition between self and other on which this debate on the national cinema depends. For the moment, Canada has one national cinema, fragmented and divided like all national cinemas, with linguistic difference as the most significant but far from impregnable boundary line. If the political order changes, the ways in which we view the national cinema will change accordingly.

I have presented Jutra as a filmmaker who speaks to these issues. For the most part, his films do not address them directly, but they unsettle the terms of the debate in ways that look forward to the postmodern and postcolonial attitudes that I have been discussing. As Linda Hutcheon has suggested, "the contradictions of both postmodern theory and practice are positioned within the system and yet work to allow its premises to be seen as fictions or ideological structures" that may be useful but do not pretend to an absolute authority. The "constant slippage" caused by this refusal of fixed meanings may create an experience that verges on the psychotic, and Jutra's films often depict characters torn between a desire for freedom and a fear of its consequences.[12] They may go "mad" or opt for the security of what the system defines as "normal," but the films imply the possibility of a "politics of difference" based on an awareness of the cultural origins of all values.

Jutra opposed the discourses of political cinema that insisted on the creation of new forms uncompromised by the supposed ideological implications of conventional film language. Realizing that no form is ever ideologically pure, he chose to work within existing forms, with the result that his films were rarely perceived as formally or politically innovative. As I have shown, their relationship to the forms that they use involves an uncertain blending of complicity and critique, which manifests itself most evidently in shifting patterns of detachment and identification that encourage the spectators to draw on their own resources.

The middle ground that Jutra's films stake out is thus more challenging and less comfortable than most accounts would suggest. It is one in which value judgments become extremely difficult, so that we are unable to decide whether the painting in *La Dame en couleurs* or the clothes in *By Design* are intended to be seen as "good" or "bad." Such judgments depend on the relations of the text to its contexts and on the relations of both to the spectator. With the exception of *Mon oncle Antoine*, Jutra's films were not highly valued by their critics, despite his reputation as a great Canadian filmmaker. For reasons that I have tried to identify, the films made many critics uncomfortable, but I hope that I have also shown that they can provide a great deal of pleasure for spectators who are willing to respond to their unstable play with codes and conventions.

FILMOGRAPHY

This filmography includes only works directed or codirected by Jutra. The most thorough filmography, including Jutra's work as writer and actor as well as his unfinished projects, was prepared by Pierre Jutras and Nicole Laurin and published in *CopieZéro* 33 (December 1987): 4–14.

1948 LE DÉMENT DU LAC JEAN-JEUNES
      (THE MADMAN OF LAKE JEAN-JEUNES)
      Director: Claude Jutra
      Cinematographer: Michel Brault
      Sound: Jacques Gagnon
      (16mm, black and white, 40 min.)

1949 MOUVEMENT PERPÉTUEL ... (PERPETUAL MOTION)
      Director: Claude Jutra
      Cinematographer: Michel Brault
      Music: Novacek's *Perpetual Motion*
      Cast: Sylvia Laroche (She), Jacques Brault (He), J.J. Pineault (The Other)
      (16mm, black and white, 15 min.)

1956 JEUNESSES MUSICALES
      Director: Claude Jutra
      Cinematographer: Lorne Batchelor
      Editor: Victor Jobin
      Musical Advisor: Maurice Blackburn
      Sound: Erik Nielsen
      Producer: Roger Blais
      Production: National Film Board
      (35mm, black and white, 43 min.)

1957 A CHAIRY TALE

Directors: Norman McLaren and Claude Jutra
Music: Ravi Shankar
Assistants: Evelyn Lambart, Herbert Taylor, Maurice Blackburn
Producer: Tom Daly
Production: National Film Board
(35mm, black and white, 10 min.)

1958 LES MAINS NETTES (CLEAN HANDS)

Screenplay: Fernand Dansereau
Director: Claude Jutra
Cinemtographers: Michel Brault, Jean Roy
Editors: David Mayerovitch, Victor Jobin
Music: Maurice Blackburn
Sound: Marcel Carrière
Producers: Guy Glover, Léonard Forest
Production: National Film Board
Cast: Denise Provost (Marguerite Courtemanche), Michel Maillot (Gérard Charbonneau), Jean Brousseau (Jean-Paul Bouchard), Teddy-Burns Goulet (M. Morin), Doris Lussier (M. de Varennes), Micheline Gérin (Mme Bouchard), Monique Joly (Monique), Lucie Mitchell (Mlle Tremblay), Roger Lebel (Ernest Rivard), George Landreau (teacher), Monique Chailler (Mme Charbonneau) (16mm, black and white, 73 min.; shown in four parts in the television series "Panoramique")

1959 ANNA LA BONNE (ANNA THE CHAMBERMAID)

Screenplay: Claude Jutra, based on a poem by Jean Cocteau
Director: Claude Jutra
Cinematographer: André Mrugalsky
Editor: Annie Tresgots
Producer: François Truffaut
Production: Les films du Carrosse
Cast: Marianne Oswald (Anna), Dorian Leigh (Mademoiselle)
(35mm, black and white, 10 min.)

—— FÉLIX LECLERC TROUBADOUR
Director: Claude Jutra
Cinematographer: Michel Brault
Editors: Camille Adam, Victor Jobin
Sound: Michel Belaieff
Producer: Léonard Forest
Production: National Film Board
(35mm, black and white, 27 min.)

—— FRED BARRY COMÉDIEN (FRED BARRY ACTOR)
Screenplay: Claude Jutra
Director: Claude Jutra
Cinematographer: Michel Brault, assisted by Michel Régnier
Editors: Camille Adam, Victor Jobin
Sound: André Hourlier, assisted by Jean-Guy Normandin
Producer: Léonard Forest
Production: National Film Board
(16mm, black and white, 21 min.)

1961 LA LUTTE (WRESTLING)
Directors: Michel Brault, Marcel Carrière, Claude Fournier, Claude Jutra
Producer: Jacques Bobet
Production: National Film Board
(16mm. Black and white, 28 min.)

—— LE NIGER JEUNE RÉPUBLIQUE (NIGER YOUNG REPUBLIC)
Director: Claude Jutra
Editors: Claude Jutra, Edouard Davidovici
Producer: Bernard Devlin
Production: National Film Board
(16mm, colour, 58 min.)

1962 QUÉBEC USA OU L'INVASION PACIFIQUE
Directors: Michel Brault, Claude Jutra
Cinematographers: Michel Brault, Bernard Gosselin
Editor: Claude Jutra, assisted by Anne Claire Poirier
Sound: Marcel Carrière
Producer: Fernand Dansereau
Production: National Film Board
(16mm, black and white, 28 min.)

1963 À TOUT PRENDRE (ALL THINGS CONSIDERED)
Screenplay: Claude Jutra
Director: Claude Jutra
Cinematographers: Michel Brault, Jean-Claude Labrecque, Bernard Gosselin
Editor: Claude Jutra
Music: Jean Cousineau, Maurice Blackburn, Serge Garant
Production: Les Films Cassiopée and Orion Films
Cast: Johanne Harelle (Johanne), Claude Jutra (Claude), Victor Désy (Victor), Tania Fédor (Claude's mother), Guy Hoffmann (the priest), Monique Joly (Monique), Monique Mercure (Barbara), Patrick Straram (Nicholas), François Tissé (an actor)
(16mm, black and white, 99 min.)

——— PETIT DISCOURS DE LA MÉTHODE
Directors: Pierre Patry, Claude Jutra
Cinematographer: Georges Dufaux
Editor: Claude Jutra
Music: Maurice Blackburn
Producer: Fernand Dansereau
Production: National Film Board
(16mm, black and white, 27 min.)

1966 COMMENT SAVOIR (KNOWING TO LEARN)

> *Director*: Claude Jutra
> *Cinematographer*: Bernard Gosselin
> *Editor*: Claude Jutra, assisted by Werner Nold
> *Sound*: Marcel Carrière
> *Animation*: Pierre Hébert
> *Commentators*: Claude Jutra, Marie Josée Genin
> *Production*: National Film Board
> (16mm, black and white, 71 min.; also released in four parts)

—— ROULI-ROULANT (THE DEVIL S TOY)

> *Director*: Claude Jutra
> *Music*: Pierre F. Brault, sung by Geneviève Bujold
> *Commentator*: Charles Denner
> *Production*: Les Films Cassiopée for the National Film Board
> (16mm, black and white, 15 min.)

1969 WOW

> *Director*: Claude Jutra
> *Cinematographer*: Gilles Gascon, assisted by André Dupont
> *Editors*: Claude Jutra, Yves Dion, Claire Boyer
> *Music*: Jim Sokin, Pierre F. Brault
> *Sound*: Claude Hazanvicius, Claude Delorme
> *Producer*: Robert Forget
> *Production*: National Film Board
> *Cast*: Danielle Bail (Babette), Philippe Dubé (Flis), Michèle Mercure (Michelle), Dave Gold (Dave), Philippe Raoul (Philippe), Monique Simard (Monique), François Jasmin (François), Marc Harvey (Marc), Pierre Charpentier (Pierre)
> (16mm, colour/black and white, 95 min.)

1971 MON ONCLE ANTOINE

Screenplay: Clément Perron, Claude Jutra

Director: Claude Jutra

Cinematographer: Michel Brault

Editors: Claude Jutra, Claire Boyer

Music: Jean Cousineau

Sound: Claude Hazanvicius

Producer: Marc Beaudet

Production: National Film Board

Cast: Jacques Gagnon (Benoît), Lyne Champagne (Carmen), Jean Duceppe (Antoine), Olivette Thibaut (Cécile), Claude Jutra (Fernand), Lionel Villeneuve (Jos Poulin), Hélène Loiselle (Mme Poulin)

(35mm, colour, 104 min.)

1973 KAMOURASKA

Screenplay: Anne Hébert, Claude Jutra

Director: Claude Jutra

Cinematographers: Michel Brault, François Protat, Jean-Charles Tremblay

Editors: Renée Lichting, Françoise London, Madeleine Guérin, Susan Kay

Music: Maurice Le Roux

Sound: Serge Beauchemin, Jacques Blain

Producer: Pierre Lamy

Production: Les Productions Carle-Lamy (Montreal), Parc Film/UPF (Paris)

Cast: Geneviève Bujold (Elisabeth d'Aulnières), Richard Jordan (Georges Nelson), Marcel Cuvelier (Jérôme Rolland), Philippe Léotard (Antoine Tassy), Suzie Baillargeon (Aurélie Caron), Huguette Oligny (Elisabeth's mother), Janine Sutto, Olivette Thibault, Marie Fresnières (Elisabeth's aunts), Camille Bernard (Mme Tassy)

(35mm, colour, 124 min.; later released in a video version of 173 min.)

1975   POUR LE MEILLEUR ET POUR LE PIRE (FOR BETTER OR FOR WORSE)

Screenplay: Claude Jutra

Director: Claude Jutra

Cinematographer: Alain Dostie

Editors: Pascale Laverrière, Dominique Frischeteau

Music: Pierre F. Brault

Sound: Jacques Blain

Producer: Pierre Lamy

Production: Les Productions Carle-Lamy

Cast: Monique Miller (Hélène), Claude Jutra (Bernard), Monique Mercure (Loulou), Pierre Dufresne (Johnny), Gisèle Trépanier (the mad woman), Dominique Senez (Martine)

(35mm, colour/black and white, 117 min.)

1976   ADA

Screenplay: Claude Jutra, from a story by Margaret Gibson

Director: Claude Jutra

Cinematographer: Ken Gregg

Editor: Toni Trow

Music: Jean Cousineau

Sound: Tom Bilewney, Eric Lingren

Producer: Ralph L. Thomas

Production: Canadian Broadcasting Corporation

Cast: Janet Amos (Ada), Anne Anglin (Jenny), Kate Reid (Jenny's mother), Jayne Eastwood (Leslie), Connie Kaidor (Alice), Sabina Maydelle (the Virgin), Kay Hawtrey (Nurse Jamie), Miles Potter (Jenny's brother)

(16mm, colour, 58 min.)

—— DREAMSPEAKER

Screenplay: Cam Hubert (Anne Cameron)
Director: Claude Jutra
Cinematographer: John Seale
Editor: Toni Trow
Music: Jean Cousineau
Producer: Ralph L. Thomas
Production: Canadian Broadcasting Corporation
Cast: Ian Tracey (Peter), George Clutesi (old man), Jacques Hubert (silent man), Robert Howay (John), John Pallone (Bill), Anna Hagan (social worker)
(16mm, colour, 75 min.)

—— QUÉBEC FÊTE JUIN 75

Directors: Jean-Claude Labrecque, Claude Jutra
Cinematographer: Jean-Claude Labrecque
Editor: Claude Jutra
Sound: Jean Rival, Esther Auger
Producer: Louise Ranger
Production: Les Films Jean-Claude Labrecque
(16mm, colour, 65 min.)

1977   ARTS CUBA

Director: Claude Jutra
Cinematographer: Henri Fiks
Editor: Toni Trow
Sound: Aerlyn Weissman
Producer: Vivienne Leebosh
Production: Octopus Films
(16mm, colour, 58 min.)

1978 SEER WAS HERE

Screenplay: Don Bailey, Claude Jutra

Director: Claude Jutra

Cinematographer: John Seale

Editor: Toni Trow

Sound: Hans Fousek, Norm Rosen

Producer: Anne Frank

Production: Canadian Broadcasting Corporation

Cast: Saul Rubinek (Seer), Robert Forsythe (Birdwall), Mina E. Mina (Bullock), Eric Paterson (the Reverend Mr Wilson), Martin Short (Dummy), David Helman (Basque), Richard Norman (Helmet)

(16mm, colour, 57 min.)

1979 THE WORDSMITH

Screenplay: Mordecai Richler

Director: Claude Jutra

Cinematographer: Vic Sarin

Editor: Arla Saare

Sound: Bill Clements

Music: Peter Mann

Producer: Robert Sherrin

Production: Canadian Broadcasting Corporation

Cast: Saul Rubinek (Mervyn), Peter Boretski (Mr Hersh), Janet Ward (Mrs Hersh), Jeremy Zeitlin (Jake), Sherry Lewis (Molly)

(16mm, colour, 72 min.)

1980 SURFACING

Screenplay: Bernard Gordon, from the novel by Margaret Atwood
Director: Claude Jutra
Cinematographer: Richard Leiterman
Editor: Toni Trow
Sound: Christian Wangler
Music: Jean Cousineau, Ann Mortifee
Producer: Beryl Fox
Production: Surfacing Film Production Inc.
Cast: Joseph Bottoms (Joe), Kathleen Beller (Kate), R.H. Thompson (David), Margaret Dragu (Anna)
(35mm, colour, 88 min.)

1981 BY DESIGN

Screenplay: Joe Wiesenfeld, Claude Jutra
Director: Claude Jutra
Cinematographer: Jean Boffety
Editor: Toni Trow
Sound: Larry Sutton
Music: Chico Hamilton
Producers: Beryl Fox, Werner Allen
Production: B.D.F. Productions
Cast: Patty Duke Astin (Helen), Sara Botsford (Angie), Saul Rubinek (Terry), Sonia Zimmer (Suzie)
(35mm, colour, 91 min.)

1984 LA DAME EN COULEURS (THE LADY OF COLOURS)
Screenplay: Claude Jutra, Louis Rinfret
Director: Claude Jutra
Cinematographer: Thomas Vamos
Editor: Claire Boyer
Sound: Richard Besse, Esther Auger
Producers: Pierre Lamy
Production: Les Productions Pierre Lamy, National Film Board
Cast: Charlotte Laurier (Agnès), Paule Baillargeon (Sister Gertrude), Gilles
Renaud (Barbouilleux), Guillaume Lemay-Thivierge (Ti-cul), Ariane Frédérique
(Gisèle), François Méthé (Sebastien), Mario Spénard (Régis), Jean-François
Lesage (Ti-Loup), Grégory Lussier (Denis), Lisette Dufour (Françoise),
Martin Guay (Mario), Rita Lafontaine (Sister Honorine), Monique Mercure
(Mother Superior), Johanne Harelle (Sister Julienne)
(35mm, colour, 111 min.)

1985 MY FATHER, MY RIVAL
Screenplay: Marisa Gioffre
Director: Claude Jutra
Cinematographer: Douglas Kieffer
Editor: Ian McBride
Sound: Stuart French
Music: Fred Mollin
Producers: Iain Paterson
Production: Scholastic Productions, Insight Production Company
Cast: Lance Guest (Scott), Wendy Crewson (Hilah), Tom Hauff (Phillip),
Helen Hughes (Gussie), Andrew Gunn (Kelly)
(16mm, colour, 50 min.)

NOTES

CHAPTER ONE

1 Fox, "Considering *À tout prendre,*" 64.
2 For a fuller discussion of the meaning of the title and the problems of translating it into English, see chapter 4.
3 Knelman, *This is Where We Came In,* 55; both Knelman in the *Globe and Mail* and Dane Lanken in the *Montreal Gazette* referred to *Mon oncle Antoine* as "the great Canadian movie."
4 After being voted the best film ever made in Quebec in a poll of film critics by *Séquences* magazine in 1980, *Mon oncle Antoine* was honoured as the best Canadian film in similar polls conducted by the Toronto Festival of Festivals in 1984 and 1993. It was also voted best Quebec film in separate polls of critics and filmmakers at the Rendez-vous du cinéma québécois in 1993.
5 Evanchuk, "Claude Jutra – Filmmaker," 34.
6 Scott, "Jutra Reached the Peak." Long before Jutra's death, John Hofsess referred to the "unremitting discouragement and public neglect" from which he had suffered; see Hofsess, *Inner Views,* 39.
7 Johnson, "Sad Fade-out," 57. In this article, Brian Johnson quoted Gilles Carle, also a filmmaker and Jutra's neighbour, who insisted that no diagnosis had been made and blamed the suicide on "severe depression" caused mainly by Jutra's professional disappointments. On the other hand, Claire Boyer, who worked with Jutra as an editor on several of his films, revealed that his memory had deteriorated to the point that he "could not remember where he had parked his car a few hours earlier" and would forget his appointments "despite memos stuck to the wall"; see Boyer, "La Mémoire du cœur," 26.
8 Baty, *American Monroe,* 10.
9 Weinmann, *Cinéma de l'imaginaire québécois,* 127.
10 Elsaesser, *Fassbinder's Germany,* 13–18.

11 A specific reference to Aquin as a "martyr" can be found in Weinmann, *Cinéma de l'imaginaire québécois*, 97; the reasons for, and responses to, Aquin's suicide are explored in Sheppard and Yanacopoulo, *Signé Hubert Aquin*. See also Jacques Godbout's 1979 film *Deux épisodes dans la vie d'Hubert Aquin*.

12 Knelman, *This Is Where We Came In*, 55.

13 Johnson, "Sad Fade-out," 57.

14 Bordwell, *The Films of Carl-Theodor Dreyer*, 9.

15 Ibid., 10.

16 After *À tout prendre*, Jutra entered into negotiations with United Artists but was "discouraged by the vacillations of that impersonal enterprise"; see Favreau, "Pour Claude Jutra." Jutra later told a reporter that he was not a "go-getter" and did not know how to interest producers in his projects; see Scully, "Une Carrière."

17 Of course, discussions of authorship in cinema should always take into account the *auteur* theory first developed by the critics of *Cahiers du cinéma* in the 1950s. Their ideas certainly affected the way Jutra saw himself as a filmmaker, but I have chosen to address these issues more fully in my discussion of specific films.

18 Jutra, quoted in Hofsess, *Inner Views*, 51.

19 Jutra, quoted in Bonneville, ed., *Le Cinéma québécois*, 449; Lamy, "Claude Jutra," 15; Jutra quoted in Johnson, "Sad Fade-out," 57.

20 Jutra, quoted in Barrière, "Pour créer," 25.

21 Knelman, *This Is Where We Came In*, 55.

22 Jutra, quoted in Brulé, "Ressac canadien." In *À tout prendre*, Claude expresses the same fear, but presumably Jutra hoped that the film itself would disprove this theory.

23 Barrière, "Pour créer," 25.

24 Jutra, quoted in Johnson, "Sad Fade-out," 57.

25 Lamy, "Claude Jutra," 16.

26 Jutra, quoted in Bonneville, ed., *Le Cinéma québécois*, 449.

27 In this respect, Jutra's "legend" is probably closer to those of gay filmmakers in Hollywood's studio era, George Cukor and Dorothy Arzner, for example, than to those of contemporaries like Fassbinder, Andy Warhol, and Luchino Visconti.

28 Hofsess, *Inner Views*, 43.

29 Bonneville, ed., *Le Cinéma québécois*, 461.

30 Jutra, quoted in Pontaut, "Claude Jutra, cinéaste." Jutra's father helped to finance the publication in 1947 of one of the major literary texts associated with this new

outlook, Gabrielle Roy's *Bonheur d'occasion* (*The Tin Flute*); see Blouin, "Un coup de vent," 49.

31 Barrière, "Pour créer," 25.

32 Knelman, *This Is Where We Came In*, 58.

33 Jutra, quoted in Goyette, "Jutra's English Films," 26.

34 Jutra, quoted in Cox, "*Kamouraska*," 48.

35 Jutra, "À pied? à joual? …," 23.

36 Jutra, quoted in Delahaye, "Le nouvel âge," 109, 111.

37 Daudelin, *Vingt ans de cinéma*, 31. *Images en boîte* was transmitted in thirteen parts beginning on 30 June 1954, and *Cinéma canadien*, also in thirteen parts, beginning on 5 July 1961. Jutra also hosted a thirty-eight-part television series on the NFB transmitted on Radio-Québec from 1977–79.

38 Baudry, "The Apparatus," 313.

39 Jutra, quoted in Delahaye, "Le nouvel age," 112.

40 Jutra, quoted in Pontaut, "Claude Jutra, cinéaste."

41 Blouin, "Un coup de vent," 49.

42 Jutra, quoted in Pontaut, "Claude Jutra, cinéaste."

43 Ibid.

44 Lamy, "Claude Jutra," 15–16.

45 I have discussed these issues at greater length in my article "Lost Bodies and Missing Persons."

46 Higson, "The Concept of National Cinema," 37.

47 O'Regan, *Australian National Cinema*, 40.

48 Elsaesser, *Fassbinder's Germany*, 10.

49 Frye, *The Bush Garden* , 220.

50 Atwood, *Survival*, 18.

51 Frye, *The Bush Garden*, iii. I used Frye's concept in my discussion of another Canadian filmmaker in "Don Owen's Obliterated Environments."

52 Morley and Robins, "Spaces of Identity," 14.

53 Higson, "The Concept of National Cinema," 46.

54 Hofsess, *Inner Views*, 41.

55 Kracauer, *From Caligari to Hitler*, 5–6.

56 Weinmann, *Cinéma de l'imaginaire québécois*, 11. As we shall see, Morin was an early admirer of *À tout prendre*.

57 Ibid., 23. Perhaps the most influential English-Canadian attempt to use this symptomatic approach was Robert Fothergill's much-quoted essay, "Coward,

Bully, or Clown: The Dream-Life of a Younger Brother," first published in 1973 and reprinted in Feldman and Nelson, eds., *Canadian Film Reader*, 234–50.

58 Harcourt, "Introduction," 372–3. Harcourt here compares Canadian to British and US television drama, but he also refers to films in both languages. In an earlier article, Harcourt had argued that the "quality of suspended judgment, of something left open at the end, of something undecided" in the NFB's Unit B documentaries is "characteristically Canadian"; see "The Innocent Eye," 72, 74.

59 Jones, *Butterfly on Rock*, 14–15.

60 The reference is to the 1950 National Film Act as cited in Morris, *The Film Companion*, 283.

61 The postwar boom in film production in Quebec is most extensively discussed in Tremblay-Daviault, *Un Cinéma orphelin*.

62 See Morris, "After Grierson."

63 Weinmann, *Cinéma de l'imaginaire québécois*, 27–66. I discuss the ideological implications of *Alexis Tremblay Habitant* in my article "Habitant and Missionary."

64 The fullest treatment of the work of Unit B can be found in Jones, *The Best Butler in the Business*. The terms "direct cinema" and "*cinéma-vérité*" are often used to differentiate approaches that claim to offer a neutral observation of reality from those that stress the engagement of the filmmakers with the reality they are filming. Unfortunately, both terms have been applied to both approaches. In keeping with common (but by no means universal) Canadian usage, I have preferred to use the term direct cinema throughout to describe all the documentary strategies that paved the way for Canadian feature film production. For further discussion, see chapter 3.

65 The direction of *La Lutte*, a study of spectators at wrestling matches, was credited to Jutra along with Michel Brault, Claude Fournier, and Marcel Carrière. The director of *À Saint-Henri* was Hubert Aquin, who was then working at the NFB, and Jutra was among many filmmakers who recorded the activities of a working-class neighbourhood in Montreal on a single day. The English-language version of this film is heavily cut, and Jacques Godbout's poetic commentary has been replaced by a more conventional and prosaic one.

66 *Seul ou avec d'autres* was directed by Denis Héroux, Denys Arcand, and Stéphane Venne with the assistance of NFB filmmakers, including Gilles Groulx and Michel Brault.

67 Other successful films from this period include *Goin' Down the Road* (Don Shebib, 1970), *Paperback Hero* (Peter Pearson, 1973), *La vraie nature de Bernadette* (Gilles Carle, 1971), and *Réjeanne Padovani* (Denys Arcand, 1973).

68 A thoughtful account of Canadian film policy can be found in Magder, *Canada's Hollywood.*

69 A brief and lucid discussion of Lacan's use of these terms can be found in Stam et al., *New Vocabularies,* 128–33.

70 Jutra, quoted in Pontaut, "Claude Jutra, cinéaste."

71 Noguez, *Essais,* 178.

72 Marsolais, *Le Cinéma canadien,* 52.

73 Daudelin, "Gilles Groulx," 121.

74 Lever, *Histoire générale,* rev. ed., 210.

75 La Rochelle and Maggi, "Situation politique," 53.

76 Jutra, quoted in Johnson, "Sad Fade-out," 57, and in Evanchuk, "Claude Jutra," 18.

77 Euvrard and Queenan, "Parlez-vous Québécois," 46. Joan Fox suggested that "French-Canadian youth" lost interest in Jutra when *À tout prendre* revealed him to be an "idiosyncratic individualist" with no apparent political commitment; see "Considering *À tout prendre,*" 64.

78 Hofsess, *Inner Views,* 45–7.

79 Knelman, *This Is Where We Came In,* 55.

80 Jutra, quoted in Blouin, "Un coup de vent," 49.

81 Jutra, quoted in Chabot, ed., *Claude Jutra,* 6, 17.

82 Jutra's letter was published in *Le Devoir,* 25 November 1972.

83 Jutra, quoted in Scully, "Une carrière."

84 Jutra, quoted in Chabot, ed., *Claude Jutra,* 18.

85 Jutra, quoted in Talbot, "Jutra entre les deux solitudes …!"

86 Jutra, quoted in Blouin, "Un coup de vent," 46, 49.

87 Jutra, quoted in Barrière, "Pour créer," 25.

88 Marsolais, *Le Cinéma canadien,* 104. I have argued against Marsolais's position in my article "Second Images."

89 Clandfield, *Canadian Film,* 65.

90 Jutra, quoted in Knelman, *This Is Where We Came In,* 58.

91 Ibid., 57.

92 Jutra, quoted in Blouin, "Un coup de vent," 46–7.

93 Ibid., 49.

94 Hall, "Minimal Selves," 44.

95 Jutra, quoted in Delahaye, "Le nouvel age," 111; Jutra, "À pied? à joual? ...," 22.

96 Jutra, quoted in Favreau, "Claude Jutra."

97 Jutra, quoted in Delahaye, "Le nouvel age," 111.

98 Knelman, *This Is Where We Came In*, 55.

99 Lyotard, *The Postmodern Condition*, 15,37. Lyotard's influential book originated as a report commissioned by the Conseil des Universités of the Quebec government. In the light of Jutra's views on technology, it is worth noting that Lyotard attributes the decline in authoritative narratives to "the blossoming of techniques and technologies since the Second World War, which has shifted emphasis from the ends of action to its means" (ibid., 37).

100 Hutcheon, *The Canadian Postmodern*, 174–5, ix. Hutcheon's book deals with English-Canadian fiction, but similar arguments about the novel in Quebec can be found in Paterson, *Postmodernism.*

101 Hutcheson, *The Canadian Postmodern*, 2.

102 Söderlind, *Margin/Alias*, 5.

103 Hutcheon, *A Poetics of Postmodernism*, 4.

104 Hutcheon, *Splitting Images*, 140.

105 Jutra, quoted in Delahaye, "Le nouvel age," 109.

106 See "The World of Wrestling," in *Mythologies*, 15–25. For Barthes's collaboration with Aquin, see MacKenzie, "The Missing Mythology."

107 Olsen, "Roland Barthes," 166; Barthes, *The Grain of the Voice*, 201, 220.

108 Sturrock, "Roland Barthes," 53–4.

109 Connor, *Postmodernist Culture*, 87, 107. Hutcheon suggests that Barthes contributed to making the fragment "one of the major postmodernist forms"; see *The Canadian Postmodern*, 84.

110 Zizek, "Rossellini," 44. In an article on recent American documentary films, Paul Arthur has identified "a documentary 'aesthetics of failure'" that calls into question the authority of the filmmakers in relation to their subjects; see "Jargons of Authenticity," 128.

111 Margaret Atwood has argued that "when Canadian writers are writing clumsy or manipulated endings, they are much less likely to manipulate in a positive than they are in a negative direction"; see *Survival*, 34–5. Despite the temptation to imitate Hollywood, much the same has been true of Canadian cinema, as I argue in my article "Second Images."

112 Marcuse, *One-Dimensional Man*, 104.

113 Hofsess, *Inner Views*, 67–9.

114 Barthes, *Roland Barthes*, 172.

CHAPTER TWO

1 Jutra, quoted in Chabot, ed., *Claude Jutra*, 14.

2 McLaren, quoted in Elley, "Rhythm 'n' Truths," 34.

3 Harcourt, "Some Relationships," 142.

4 Newman, quoted in Elley, "Rhythm 'n' Truths", 32.

5 Harcourt, "Some Relationships," 138.

6 Jones, *Movies and Memoranda*, 77.

7 Lamy, "Claude Jutra," 18.

8 McLaren, quoted in Elley, "Rhythm 'n' Truths," 36.

9 Jutra, quoted in Bonneville, ed., *Le Cinéma québécois*, 447.

10 Noguez, *Essais*, 143.

11 Dansereau, quoted in Lafrance, *Cinéma d'ici*, 101.

12 Jodoin, quoted in ibid., 43.

13 Jutra, quoted in ibid., 76.

14 Jutra, quoted in Bonneville, ed., *Le Cinéma québécois*, 442.

15 Beaulieu, "À tout prendre," 19.

16 Jutra, quoted in Pontaut, "Claude Jutra, cinéaste."

17 Beaulieu, "À tout prendre," 21.

18 Jutra, quoted in Pontaut, "Claude Jutra, cinéaste."

19 Ibid.

20 Morris, "After Grierson," 185.

21 Ibid., 187.

22 Brault, quoted in Bonneville, ed., *Le Cinéma québécois*, 131.

23 James, *Film as a National Art*, 307.

24 Mills, *White Collar*, xvi, 349.

25 Ibid., 349.

26 Brault, quoted in Bonneville, ed., *Le Cinéma québécois*, 131.

27 Throughout this book I will use the term "classical narrative cinema" as a convenient shorthand for a set of norms and conventions that became the basis for what was recognized as film "language" in commercial filmmaking in Hollywood and elsewhere. For a full discussion of the range of choices and constraints covered by the term, see Bordwell, *Narration*, 156–204. One of the most

important norms of classical narrative cinema is the shot/reverse shot structure, often used in dialogue sequences, in which a shot of one character looking off screen is followed by a shot of another character looking in the opposite direction.

28 Brault, quoted in Bonneville, ed., *Le Cinéma québécois*, 131.

29 Rouch, quoted in Cameron and Shivas, "Cinéma-vérité," 23.

30 James, *Film as a National Art*, 312. The films produced under the "Profils et pay-sages" title were presented on television as part of the ongoing series "Temps present" (1957–64), which would later include the key direct cinema films produced by the NFB's French Unit.

CHAPTER THREE

1 Jutra, "En courant derrière Rouch."

2 Daudelin, *Vingt ans de cinéma*, 32.

3 Jutra, "Anna La Bonne," 10.

4 Jutra, "En courant derrière Rouch: 1," 33.

5 Marsolais, *L'Aventure du cinéma direct*, 180.

6 Comolli and Narboni, "Cinema/Ideology/Criticism," 28.

7 Rouch, quoted in Yakir, "*Ciné-transe*," 7–8. In the United States, "direct cinema" more often refers to the observational approach and "*cinéma-vérité*" to films that acknowledge the impact of the filmmakers on the subjects of the film.

8 Lamy, "Claude Jutra," 18. "Candid Eye" was the title of a series of thirteen Unit B documentaries broadcast by the CBC in 1958 and 1959; see Morris, *The Film Companion*, 53–4.

9 Jutra, quoted in Lafrance, *Cinéma d'ici*, 74–5; Rouch, "The Camera and Man," 56.

10 Rouch thought the shot was Brault's, but Brault himself has described how Wolf Koenig picked up the camera and held it just behind the guard's gun as he walked towards the armoured car; see Jones, *The Best Butler in the Business*, 107.

11 Rouch, "The Camera and Man," 57.

12 Cameron and Shivas, "Cinéma-vérité," 12–13.

13 An excellent and thorough discussion of the ways in which perspective has shaped attitudes to images and sight can be found in Jay, *Downcast Eyes*.

14 Rouch, "The Camera and Man," 56.

15 Rouch, quoted in Yakir, "*Ciné-transe*," 11.

16 Jutra, "En courant derrière Rouch: 1," 32.

17 Jutra, quoted in Lafrance, *Cinéma d'ici*, 94.

18 Jutra, "En courant derrière Rouch: 3," 39.

19 Elder, "On the Candid-Eye Movement," 93.

20 Jutra, quoted in Daudelin and Patenaude, "Michel Brault," 7.

21 Ibid.

22 Delahaye and Rivette, "Entretien avec Claude Lévi-Strauss," 26.

23 Fieschi, "Slippages of Fiction," 67.

24 Ibid., 69, 73.

25 Eaton, "Production," 43.

26 Jutra, quoted in Bonneville, ed., *Le Cinéma québécois*, 447.

27 Jutra, "En courant derrière Rouch: 2," 32.

28 Véronneau, "1956–1960," 17.

29 Daudelin, *Vingt ans de cinéma*, 32.

30 Brulé, "Ressac canadien."

31 *La Presse*, "Le Niger."

32 In this respect, the film anticipates the more extreme depiction of the plight of francophones in Quebec in Pierre Vallières' *White Niggers of America*, first published in 1968.

33 *La Presse*, "Le Niger."

34 Rohmer and Marcorelles, "Entretien avec Jean Rouch," 22. The abbreviated English-language version of *Pour la suite du monde* was released as *Moontrap*, a title that eliminates the connotations of tradition and continuity in the original.

35 Lefebvre and Pilon, "L'Équipe française," 45–6.

36 Ibid., 47–53.

37 Clandfield, "From the Picturesque," 51.

38 Ibid.

39 Carle, quoted in Marsolais, *Le Cinéma canadien*, 64.

40 Clandfield, "From the Picturesque," 51.

41 Ibid., 53; Jutra described his role in making this film in Lafrance, *Cinéma d'ici*, 82–3.

42 Daudelin, *Vingt ans de cinéma*, 32–3.

43 Fournier, "*La Lutte*," 19.

44 Morris, *The Film Companion*, 2.

CHAPTER FOUR

1 Jutra, "Les 101 questions," 24.

2 Jutra, quoted in Bonneville, ed., *Le Cinéma québécois*, 449.

3 Lacan, "Television," 7.

4 Young, "Review," 156.

5 Noguez, *Essais*, 33; Marsolais, "Entretien avec Jean Rouch," 25.

6 Jutra, quoted in Delahaye, "Le nouvel age," 110.

7 Ibid., 109–10.

8 *La Presse*, "*À tout prendre*."

9 Jutra, quoted in Chabot, ed., *Claude Jutra*, 9.

10 Ibid., 11.

11 Ibid., 10.

12 Young, "Review," 155.

13 Jutra, quoted in Chabot, ed., *Claude Jutra*, 9–10.

14 Jutra, quoted in Pontaut, "Claude Jutra et Pierre Patry."

15 Marcorelles, "Lettre de Montréal," 47.

16 René Prédal, *Jeune cinéma canadien*, 63.

17 Simon, *Private Screenings*, 256–7.

18 Young, "Review," 153, 155.

19 Jutra, "Les 101 questions," 25.

20 Patenaude, "*À tout prendre*," 43.

21 Jutra, quoted in Chabot, ed., *Claude Jutra*, 6.

22 Basile, "*À tout prendre*."

23 Marsolais, *Le Cinéma canadien*, 84.

24 Bonneville, "Le Cinéma canadien," 14.

25 Arcand, "Cinéma et sexualité," 94, 96.

26 Jutra, quoted in Young, "Review," 155.

27 Carrière, "Les Images de femmes," 64.

28 Crowther, "*Take It All*."

29 See, for example, Marsolais, *Le Cinéma canadien*, 82.

30 In a later sequence, the camera does move towards an open window to peer in on Johanne, who welcomes it, but this may be a subjective shot from Claude's viewpoint.

31 Fox, "Considering *À tout prendre*," 63–4.

32 Marcorelles, "Lettre de Montréal," 47.

33 De Laurot, "From Logos to Lens," 580–1.

34 Lefebvre, "La Crise du langage," 27. Although Lefebvre does mention *Nobody Waved Good-bye* in his conclusion, the article deals essentially with the Quebec situation.

35 Ibid., 28–9.

36 Ibid., 29.

37 Daudelin, "Gilles Groulx," 120.

38 Jutra, quoted in Bonneville, ed., *Le Cinéma québécois*, 449.

39 Jutra, "Les 101 questions," 26.

40 Constanzo, "The Persistence of Proust," 169.

41 Marsolais, *Le Cinéma canadien*, 80.

42 Patenaude, "*À tout prendre*," 42; Marsolais, *Le Cinéma canadien*, 84.

43 Jutra, "En courant derrière Rouch: 2," 26.

44 Fox, "Considering *À tout prendre*," 64.

45 Moffat, "*À tout prendre*," 154.

46 Fox, "Considering *À tout prendre*," 64.

47 These responsibilities are, of course, heightened by the prospect of becoming a
father, a version of adulthood that Claude sees as a trap. His refusal of fatherhood may be partially attributed to his discovery of his homosexuality, but it is
given a cultural dimension through its link to the motif of the absent father in
Quebec literature (soon to become equally prevalent in the new cinema).

CHAPTER FIVE

1 *La Presse*, "Claude Jutra: Tout prendre!"

2 Favreau, "Pour Claude Jutra." Columbia had, however, acquired international
distribution rights for *À tout prendre*; see, Dorland, *So Close to the State/s*, 95.

3 Jutra, quoted in *La Presse*, "Claude Jutra: Tout prendre!"

4 Tadros, "*Wow* de Claude Jutra."

5 Ibid.

6 Blumer, "*Wow*," 28.

7 Cameron, ed., *Second Wave*, 5.

8 Demers, "L'Alternative," 24.

9 Carrière, "Les Images de femmes," 95; Jutra, quoted in Hofsess, *Inner Views*, 44.

10 Favreau, "Claude Jutra."

11 Jutra, quoted in Tadros, "Claude Jutra."

12 Jutra, quoted in Delahaye, "Le nouvel age," 113.

13 Ibid.

14 Jutra, quoted in Tadros, "Claude Jutra."

15 Tadros, "*Wow* de Claude Jutra."

16 Carrière, "Les Images de femmes," 95.

17 Blumer, "*Wow*," 28.

18 Tadros, "*Wow* de Claude Jutra."

19 Jutra, quoted in Delahaye, "Le nouvel age," 113.

20 Lever, *Cinéma et société québécoise*, 149.

21 Jutra, quoted in *La Presse*, "Claude Jutra: Tout prendre!"

22 Jutra, quoted in Chabot, ed., *Claude Jutra*, 9.

23 Jutra, quoted in Bonneville, ed., *Le Cinéma québécois*, 452–3.

24 Tadros, "*Wow* de Claude Jutra"; Blumer, "*Wow*," 28.

25 Jutra, quoted in Tadros, "Claude Jutra."

26 Noguez, *Essais*, 133.

27 Jutra, quoted in *La Presse*, "Claude Jutra: Tout prendre!"

28 Jutra, quoted in Chabot, *Claude Jutra*, 16.

29 Jutra, quoted in Favreau, "Claude Jutra."

30 Jutra, quoted in Chabot, ed., *Claude Jutra*, 15.

31 Jutra, quoted in *La Presse*, "Claude Jutra: Tout prendre!"

32 Jutra, quoted in Bonneville, ed., *Le Cinéma québécois*, 451.

33 Noguez, *Essais*, 130–1, 134.

34 Ibid., 127–9.

35 Tadros, "*Wow* de Claude Jutra."

36 Noguez, *Essais*, 130.

37 Jutra, quoted in Chabot, ed., *Claude Jutra*, 13, and in Tadros, "Claude Jutra."

38 Jutra, quoted in Tadros, "Claude Jutra."

39 Jutra, quoted in *La Presse*, "Claude Jutra: Tout prendre!"

40 Jutra, quoted in Tadros, "Claude Jutra."

41 Tadros, "*Wow* de Claude Jutra."

42 Jutra, quoted in Tadros, "Claude Jutra."

43 Jutra, quoted in Chabot, ed., *Claude Jutra*, 15.

44 Ibid., 13.

45 Jutra, quoted in Tadros, "Claude Jutra."

46 Jutra, quoted in Favreau, "Pour Claude Jutra."

47 Blumer, "*Wow*," 28.

48 McLuhan argued that print and film are "hot" media, densely saturated with information that audiences must simply absorb, while "cool" media, such as television, are low density and invite viewers to fill in the gaps in the information provided; see, especially, *Understanding Media*, chapter 2.

49 Meyrowitz, *No Sense of Place*, 226.

50 Morris, *The Film Companion*, 99.

51 Richardson, quoted in Morris, *The Film Companion*, 60–1.

52 Barthes, *Image Music Text*, 147–8.

53 Holub, *Jürgen Habermas*, 108.

CHAPTER SIX

1 Tadros, "Claude Jutra, Clément Perron."

2 Evans, *In the National Interest*, 208.

3 Knelman, *This Is Where We Came In*, 51.

4 Jutra, quoted in Bonneville, ed., *Le Cinéma québécois*, 454, 459.

5 Fontaine, "Un moment," 4.

6 Beard, "*Mon Oncle Antoine*," 12.

7 Viswanathan, "Approche pédagogique," 856.

8 Tadros, "À la découverte."

9 Knelman, *This Is Where We Came In*, 57, 51.

10 Noguez, *Essais*, 207.

11 Harcourt, "Introduction," 372.

12 *La Presse*, "Claude Jutra: Tout prendre!"

13 Jutra quoted in Bujold et al., "Interviews," 48.

14 Weinberg, "Reflections," 33.

15 Elder, "Claude Jutra's *Mon oncle Antoine*," 194–5.

16 Tadros, "À la découverte."

17 Leduc, "La Québécitude," 13.

18 See, for example, Houle and Julien, eds., *Dictionnaire*, 191, and Lever, *Histoire générale*, rev. ed., 275.

19 Tadros, "À la découverte."

20 Houle and Julien, eds., *Dictionnaire*, 191.

21 Viswanathan, "Approche pédagogique," 851.

22 Elder, "Claude Jutra's *Mon oncle Antoine*," 198.

23 Leduc, "La Québécitude," 13.

24 Jutra, quoted in Bonneville, ed., *Le Cinéma québécois*, 457.

25 Therrien, "L'Éros du regard," 38. Laura Mulvey's article "Visual Pleasure and Narrative Cinema" can be found in many anthologies, including Rosen, ed., *Narrative, Apparatus, Ideology*, 198–209.

26 Elder, "Claude Jutra's *Mon oncle Antoine*," 197.

27 Even, "Un Antoine Doinel québécois."

28 Atwood, *Survival*, 222–3.

29 Weinmann, *Cinéma de l'imaginaire québécois*, 88.

30 Leduc, "La Québécitude," 13.

31 Jutra, quoted in Bonneville, ed., *Le Cinéma québécois*, 455.

32 Jutra, quoted in Tadros, "Claude Jutra."

33 Bonneville, "Hommage à Claude Jutra," 14.

34 Weinmann, *Cinéma de l'imaginaire québécois*, 81.

35 Weinberg, "Reflections," 33.

36 Weinmann, *Cinéma de l'imaginaire québécois*, 73.

37 Jutra, quoted in Even, "Un Antoine Doinel québécois."

38 Knelman, *This Is Where We Came In*, 47–8.

39 Fontaine, "Un moment," 4–5.

40 Jutra, quoted in Even, "Un Antoine Doinel québécois."

41 Tadros, "Claude Jutra."

42 Even, "Un Antoine Doinel québécois."

43 Jutra, quoted in Even, "Un Antoine Doinel québécois."

44 Jutra, quoted in Tadros, "Claude Jutra."

45 Jutra, quoted in Even, "Un Antoine Doinel québécois."

CHAPTER SEVEN

1 I have discussed the Canadian genre films of this period in "The Body Snatchers."

2 Jutra, quoted in Talbot, "Jutra entre les deux solitudes …!"

3 Turner, "The Genres are American," 104–5.

4 Ibid., 105.

5 Perreault, "À la recherche de l'enfance."

6 Lamy, "Claude Jutra," 17; Jutra, quoted in Hofsess, *Inner Views*, 51.

7 Coulombe and Jean, eds., *Dictionnaire*, 281.

8 Thompson, "*Kamouraska*," 26.

9 Lord Durham, quoted in Wade, *The French Canadians*, vol. 1, 212.

10 Hébert, *Kamouraska*, 44.

11 Jutra, quoted in Perreault, "Une grosse machine."

12 Hofsess, *Inner Views*, 45.

13 Houle and Julien, eds., *Dictionnaire*, 147.

14 Scully, "L'œuvre"; Perreault, "À la recherche de l'enfance."

15 Vallières, "Les Critiques."

16 Evanchuk, "An Innerview," 22.

17 Jutra, quoted in Perreault, "À la recherche de l'enfance."

18 Higson, "Re-presenting the National Past," 122.

19 Jutra, quoted in Perreault, "Une grosse machine."

20 Jutra, quoted in Perreault, "À la recherche de l'enfance."

21 Barthes, *Mythologies*, 129.

22 Buck-Morss, *The Dialectics of Seeing*, 78.

23 Scully, La superproduction"; Knelman, *This Is Where We Came In*, 52.

24 Shuster, "*Kamouraska*," 28.

25 Lefebvre, "La cohérence," 44.

26 Knelman, *This Is Where We Came In*, 53.

27 Lamy, "Claude Jutra," 17.

28 Hébert, quoted in Tadros, "L'œuvre écrite."

29 Petric, "Le cinéma québécois," 38.

30 Jutra, quoted in Tadros, "L'œuvre écrite." The comparison with *Gone with the Wind* appeared in several articles by Robert Guy Scully.

31 Jutra, quoted in Perreault, "À la recherche de l'enfance."

32 Evanchuk, "An Innerview," 22.

33 Russell, *Anne Hébert*, 135n.38.

34 Harvey, *Une écriture*, 12–13.

35 Shuster, "*Kamouraska*," 28.

36 Scully, "L'œuvre."

37 Scully, "La superproduction."

38 Harvey, *Une écriture*, 115, 9.

39 Hébert, quoted in Tadros, "L'œuvre écrite."

40 Jutra, quoted in Tadros, "Une espèce de joie," 16.

41 Jutra, quoted in Perreault, "Une grosse machine."

42 Perreault, "Copie trop conforme."

43 Fulford, *Marshall Delaney at the Movies*, 74–5.

44 Jutra, quoted in Perreault, "Une grosse machine."

45 Jutra, quoted in Tadros, "Une espèce de joie."

46 Perreault, "Copie trop conforme."

47 Jutra, quoted in Bujold et al., "Interviews," 49.

48 Jutra, quoted in Tadros, "Une espèce de joie," 19. Jutra replaced the original music by Maurice Le Roux with a new score by André Gagnon when he prepared the video version.

49 Jutra, quoted in Perreault, "Une grosse machine."

50 Bazin, *What Is Cinema?*, 13.

51 Baudry, "The Apparatus," 311.

52 Hébert, *Kamouraska*, 7–11.

53 Tadros, "L'œuvre écrite."

54 Hébert, *Kamouraska*, 9–10.

55 Ibid., 12.

56 Jutra, quoted in Tadros, "Une espèce de joie," 16.

57 Perreault, "Copie trop conforme."

58 Hébert, quoted in Tadros, "L'œuvre écrite."

59 Jutra, quoted in Tadros, "Une espèce de joie," 19, 16.

60 Tadros, "*Kamouraska*."

61 Hébert, quoted in Tadros, "L'œuvre écrite."

62 Vallières, "Les Critiques."

63 Jutra, quoted in Perreault, "À la recherche de l'enfance."

64 Hofsess, *Inner Views*, 47–8.

65 Knelman, *This Is Where We Came In*, 53.

66 The intrusion of English into the French text also occurs in the novel but the effect is, of course, lost in the translation, as in the dubbed version of the film (in which it was felt necessary to correct the clerk's pronunciation).

67 Hofsess, *Inner Views*, 45–7.

68 Jutra, quoted in Perreault, "À la recherche de l'enfance."

CHAPTER EIGHT

1 Perreault, "Jutra."

2 Jutra, quoted in Laurendeau, "De *Pour la meilleur*," 6–7.

3 *La Presse*, "Cinq long métrages québécois."

4 Jutra, quoted in Delahaye, "Le nouvel age," 112.

5 Ibid.

6 Bonneville, ed., "*Le Cinéma québécois*," 462.

7 Elia, "*Pour le meilleur*," 26–7.

8 Edell, "Films," 46.

9 Denton, "Claude Jutra's *Pour le meilleur*," 54.

10 Gay and Laurendeau, "Claude Jutra," 12.

11 Coulombe and Jean, eds., *Dictionnaire*, 282.

12 The "unstable mixture" may owe something to Bergman's farcical but dark comedy, *Now about All These Women* (1964), which was also very unsettling for many critics.

13 See Dyer, "Entertainment and Utopia."

14 Albee's play was enormously successful and was quickly and faithfully adapted in Mike Nichols's film version (1966), starring Elizabeth Taylor and Richard Burton.

15 Jutra, quoted in Laurendeau, "De *Pour la meilleur*," 7.

16 See, for example, Leroux, "*Pour la meilleur*", and Elia, "*Pour le meilleur*," 27.

17 Jutra, quoted in Laurendeau, "De *Pour la meilleur*," 6.

18 Gay and Laurendeau, "Claude Jutra," 11.

19 Jutra, quoted in Laurendeau, "De *Pour la meilleur*," 6.

20 Gay and Laurendeau, "Claude Jutra," 11.

21 Ibid., 13.

22 Jutra, quoted in Laurendeau, "De *Pour la meilleur*," 6.

23 Leroux, "*Pour la meilleur*."

24 Benjamin, *Illuminations*, 239–41.

25 Jutra, quoted in Laurendeau, "De *Pour la meilleur*," 6.

26 Ibid.

27 Gay and Laurendeau, "Claude Jutra," 13.

28 Brecht, "Literalization," 44.

29 Gay and Laurendeau, "Claude Jutra," 11; Leroux, "*Pour la meilleur*."

30 Coulombe and Jean, eds., *Dictionnaire*, 281.

31 Jutra, quoted in Laurendeau, "De *Pour la meilleur*," 6.

32 Leroux, "*Pour la meilleur*."

33 Edell, "Films," 47.

34 Coulombe and Jean, eds., *Dictionnaire*, 281.

35 Albee has rejected this interpretation; see Rutenberg, *Edward Albee*, 234–5. It is perhaps worth noting that "Rio Rita" may be an allusion not only to Hollywood musicals but also to the "homosexual navvy" who goes by that name in Brendan Behan's play *The Hostage* (1958).

CHAPTER NINE

1 Morris, *The Film Companion*, 55.

2 Henley, "On the Record," 18.

3 Gervais, "Lightyears Ahead," 35.

4 Henley, "On the Record," 19.

5 Gervais, "Lightyears Ahead," 35.

6 See Feldman, "Footnote to Fact," 344.

7 Thomas, "Comment Claude Jutra …," 34.

8 Knelman, *This Is Where We Came In*, 61–2.

9 Goyette, "Jutra's English Films," 25.

10 Gervais, "Lightyears Ahead," 36.

11 Goyette, "Jutra's English Films," 26.

12 Barrière, "Pour créer."

13 Knelman, *This Is Where We Came In*, 61.

14 Laing, *The Politics of Experience*, 100.

15 Gibson, *The Butterfly Ward*, 22.

16 Cousineau, "Un très beau film."

17 Reif, quoted in Erickson, "To Be a Writer," 8.

18 Hubert, *Dreamspeaker*, 1, 45, 52.

19 Ibid., 1, 3–4.

20 Ibid., 45.

21 Ibid., 2–3.

22 Ibid., 35–6, 76–7.

23 Ibid., 26, 28.

24 Miller, *Turn Up the Contrast*, 241.

25 Hubert, *Dreamspeaker*, 85.

26 Morris, *The Film Companion*, 90.

CHAPTER TEN

1 Thomas, "Comment Claude Jutra …," 34.

2 Conlogue, "Jutra surfaces."

3 Hofsess, *Inner Views*, 70.

4 Coburn, "Thumbs Up," 19.

5 Hynam, "Beryl Fox," 27.

6 Conlogue, "Jutra surfaces."

7 Fox, quoted in Coburn, "Thumbs Up," 19.

8 Knelman, "Mum's the Word," 22.

9 Frye, *The Bush Garden*, iii.

10 Atwood, *Surfacing*, 59.

11 Ibid., 129.

12 Atwood, quoted in Grace, "Articulating the 'Space Between,'" 11.

13 Fox, quoted in Coburn, "Thumbs Up," 19.

14 Atwood, *Surfacing*, 168, 192.

15 Ibid., 192.

16 Jacobowitz, "*Surfacing*," 35.

17 Ibid.

18 Ibid.

19 Atwood, *Surfacing*, 116.

20 There are two versions of this sequence: one in which Anna dances naked, and another in which she wears a brief bikini, the latter version filmed apparently with television sales in mind.

21 Rao, *Strategies for Identity*, 41.

22 Hynam, "Beryl Fox," 26.

23 Bartosh, "In Progress," 41.

24 Szporer, "Claude Jutra's *By Design*," 43.

25 Knelman, "Mum's the Word," 21, 23.

26 Kael, *Taking It All In*, 421.

27 Knelman, "Mum's the Word," 22–3; Pratley, "Canada," 89.

28 Kael, *Taking It All In*, 421–3.

29 Szporer, "Claude Jutra's *By Design*," 43.

30 Schupp, "*By Design*," 29.

31 Kael, *Taking It All In*, 421, 424.

32 Ibid., 423.

33 Ibid.

34 Knelman, "Mum's the Word," 23.

CHAPTER ELEVEN

1 Johnson, "Sad Fade-out," 57.

2 Dorland, "*La Dame en couleurs*," 27.

3 Lever, *Histoire générale*, (1988) 325. The passage quoted appears as a caption to a still from the film omitted from the revised edition; similar comments, however, are found in the revised text, 352. Dorland also thought that there were continuity problems but attributed them to the effects of editing an original three-hour version.

4 Lockerbie, "Le cinéma québécois," 17.

5 Rinfret, "La complicité d'un magicien," 32.

6 Jean, *Le Cinéma québécois*, 282.

7 The appearance of Johanne Harelle and Monique Mercure in small roles as two of the nuns adds to the sense of a film designed to evoke memories of the director's earlier work. The two women had appeared together in *À tout prendre*, and Mercure had supporting roles in *Mon oncle Antoine* and *Pour le meilleur et pour le pire*.

8 Goyette, "Jutra's English Films," 26.

9 Corbeil, "Jutra Film a Gem."

10 Dorland, "*La Dame en couleurs*," 27.

11 Beaulieu, "*La Dame en couleurs*," 82.

12 Jean-Claude Lauzon's *Léolo* (1992), for example, deals with a young boy's attempt to escape his grotesque working-class family by constructing an elaborate fantasy world in which he is really Italian.

13 See, for example, Marie-Claire Blais, *Une Saison dans la vie d'Emmanuel* (1965), translated by Derek Coltman as *A Season in the Life of Emmanuel* (New York: Farrar, Straus and Giroux, 1966); Réjean Ducharme, *L'Avalée des avalés* (1967), translated by Barbara Bray as *The Swallower Swallowed* (London: Hamish Hamilton, 1968), and André Langevin, *Une Chaîne dans le parc* (1974), translated by Alan Brown as *Orphan Street* (Toronto: McClelland and Stewart, 1976).

14 Quigley, *The Child Hero*, 129.

15 Dorland, "*La Dame en couleurs*," 27.

16 Lever, *Histoire générale*, rev. ed., 376. Denis Bellemare also compared Jutra's film to *La Petite Aurore* in "La mélancolie et le banal," 9.

17 Tremblay-Daviault, *Un Cinéma orphelin*.

18 Beaulieu, "*La Dame en couleurs*," 82.

19 Beaulieu, "À tout prendre," 23.

20 Beaulieu, "*La Dame en couleurs*," 82.

21 Dorland, "*La Dame en couleurs*," 27–8.

22 Corbeil, "Jutra Film a Gem."

23 Beaulieu, "*La Dame en couleurs*," 82.

24 Jutra, quoted in Blouin, "Un coup de vent," 49.

25 Dorland, "*La Dame en couleurs*," 27.

26 Beaulieu, "*La Dame en couleurs*," 82.

27 Lockerbie, "Le cinéma québécois," 11, 19.

28 Ibid., 17.

29 Dorland, "*La Dame en couleurs*," 28.

1 Brûlé, "Ressac canadien."
2 Dorland, *So Close to the State/s,* 7.
3 Ibid., 6; Feldman and Nelson, eds., *Canadian Film Reader,* x.
4 Jutra, quoted in Knelman, *This Is Where We Came In,* 58.
5 Vallières, *White Niggers of America,"* 17.
6 Fothergill, "Coward, Bully, or Clown, 246.
7 Feldman and Nelson, eds., *Canadian Film Reader,* ix.
8 Elsaesser, "Chronicle of a Death Retold," 166.
9 Hall, quoted in Grossberg, ed., "On Postmodernism," 132. Parts of this paragraph are taken from a longer discussion of these issues in my article "Lost Bodies and Missing Persons."
10 Hall, "Minimal Selves," 45.
11 Harcourt, "Faces Changing Colour," 7–8.
12 Hutcheon, *The Poetics of Postmodernism,* 13, 20.

BIBLIOGRAPHY

Arcand, Denys. "Cinéma et sexualité." *Parti pris* 9–11 (Summer 1964): 90–7.

Arthur, Paul. "Jargons of Authenticity (Three American Moments)." In *Theorizing Documentary*, edited by Michael Renov, 108–34. New York: Routledge, 1993.

Atwood, Margaret. *Surfacing*. New York: Simon and Schuster, 1972.

– *Survival: A Thematic Guide to Canadian Literature*. Toronto: Anansi, 1972.

Barrière, Louise. "Pour créer Claude Jutra ne se limite pas au cinéma." *Téléspec* (31 March 1977).

Barthes, Roland. *Mythologies*. Trans. Annette Lavers. London: Jonathan Cape, 1972.

– *Image Music Text*. Trans. Stephen Heath. London: Fontana, 1977.

– *Roland Barthes By Roland Barthes*. Trans. Richard Howard. New York: Hill and Wang,, 1977.

– *The Grain of the Voice: Interviews 1962–1980*. Trans. Linda Coverdale. Berkeley: University of California Press, 1985.

Bartosh, Glenda. "In Progress: *By Design*." *Cinema Canada* 73 (April 1981): 41.

Basile, Jean. "*À tout prendre*, de Jutra, au Festival." *Le Devoir* (Montreal), 12 August 1963.

Baty, S. Paige. *American Monroe: The Making of a Body Politic*. Berkeley: University of California Press, 1995.

Baudry, Jean. "The Apparatus: Metapsychological Approaches to the Impression of Reality in Cinema." In *Narrative, Apparatus, Ideology: A Film Theory Reader*, edited by Philip Rosen, 299–318. New York: Columbia University Press, 1986.

Bazin, André. *What is Cinema?* Trans. Hugh Gray. Berkeley: University of California Press, 1967.

Beard, David. "*Mon Oncle Antoine: Silent Night*." *Canadian Forum* (April 1972): 12–13.

Beaulieu, Janick. "*Mon oncle Antoine*." *Séquences* 67 (December 1971): 14–18.

– "*La Dame en couleurs*." *Séquences* 120 (April 1985): 81–2.

– "À tout prendre, les films de Claude Jutra sont là pour qu'on en garde mémoire." *Séquences* 131 (October 1987): 19–23.

Bellemare, Denis. "La mélancolie et le banal." *Dérives* 52 (1986): 7–24.

Benjamin, Walter. *Illuminations.* Trans. Harry Zohn. New York: Schocken Books, 1968.

Bhabha, Homi K., et al. *The Real Me: Post-Modernism and the Question of Identity.* London: Institute of Contemporary Arts, 1987.

Billard, Jean Antonin. "À Claude Jutra." *24 Images* 36 (1987): 52–3.

Blouin, Jean. "Un coup de vent nommé Claude Jutra." *L'Actualité* 5, no. 1 (January 1980): 45–9.

Blumer, Ronald. "*Wow.*" *Take One* 2, no. 5 (May 1970): 28.

– "*Mon oncle Antoine.*" *Take One* 3, no. 1 (December 1971): 25.

Bonneville, Léo. "Le Cinéma canadien à l'heure de la révolution québécoise." *Séquences* 40 (February 1965): 12–19.

– "Hommage à Claude Jutra." *Séquences* 131 (October 1987): 14.

Bonneville, Léo, ed. *Le Cinéma québécois par ceux qui le font.* Montreal: Éditions Paulines, 1979.

Bordwell, David. *The Films of Carl-Theodor Dreyer.* Berkeley: University of California Press, 1981.

– *Narration in the Fiction Film.* Madison: University of Wisconsin Press, 1985.

Boyer, Claire. "La Mémoire du cœur." *CopieZéro* 33 (September 1987): 26.

Brecht, Bertolt. "The Literalization of the Theatre (Notes to the *Threepenny Opera*)." In *Brecht on Theatre*, edited by John Willet, 43–7. New York: Hill and Wang, 1964.

Brulé, Michel. "Ressac canadien de la nouvelle vague." *Le Nouveau Journal* (Montreal), 3 March 1962.

Buck-Morss, Susan. *The Dialectics of Seeing: Walter Benjamin and the Arcades Project.* Cambridge, MA: MIT Press, 1991.

Bujold, Geneviève, and Claude Jutra. "Entretiens." *Cinéma Québec* 2, nos. 6–7 (March-April 1973): 12–19.

Bujold, Geneviève, Michel Brault, and Claude Jutra. "Interviews." *Cinema Canada* 7 (April-May 1973): 42–50.

Cameron, Ian, ed. *Second Wave: Newer than New Wave Names in World Cinema.* London: Studio Vista, 1970.

Cameron, Ian, and Mark Shivas. "Cinéma-vérité." *Movie* 8 (1963): 12–15.

Carrière, Louise. "Les images de femmes dans le cinéma masculin: 1960–1983." In *Femmes et cinéma québécois*, edited by Louise Carrière, 53–112. Montreal: Boréal Express, 1983.

Carrière, Louise, ed. *Femmes et cinéma québécois.* Montreal: Boréal Express, 1983.

Chabot, Claude, and Denise Pérusse, eds. *Cinéma et sexualité.* Quebec City: Prospec, 1988.

Chabot, Claude, Michel Larouche, Denise Pérusse, and Pierre Véronneau, eds. *Le Cinéma Québécois des Années 80*. Montreal: Cinémathèque Québécoise, 1989.

Chabot, Jean, ed. *Claude Jutra*. Montreal: Conseil québécois pour la diffusion du cinéma, 1970.

Cholokian, Vartkes. "*Pour le meilleur et pour le pire*." *Cinéma Québec* 4, nos. 9–10 (1976): 81.

– "Un cinéaste canadien: Claude Jutra." *Séquences* 25 (April 1961): 29–30.

Clandfield, David. "From the Picturesque to the Familiar: Films of the French Unit at the NFB (1958–1964)." *Ciné-Tracts* 4 (Spring-Summer 1978): 50–62.

– *Canadian Film*. Toronto: Oxford University Press, 1987.

Coburn, Teri. "Thumbs Up – And All Is Surfacing." *Cinema Canada* 58 (September 1979): 15–19.

Comolli, Jean-Luc, and Jean Narboni. "Cinema/Ideology/Criticism." In *Movies and Methods*, edited by Bill Nichols, 22–30. Berkeley: University of California Press, 1976.

Conlogue, Ray. "Jutra Surfaces with his First English Film." *Globe and Mail* (Toronto), 26 October 1981.

Connor, Steven. *Postmodernist Culture: An Introduction to Theories of the Contemporary*. Oxford: Basil Blackwell, 1989.

Constanzo, William V. "The Persistence of Proust, the Resistance of Film." *Literature/ Film Quarterly* 15, no. 3 (1987): 169–74.

Corbeil, Carole. "Jutra Film a Gem Despite Flaws." *Globe and Mail* (Toronto), 12 September 1985.

Coulombe, Michel, and Marcel Jean (eds.). *Le Dictionnaire du cinéma québécois*. Montreal: Boréal, 1991.

Cousineau, Louise. "Un très beau film de Jutra est à l'affiche ce week-end." *La Presse* (Montreal), 22 September 1978.

Cox, Kirwan. "*Kamouraska*: Interview with Claude Jutra." *Cinema Canada* 7 (April–May 1973): 47–50.

Crowther, Bosley. "*Take It All*." *New York Times*, 26 April 1966.

Daudelin, Robert. *Vingt ans de cinéma au Canada français*. Quebec City: Ministère des Affaires culturelles, 1967.

– "Gilles Groulx." In *Second Wave: Newer than New Wave Names in World Cinema*, edited by Ian Cameron, 120–3. London: Studio Vista, 1970.

Daudelin, Robert, and Michel Patenaude. "Michel Brault et Claude Jutra racontent Jean Rouch." *Objectif* 3 (December 1960): 3–12.

Delahaye, Michel. "Le nouvel âge: entretien avec Claude Jutra." *Cahiers du cinéma* 200–1 (April–May 1968): 109–13.

Delahaye, Michel, and Jacques Rivette. "Entetien avec Claude Lévi-Strauss." *Cahiers du cinéma* 156 (June 1964): 19–29.

De Laurot, Yves. "From Logos to Lens." In *Movies and Methods*, edited by Bill Nichols, 578–82. Berkeley: University of California Press, 1976.

Demers, Pierre. "L'Alternative: Un réseau de cinémas parallèles." *Cinéma Québec* 1, no. 2 (Summer 1971): 22–7.

Denton, Clive. "Claude Jutra's *Pour le meilleur et pour le pire.*" *Cinema Canada* 23 (November 1975): 54.

Dorland, Michael. "Claude Jutra's *La Dame en couleurs.*" *Cinema Canada* 116 (March 1985): 27–8.

– *So Close to the State/s: The Emergence of Canadian Feature Film Policy.* Toronto: University of Toronto Press, 1998.

Dyer, Richard. "Entertainment and Utopia." *Movie* 24 (Spring 1977): 2–13.

Eaton, Mick. "The Production of Cinematic Reality." In *Anthropology-Reality-Cinema: The Films of Jean Rouch*, edited by Mick Eaton, 40–53. London: British Film Institute, 1979.

Eaton, Mick, ed. *Anthropology-Reality-Cinema: The Films of Jean Rouch.* London: British Film Institute, 1979.

Edell, Frederick. "Films." *Canadian Dimension* 11, no. 4 (March 1976): 46–7.

Elder, Bruce. "Claude Jutra's *Mon oncle Antoine.*" In *Canadian Film Reader*, edited by Seth Feldman and Joyce Nelson, 194–9. Toronto: Peter Martin Associates, 1977

– "On the Candid-Eye Movement." In *Canadian Film Reader*, edited by Seth Feldman and Joyce Nelson, 86–94. Toronto: Peter Martin Associates, 1977

Elia, Maurice. "*Pour le meilleur et pour le pire.*" *Séquences* 84 (April 1976): 26–7.

Elley, Derek. "Rhythm 'n' Truths." *Films and Filming* 20, no. 9 (June 1974): 30–6.

Elsaesser, Thomas. "Chronicle of a Death Retold." *Monthly Film Bulletin* 54 (June 1987): 164–7

– *Fassbinder's Germany: History Identity Subject.* Amsterdam: Amsterdam University Press, 1996.

Erickson, Jim. "To Be a Writer: Write! Anne Cameron." *Cinema Canada* 48 (June 1978): 6–8.

Euvrard, Michel, and Bernard Queenan. "Parlez-vous Québécois?" *Film Comment* 16, no. 2 (March–April 1980): 45–8.

Evanchuk, P.M. "Claude Jutra – Filmmaker." *Motion* (January–February 1974): 32–4.

– "Claude Jutra." *Motion* (May–June 1974): 17–18.

– "An Innerview of Michel Brault." *Motion* (January-March 1975): 12–22, 31.

Evans, Gary. *In the National Interest: A Chronicle of the National Film Board of Canada from 1949–1989.* Toronto: University of Toronto Press, 1991.

Even, Martin. "Un Antoine Doinel québécois." *Le Devoir* (Montreal), 10 February 1973.

Favreau, Michèle. "Pour Claude Jutra, le cinéma n'existe pas." *La Presse* (Montreal), 18 September 1965.

– "Claude Jutra ou les confidences d'un professeur de cinéma." *La Presse* (Montreal), 16 July 1966.

Feldman, Seth. "Footnote to Fact: The Docudrama." In *Film Genre Reader*, edited by Barry Keith Grant, 344–56. Austin: University of Texas Press, 1986.

Feldman, Seth, ed. *Take Two.* Toronto: Irwin Publishing, 1984.

Feldman, Seth, and Joyce Nelson, eds. *Canadian Film Reader.* Toronto: Peter Martin Associates, 1977.

Fieschi, Jean-André. "Slippages of Fiction: Some Notes on the Cinema of Jean Rouch." In *Anthropology-Reality-Cinema: The Films of Jean Rouch*, edited by Mick Eaton, 67–77. London: British Film Institute, 1979.

Fontaine, Henriette. "Un moment de notre passé pour mieux voir notre présent." *Cinéma Québec* 1, no. 10 (July-August 1972): 4–5.

Fothergill, Robert. "Coward, Bully, or Clown: The Dream-Life of a Younger Brother." In *Canadian Film Reader*, edited by Seth Feldman and Joyce Nelson, 234–50. Toronto: Peter Martin Associates, 1977.

Fournier, Claude. "*La Lutte* ou la fin des combats en équipe." *CopieZéro* 33 (September 1987): 19.

Fox, Joan. "Considering *À tout prendre.*" *Canadian Forum* (June 1965): 63–4.

Friedman, Lester, ed. *Fires Were Started: British Cinema and Thatcherism.* Minneapolis: University of Minnesota Press, 1993.

Frye, Northrop. *The Bush Garden: Essays on the Canadian Imagination.* Toronto: Anansi, 1971.

Fulford, Robert. *Marshall Delaney at the Movies.* Toronto: Peter Martin Associates, 1974.

Gay, Richard, and Francine Laurendeau. "Claude Jutra et la vie de couple: le pour et le contre." *Cinéma Québec* 4, no. 8 (1975): 10–14.

Gervais, Marc. "Lightyears Ahead: For the Record." *Cinema Canada* 36 (March 1977): 34–6.

Gibson, Margaret. *The Butterfly Ward.* Ottawa: Oberon Press, 1976.

Goyette, Louis. "Jutra's English Films in Focus." *Cinema Canada* 142 (June 1987): 25–7.

Grace, Sherrill E. "Articulating the 'Space Between': Atwood's Untold Stories and Fresh Beginnings." In *Margaret Atwood: Language, Text, and System*, edited by Sherrill E. Grace, and Lorraine Weir. Vancouver: University of British Columbia Press, 1983.

Grace, Sherrill E., and Lorraine Weir, eds. *Margaret Atwood: Language, Text, and System*. Vancouver: University of British Columbia Press, 1983.

Grant, Barry Keith, ed. *Film Genre Reader*. Austin: University of Texas Press, 1986.

Grossberg, Lawrence, ed. "On Postmodernism and Articulation: An Interview with Stuart Hall." In *Stuart Hall: Critical Dialogues in Cultural Studies*, edited by David Morley and Kuan-Hsing Chen, 131–50. London: Routledge, 1996.

Hall, Stuart. "Minimal Selves." In Homi K. Bhabha et al. *The Real Me: Post-Modernism and the Question of Identity*, 44–6. London: Institute of Contemporary Arts, 1987.

Harcourt, Peter. "The Innocent Eye: An Aspect of the Work of the National Film Board of Canada." In *Canadian Film Reader*, edited by Seth Feldman and Joyce Nelson, 67–77. Toronto: Peter Martin Associates, 1977.

– "Introduction." In *Canadian Film Reader*, edited by Seth Feldman and Joyce Nelson, 370–6. Toronto: Peter Martin Associates, 1977.

– "Some Relationships between the NFB Animation Department and the Documentary." In Peter Ohlin et al. *John Grierson and the NFB*, 136–46. Toronto: ECW Press, 1984.

– "Faces Changing Colour Changing Canon." *CineAction* 45 (February 1998): 2–9.

Hervey, Robert. *Une Écriture de la passion*. LaSalle: Hurtubise, 1982.

Hébert, Anne. *Kamouraska*. Trans. Norman Shapiro. Toronto: General Publishing, 1973.

Henley, Gail. "On the Record: *For the Record*'s 10 Distinctive Years." *Cinema Canada* 117 (April 1985): 18–21.

Higson, Andrew. "The Concept of National Cinema." *Screen* 30, no. 4 (Autumn 1989): 36–46.

– "Re-presenting the National Past: Nostalgia and Pastiche in the Heritage Film." In *Fires Were Started: British Cinema and Thatcherism*, edited by Lester Friedman. Minneapolis: University of Minnesota Press, 1993.

Hofsess, John. "The Emergence of Claude Jutra." *Maclean's* 86, no. 8 (August 1973): 42–3, 66, 68, 70–1.

– *Inner Views: Ten Canadian Film-makers*. Toronto: McGraw-Hill Ryerson, 1975.

Holub, Robert C. *Jürgen Habermas: Critic in the Public Sphere*. London: Routledge, 1991.

Houle, Michel, and Alain Julien, eds. *Dictionnaire du cinéma québécois*. Montreal: Fides, 1978.

Hubert, Cam. *Dreamspeaker*. New York: Avon Books, 1980.

Hutcheon, Linda. *The Canadian Postmodern: A Study of Contemporary English-Canadian Fiction.* Toronto: Oxford University Press, 1988.

– *A Poetics of Postmodernism: History, Theory, Fiction.* New York: Routledge, 1988.

– *Splitting Images: Contemporary Canadian Ironies.* Toronto: Oxford University Press, 1991.

Hynam, Penelope. "Beryl Fox: An Interview." *Cinema Canada* 73 (April 1981): 26–30.

Jacobowitz, Florence. "*Surfacing.*" *Cinema Canada* 80 (December–January 1981–82): 35.

James, C. Rodney. *Film as a National Art: NFB of Canada and the Film Board Idea.* New York: Arno Press, 1977.

Jay, Martin. *Downcast Eyes: The Denigration of Vision in Twentieth-Century French Thought.* Berkeley: University of California Press, 1993.

Jean, Marcel. *Le Cinéma québécois.* Montreal: Boréal, 1991.

Johnson, Brian D. "Sad Fade-out for a Cinematic Master." *Maclean's* 100, no. 18 (4 May 1987): 57.

Jones, D.B. *Movies and Memoranda: An Interpretative History of the National Film Board of Canada.* Ottawa: Canadian Film Institute, 1981.

– *The Best Butler in the Business: Tom Daly of the National Film Board of Canada.* Toronto: University of Toronto Press, 1996.

Jones, D.G. *Butterfly on Rock: Images in Canadian Literature.* Toronto: University of Toronto Press, 1970.

Jutra, Claude. "Anna La Bonne." *Objectif* 2 (November 1960): 10–14.

– "En courant derrière Rouch: 1." *Cahiers du cinéma* 112 (November 1960): 32–43.

– "En courant derrière Rouch: 2." *Cahiers du cinéma* 115 (January 1961): 23–33.

– "En courant derrière Rouch: 3." *Cahiers du cinéma* 116 (February 1961): 39–44.

– "Les 101 questions: *À tout prendre.*" *Objectif* 37 (November–December 1966): 24–30.

– "À force de chanter pis de parler ensemble...." *Le Devoir* (Montreal), 25 November 1972.

– "A pied? à joual? ... ou en ski-doo?" *Cinéma Québec* 2, no. 9 (1973): 22–3.

– "Dans trois villes Russes ... du cinéma Canadien." *Cinéma Québec* 4, nos. 9–10 (1976): 14–17.

– *Mon oncle Antoine.* Montreal: Art Global, 1979.

Kael, Pauline. *Taking It All In.* New York: Holt, Rinehart and Winston, 1984.

Kelman, Paul. "Jutra on the Tube." *Cinema Canada* 53 (March 1979): 21–4.

Knelman, Martin. "The Great Canadian Movie but Can It Find an Audience." *Globe and Mail* (Toronto), 25 September 1971.

– *This is Where We Came In: The Career and Character of Canadian Film.* Toronto: McClelland and Stewart, 1977.

– "Mum's the Word." In *Take Two*, edited by Seth Feldman, 21–3. Toronto: Irwin Publishing, 1984.

Koller, George Csaba, and Peter Wronski. "Jutra in Two Takes." *Cinema Canada* 23 (November 1975): 30–4.

Kracauer, Siegfried. *From Caligari to Hitler: A Psychological History of the German Film.* Princeton: Princeton University Press, 1966.

La Rochelle, Réal, and Gilbert Maggi. "Situation politique du cinéma québécois." *Champ libre* 1 (July 1971): 53–66.

Lacan, Jacques. "Television." *October* 40 (Spring 1987): 7–50.

Lafrance, André. *Cinéma d'ici.* Montreal: Leméac, 1973.

Laing, R.D. *The Politics of Experience and the Bird of Paradise.* Harmondsworth: Penguin, 1967.

Lamy, Pierre. "Claude Jutra." *Séquences* 131 (October 1987): 15–18.

Lanken, Dane. "Jutra's *Mon oncle Antoine* Worth the Long Wait." *Montreal Gazette*, 19 November 1971.

Laurendeau, Francine. "De *Pour le meilleur et pour le pire* à la loi-cadre." *Cinéma Québec* 4, no. 7 (1975): 5–9.

Leach, Jim. "Don Owen's Obliterated Environments." *Dalhousie Review* 60, no. 2 (Summer 1980): 277–89.

– "Second Images: Reflections on the Canadian Cinema(s) in the Seventies." In *Take Two*, edited by Seth Feldman, 100–10. Toronto: Irwin Publishing, 1984.

– "The Body Snatchers: Genre and Canadian Cinema." In *Film Genre Reader*, edited by Barry Keith Grant, 357–69. Austin: University of Texas Press, 1986.

– "Habitant and Missionary: Ideology and the Voice-of-God in Two 1943 Films on Quebec." *Journal of Canadian Studies*, 25, no. 4 (Winter 1990–91): 100–10.

– "Lost Bodies and Missing Persons: Canadian Cinema(s) in the Age of Multi-National Representations." *Post Script* 18, no. 2 (Winter-Spring 1999): 5–18.

Leduc, Jean. "La Québécitude, maladie à virus?" *Cinéma Québec* 1, no. 8 (March–April 1972): 13.

Lefebvre, Jean Pierre. "La Crise du langage et le cinéma canadien." *Objectif* 32 (April-May 1965): 27–36.

– "La Cohérence, dans le cinéma québécois." *Cinéma Québec* 4, nos. 9–10 (1976): 42–5.

Lefebvre, Jean Pierre, and Jean-Claude Pilon. "L'Équipe française souffre-t-elle de 'Roucheole'?" *Objectif* 15–16 (August 1962): 45–53.

Leroux, André. "*Pour le meilleur ou pour le pire*: l'ennui au compte-goutte." *Le Devoir* (Montreal), 11 October 1975.

– "Au hasard des malchances …!" *Le Devoir* (Montreal), 14 October 1975.

Lever, Yves. *Cinéma et société québécoise*. Montreal: Éditions du Jour, 1972.

– *Histoire du cinéma au Québec*. Quebec City: Direction générale de l'enseignement collégial, 1983.

– *Histoire générale du cinéma au Québec*. Montreal: Boréal, 1988. Rev. ed. Montreal: Boréal, 1995.

Lockerbie, Ian, "Le Cinéma Québécois: une allégorie de la conscience collective." In *Le Cinéma Québécois des Années 80*, edited by Claude Chabot et al., 8–21. Montreal: Cinémathèque Québécoise, 1989.

– "Regarder la mort en face," *Cinébulles* 15, no. 2 (Summer 1996): 46–9.

Lyotard, Jean-François. *The Postmodern Condition: A Report on Knowledge*. Trans. Geoff Bennington and Brian Massumi. Minneapolis: University of Minnesota Press, 1984.

MacKenzie, Scott. "The Missing Mythology: Barthes in Québec." *Canadian Journal of Film Studies* 6, no. 2 (Fall 1998): 65–74.

Magder, Ted. *Canada's Hollywood: The Canadian State and Feature Films*. Toronto: University of Toronto Press, 1993.

Major, Ginette. *Le Cinéma québécois à la recherche d'un public*. Montreal: Les Presses de l'Université de Montréal, 1982.

Marcorelles, Louis. "Lettre de Montréal." *Cahiers du cinéma* 149 (November 1963): 45–7.

Marcuse, Herbert. *One-Dimensional Man: Studies in the Ideology of Advanced Industrial Society*. 2d ed. Boston: Beacon Press, 1991.

Marsolais, Gilles. *Le Cinéma canadien*. Montreal: Éditions du Jour, 1968.

– *L'Aventure du cinéma direct*. Paris: Seghers, 1974.

– "Entretien avec Jean Rouch." *24 Images* 46 (November–December 1989): 23–5.

Maulucci, Anthony S. "Comment on Cannes." *Motion* 4, no. 2 (1975): 36–8.

McLuhan, Marshall. *Understanding Media: The Extensions of Man*. New York: McGraw-Hill, 1964.

Meyrowitz, Joshua. *No Sense of Place: The Impact of Electronic Media on Social Behavior*. New York: Oxford University Press, 1985.

Miller, Mary Jane. *Turn Up the Contrast: CBC Television Drama since 1952*. Vancouver: University of British Columbia Press, 1987.

Mills, C. Wright. *White Collar: The American Middle Classes*. New York: Oxford University Press, 1962.

Moffat, Alain-Napoléon. "*À tout prendre* de Claude Jutra: Le docu-drame de la confession." *Québec Studies* 12 (1991): 147–54.

Morley, David, and Kuan-Hsing Chen, eds. *Stuart Hall: Critical Dialogues in Cultural Studies*. London: Routledge, 1996.

Morley, David, and Kevin Robins. "Spaces of Identity: Communications Technologies and the Reconfiguration of Europe." *Screen* 30, no. 4 (Autumn 1989): 10–34.

Morris, Peter. *The Film Companion*. Toronto: Irwin Publishing, 1984.

– "After Grierson: The National Film Board 1945–53." In *Take Two*, edited by Seth Feldman, 182–94. Toronto: Irwin Publishing, 1984.

Nichols, Bill, ed. *Movies and Methods*. Berkeley: University of California Press, 1976.

Noguez, Dominique. "*Wow*, de Claude Jutra." *Vie des arts* 59 (Summer 1970): 40–3.

– *Essais sur le cinéma québécois*. Montreal: Éditions du Jour, 1970.

O'Regan, Tom. *Australian National Cinema*. London: Routledge, 1996.

Ohlin, Peter et al. *John Grierson and the NFB*. Toronto: ECW Press, 1984.

Olsen, Bjornar. "Roland Barthes." In *Reading Material Culture: Structuralism, Hermeneutics and Post-Structuralism*, edited by Christopher Tilley, 163–205. Oxford: Basil Blackwell, 1990.

Patenaude, Michel. "*À tout prendre*." *Objectif* 23–4 (October 1963): 41–3.

Paterson, Janet M. *Postmodernism and the Quebec Novel*. Trans. David Homel and Charles Phillips. Toronto: University of Toronto Press, 1994.

Perreault, Luc. "Une grosse machine appelée *Kamouraska*." *La Presse* (Montreal), 13 May 1972.

– "À la recherche de l'enfance." *La Presse* (Montreal), 31 March 1973.

– "Copie trop conforme." *La Presse* (Montreal), 31 March 1973.

– "Jutra: le public n'est pas avec nous." *La Presse* (Montreal), 4 October 1975.

Petric, Vlada. "Le cinéma québécois au carrefour: An Oblique View by a Foreigner." *Parachute* (Spring 1978): 37–9.

Pevere, Geoff. "Letter from Canada." *Film Comment* 28, no. 2 (March–April 1992): 61–5.

Pontaut, Alain. "Claude Jutra et Pierre Patry tentent l'aventure du long métrage." *La Presse* (Montreal), 20 July 1963.

– "Claude Jutra, cinéaste." *La Presse* (Montreal), 9 May 1964

Pratley, Gerald. "*Mon oncle Antoine*." *International Film Guide* (1972): 72.

– "Canada." *International Film Guide* (1982): 86–9.

Prédal, René. *Jeune cinéma canadien*. Lyon: Premier Plan, 1967.

La Presse. "*À tout prendre*: strip-tease moral et maîtrise technique." 16 May 1964.

– "Cinq long métrages québécois." 27 August 1966.

- "Claude Jutra: Tout prendre!" 28 March 1970.
- "*Le Niger*, de Claude Jutra: un excellent documentaire." 17 March 1962.
Quigley, Theresia. *The Child Hero in the Canadian Novel*. Toronto: NC Press, 1991.
Rao, Eleonora. *Strategies for Identity: The Fiction of Margaret Atwood*. New York: Peter Lang, 1993.
Renov, Michael, ed. *Theorizing Documentary*. New York: Routledge, 1993.
Rinfret, Louise. "La complicité d'un magicien." *CopieZéro* 33 (September 1987): 32–3.
Rochon, Gaétan, and Marie-Claire Lanctôt. "*Comment savoir*." *Objectif* 38 (May 1967): 21–4.
Rohmer, Éric, and Louis Marcorelles. "Entretien avec Jean Rouch." *Cahiers du cinéma* 144 (June 1963): 16–22.
Rosen, Philip, ed. *Narrative, Apparatus, Ideology: A Film Theory Reader*. New York: Columbia University Press, 1986.
Rouch, Jean. "The Camera and Man." In *Anthropology-Reality-Cinema: The Films of Jean Rouch*, edited by Mick Eaton, 54–63. London: British Film Institute, 1979.
Russell, Delbert W. *Anne Hébert*. Boston: Twayne, 1983.
Rutenberg, Michael E. *Edward Albee: Playwright in Protest*. New York: Avon Books, 1969.
Schupp, Patrick. "*By Design*." *Séquences* 112 (April 1983): 29.
Scott, Jay. "Jutra Reached the Peak of Canadian Filmmaking." *Globe and Mail* (Toronto), (24 April 1987).
Scully, Robert Guy. "Le Tournage de *Kamouraska*." *Le Devoir* (Montreal), 26 August 1972.
- "Une Carrière." *Le Devoir* (Montreal), 2 December 1972.
- "L'œuvre de notre grande bourgeoisie." *Le Devoir* (Montreal), 31 March 1973.
- "La superproduction." *Le Devoir* (Montreal), 7 April 1973.
Sheppard, Gordon, and Andrée Yanacopoulo. *Signé Hubert Aquin: Enquête sur le suicide d'un écrivain*. Montreal: Boréal, 1985.
Shuster, Nat. "*Kamouraska*: Wuthering Heights on the St. Lawrence." *Motion* (November–December 1973): 28–9.
Simon, John. *Private Screenings*. New York: Berkley Publishing, 1967.
Socken, Paul G. "*Mon Oncle* Revisited." *Cinema Canada* 49–50 (September–October 1978): 26–7.
Söderlind, Sylvia. *Margin/Alias: Language and Alienation in Canadian and Québécois Fiction*. Toronto: University of Toronto Press, 1991.
Stam, Robert, Robert Burgoyne, and Sandy Flitterman-Lewis, *New Vocabularies in Film Semiotics: Structuralism, Post-Structuralism and Beyond*. London: Routledge, 1992.

Sturrock, John. "Roland Barthes." In *Structuralism and Since: From Lévi-Strauss to Derrida*, edited by John Sturrock, 52–80. Oxford: Oxford University Press, 1979.

Sturrock, John, ed. *Structuralism and Since: From Lévi-Strauss to Derrida*. Oxford: Oxford University Press, 1979.

Szporer, Philip. "Claude Jutra's *By Design*." *Cinema Canada* 92 (January 1983): 43.

Tadros, Jean-Pierre. "Claude Jutra." *Le Devoir* (Montreal), 21 March 1970.

– "*Wow* de Claude Jutra." *Le Devoir* (Montreal), 28 March 1970.

– "Claude Jutra, Clément Perron et Thetford Mines." *Le Devoir* (Montreal), 6 June 1970.

– "À la découverte de Claude Jutra, acteur." *Le Devoir* (Montreal), 20 November 1971.

– "*Mon oncle Antoine* et la poésie du quotidien." *Le Devoir* (Montreal), 20 November 1971.

– "Une Espèce de joie dans la création: une interview avec Claude Jutra." *Cinéma Québec* 2, nos. 6–7 (March-April 1973): 15–19.

– "*Kamouraska*, une certaine perfection." *Le Devoir* (Montreal), 6 April 1973.

– "L'œuvre écrite." *Le Devoir* (Montreal), 7 April 1973.

Talbot, Michelle. "Jutra entre les deux solitudes …!" *Dimanche-Matin* (Montreal), 24 September 1978.

Thériault, Jacques. "Claude Jutra: Une vie à deux." *Le Devoir* (Montreal), 4 October 1975.

Therrien, Denyse. "L'éros du regard." In *Cinéma et sexualité*, edited by Claude Chabot and Denise Pérusse, 34–41. Montreal: Prospec, 1988.

Thomas, Ralph L. "Comment Claude Jutra en vint à travailler au Canada anglais." *CopieZéro* 33 (September 1987): 34.

Thompson, Patricia. "*Kamouraska* (1972–1983)." *Cinema Canada* 103 (January 1984): 26.

Tilley, Christopher, ed. *Reading Material Culture: Structuralism, Hermeneutics and Post-Structuralism*. Oxford: Basil Blackwell, 1990.

Tremblay-Daviault, Christiane. *Un cinéma orphelin: Structures mentales et sociales du cinéma québècois*. Montreal: Québec/Amérique, 1981.

Turner, Graeme. "The Genres are American: Australian Narrative, Australian Film, and the Problem of Genre." *Literature/Film Quarterly* 21, no. 2 (1993): 102–11.

Vallières, Pierre. *White Niggers of America*. Trans. Joan Pinkham. Toronto: McLelland and Stewart, 1971.

– "Les Critiques face à *Kamouraska*." *Le Devoir* (Montreal), 12 May 1973.

Véronneau, Pierre. "1956–1960 – Entre l'espoir et la colère." *CopieZéro* 33 (September 1987): 17.

Véronneau, Pierre, and Piers Handling, eds. *Self Portrait: Essays on the Canadian and Quebec Cinemas*. Ottawa: Canadian Film Institute, 1980.

Viswanathan, Jacqueline. "Approche pédagogique d'un classique du cinéma québécois: *Mon oncle Antoine*." *The French Review* 63, no. 5 (April 1990): 849–58.

Wade, Mason. *The French Canadians 1760–1967*. Revised ed. in two vols. Toronto: Macmillan, 1968.

Weinberg, Herman G. "Reflections on the Current Scene." *Take One* 3, no. 3 (April 1972): 32–3.

Weinmann, Heinz. *Cinéma de l'imaginaire québécois: De La Petite Aurore à Jésus de Montréal*. Montreal: L'Hexagone, 1990.

Willet John, ed. *Brecht on Theatre*. New York: Hill and Wang, 1964.

Yacowar, Maurice. "The Canadian as Ethnic Minority." *Film Quarterly* (Winter 1986–87): 13–19.

Yakir, Dan. "*Ciné-transe*: The Vision of Jean Rouch." *Film Quarterly* 31, no. 3 (Spring 1978): 2–11.

Young, Colin. "Review of *À tout prendre*." In *Canadian Film Reader*, edited by Seth Feldman and Joyce Nelson, 153–6. Toronto: Peter Martin Associates, 1977.

Young, Robert, ed. *Untying the Text: A Post-Structuralist Reader*. Boston: Routledge and Kegan Paul, 1981.

Zizek, Slavoj. "Rossellini: Woman as Symptom of Man." *October* 54 (Fall 1990): 18–44.

INDEX OF FILM TITLES

INDEX